The **Busines**

UPPER-INTERMEDIATE Student's Book

John Allison & Jeremy Townend with Paul Emmerson

The Business
UPPER-INTERMEDIATE

To the student

The objective of *The* Business is to help you learn two things: how to do business in English and the language you need to do it. The new language and structures are presented in the Student's Book whilst the DVD-ROM provides language practice and extension.

Here is a summary of what you will find in each.

Student's Book

The modules

The Student's Book contains 48 modules in eight units. Each unit deals with a key sector of activity in the business world. There are six different types of module:

1 About business

These modules contain information and language for the topic area of each unit. The focus is on understanding the topic and the general sense of the texts – don't worry too much about details such as new vocabulary.

2 Vocabulary

These modules build on the important words and phrases associated with the topic and provide thorough practice.

3 Grammar

The first part of these modules – Test yourself – tests your knowledge of important grammatical structures. Do this before and / or after the practice activities in the second part. If necessary, refer to the Grammar and practice section at the back of the book for help.

4 Speaking

These modules develop understanding and speaking skills in typical business situations. Good and bad examples are given for comparison, and the speaking activities allow you to practise key phrases and skills in realistic situations with other people.

5 Writing

These modules provide practice for the most important types of document you will need to write at work. Model texts are examined and used as a basis to write your own.

6 Case study

The case studies provide an opportunity to apply all the language, skills and ideas you have worked on in the unit. They present authentic problem-solving situations similar those you will meet in business.

Internet research

Every module includes an Internet research task. The Internet provides almost unlimited resources for improving your English and learning more about business. These tasks direct you to interesting background and details on topics related to each module. The tasks can be done before or after working on the module.

Other features

In addition to the eight main units, the Student's Book contains the following:

Reviews

These units can be used in three ways: to consolidate your work on the units, to catch up quickly if you have missed a lesson, and to revise before tests or exams.

Additional material

This section contains all the extra materials you need to do pair or group work activities.

Grammar and practice

The section gives a very useful summary of rules with clear examples, but also provides further practice of the essential grammar points in this level of the course.

Recordings

Full scripts of all the audio recordings are given, allowing you to study the audio dialogues in detail. However, try not to rely on reading them to understand the listenings – very often, you don't need to understand every word, just the main ideas.

Wordlist

In the modules, words which you may not know are in grey; you will find definitions in the wordlist, often with examples. Words in red are high-frequency items, which you should try to learn and use. The others, in black, are words you just need to understand.

The DVD-ROM

The DVD-ROM is designed to help you continue improving your English on your own, away from the classroom. It includes an interactive workbook which, like the Review units in the Student's Book, can be used in three ways: to improve your listening, grammar, vocabulary and pronunciation; to catch up on lessons you have missed; to revise for tests and exams.

Interactive workbook

This includes everything you would normally find in a workbook, and more; activities for vocabulary, grammar, pronunciation, writing and listening practice.

Video

Each unit includes an episode of a mini-drama illustrating the communication and people skills practised in each unit, with exercises to practise the functional language used in the video.

Business dilemmas

There are four problem-solving games to allow you to review and practise functional language from the Student's Book. Try doing these with a partner to practise discussing problems and solutions.

Tests

Four tests, one for every two units, allow you to check your progress through the DVD-ROM. If you do well on a test, you get 'promoted'; if you do well on all four tests, you become CEO!

Business documents

There is a model document for each unit, including letters, invoices, CVs, etc. Each document includes annotations explaining the structure and key phrases, and a follow-up activity tests understanding of this.

Grammar reference

You can refer this section any time for helpful grammar rules and examples.

Class audio

This section of the DVD-ROM contains all the audio recordings from the Student's Book, together with scrollable scripts.

Downloadables

The DVD-ROM includes a set of downloadable files for use outside the DVD-ROM or away from your computer. There is a downloadable and printable PDF of the answers to the Student's Book exercises; a Word file containing the text of each Business document; and MP3 files of all the Student's Book audio that you can transfer to your MP3 player or iPod for listening on the move.

We sincerely hope you will enjoy working with *The* Business.
Good luck!

John Allison
Jeremy Townend
Paul Emmerson

Contents

	About business	Vocabulary	Grammar
1 **Building a career** PAGE 6	1.1 The education business	1.2 Education and career	1.3 Tense review
2 **Information** PAGE 18	2.1 IT solutions	2.2 Information systems and communication	2.3 Comparing solutions and getting help
Reviews 1 and 2	PAGES 30–31		
3 **Quality** PAGE 32	3.1 What quality means	3.2 Quality and standards	3.3 Passive structures and *have something done*
4 **Feedback** PAGE 44	4.1 The project team	4.2 Managing people and projects	4.3 Regulations, speculation and habits
Reviews 3 and 4	PAGES 56–57		
5 **Selling more** PAGE 58	5.1 Viral marketing	5.2 The marketing mix	5.3 Questions for persuading
6 **New business** PAGE 70	6.1 Self-financing	6.2 Funding a start-up	6.3 Future perfect and future continuous
Reviews 5 and 6	PAGES 82–83		
7 **Financial control** PAGE 84	7.1 Accountants	7.2 Financial documents and regulation	7.3 Cause and effect, ability, articles
8 **Fair trade** PAGE 96	8.1 Fair trade or free trade	8.2 Contracts and corporate ethics	8.3 Obligation and permission, inversion
Reviews 7 and 8	PAGES 108–109		
Additional material	PAGES 110–115		
Grammar and practice	PAGES 116–131		
Recordings	PAGES 132–143		
Wordlist	PAGES 144–150		

Speaking	Writing	Case study
1.4 Giving reasons in interviews	1.5 Cover letters	1.6 Mangalia Business School
2.4 Telephoning	2.5 Memos	2.6 Meteor Bank
3.4 Delivering presentations	3.5 Procedures and instructions	3.6 Zaluski Strawberries
4.4 Coaching	4.5 Reports	4.6 Trident Overseas
5.4 Dealing with objections	5.5 Mail shots and sales letters	5.6 Backchat Communications
6.4 Taking questions in presentations	6.5 An executive summary	6.6 Angels or demons
7.4 Communicating in meetings	7.5 Minutes	7.6 Car-Glazer
8.4 Negotiating a compromise	8.5 Assertive writing	8.6 Green Hills Coffee

The *Wordlist* is a module-by-module glossary of all the words in grey in this coursebook.

1 | Building a career

Discussion

1 Decide which of these factors would be most important to you in choosing a business course. Order them from 1 = most important to 10 = least important.

- [ ] quality and reputation of faculty
- [ ] quality and experience of fellow students
- [ ] help with finding top jobs
- [ ] location
- [ ] alumni network
- [ ] cost
- [ ] innovative curriculum
- [ ] sports and social facilities
- [ ] earning potential
- [ ] accommodation service

Predicting and reading

2 Read the title of the article opposite. Which of these marketing techniques do you think are used?

- [ ] telemarketing
- [ ] TV advertising
- [ ] discounts for early booking
- [ ] weekends at Harvard
- [ ] mail shots
- [ ] travelling shows
- [ ] free holidays
- [ ] sponsorship

3 Read the article and check your predictions.

Scan reading

4 Find what these numbers from the article refer to.

a 23,000   c 80%   e 35   g 60,000
b 9%   d 10%   f 43,700   h 8000

Reading for detail

5 Read the article again and complete the chart.

Listening and discussion

6 🎧 1:01 Listen to four students reacting to the article. Match each speaker 1–4 with the correct summary a–d.

a Universities should be accessible to everyone.
b Universities reinforce an unequal system.
c Universities are right to be commercial.
d Universities are right to be selective.

7 Discuss your own reactions to the article and your opinions on elitism in education.

The Harvard battle plan

Phase 1

1 Purchase _____ from examination boards.
2 Send _____ to high school juniors.
3 Visit _____ and travel to other countries.
4 Send out _____ to identify possible candidates.

Phase 2

5 Sort applications and give a score from _____ .
6 Local _____ discuss the case for and against each candidate.

Phase 3

7 _____ lobby successful candidates by phone.
8 Invite applicants to spend _____ at Harvard in _____ .

How Harvard gets its best and brightest

SURE, students work hard to get into this elite college. But so does the admissions committee, assures Dean Bill Fitzsimmons.

In the US, few competitions are more cutthroat than the college admissions game. And every year it grows more intense as an ever-larger pool of high school seniors apply for one of the coveted spots at the nation's top colleges. Meanwhile, the elite colleges have been stepping up their efforts to attract the best and brightest students – the prized pupils who will help increase the prestige of their campuses.

You might assume that Harvard College – blessed with higher education's greatest brand name and an endowment second to none – could afford to remain relatively aloof from this battle. But in reality, 'There is no place that works harder than we do,' says William R 'Bill' Fitzsimmons, Harvard's veteran dean of admissions.

For the new academic year, which will start in September, Harvard received a near-record 23,000 applications. Of these, it accepted a mere 2,100 – or just 9% – ranking it as the nation's most selective college. Even more impressive, some 80% of the chosen ultimately decided to attend Harvard – a rate that is easily the highest among colleges and universities.

The real surprise, however, is how hard Harvard works behind the scenes to achieve these amazing results. From his corner office in Byerly Hall, Fitzsimmons oversees a carefully considered three-part battle plan. The first phase begins in the spring, when Harvard mails letters to a staggering 70,000-or-so high school juniors – all with stellar test scores – suggesting they consider applying to America's best-known college. Harvard buys their names from the examination boards which administer aptitude and college-admission tests.

Each year, Harvard's admissions team tours 140 US cities, as well as hundreds of other places in Latin America, Europe, Africa and the Far East. This year, 10% of the admitted students came from abroad. In addition to his staff of 35, Fitzsimmons enlists Harvard's coaches and professors to look for talent. The math department, for instance, starts to identify budding math geniuses by keeping a close eye on kids doing well in math contests.

Harvard students also get into the act. Since 2003, Harvard has hired fifteen to twenty low-income students to call and email promising low-income high school students. Their job: to counter the 'impression that Harvard is only for the rich and elite,' says Fitzsimmons. In fact, under Harvard's relatively new financial aid policies, parents who make less than $60,000 a year aren't expected to pay anything toward the annual $43,700 fee for tuition, room and board. Fitzsimmons also sends an army of some 8,000 alumni volunteers to tour the country to identify and recruit promising high school students by holding shows where they live. Later, they also interview nearly all applicants.

By then, Fitzsimmons will be deep into the second phase of his battle plan: sifting through the thousands of applicants. Every application is rated on a scale of one (the best ever) to six (the worst ever). Then, in February, the applications are divided up geographically among twenty subcommittees. 'We present the case for each applicant like a lawyer would,' says Fitzsimmons. 'This is the polar opposite of a computer process and because we have so many people involved, there are lots of checks and balances.'

Once the final decisions have been made, Fitzsimmons and his team move to phase three: an all-out push to convince the chosen few to attend Harvard. Professors, alumni and students are all recruited to start calling the admitted. And in mid to late April over half of those who were accepted typically show up at Harvard for an elaborate weekend.

The Harvard pitch is clearly effective. 'What we aim to do is to get the very best faculty together with the very best students,' Fitzsimmons says. 'Our hope is that these synergies will develop the talents of these students to a much greater degree and that they will then give back a lot more to America and the world.' That belief may sound corny, but it's clearly helped drive Harvard to go to enormous lengths to find the best and brightest.

1 | Building a career

Brainstorming

1 Think of as many good reasons as possible for studying business.

2 The letter below discusses reasons for attending business school. Choose one verb for each of 1–10 to complete the letter with the correct collocations.

Dear Sonia,

You asked my advice about going to business school. Well, don't miss out on a wonderful opportunity to (1) **gain/boost/make** knowledge and to (2) **make/acquire/do** skills which will serve you for a lifetime. As well as (3) **gaining/receiving/improving** your employability and (4) **having/boosting/making** your future earnings, you'll (5) **get/have/obtain** lots of fun (6) **going to/doing/getting** parties and (7) **doing/making/learning** friends. If you choose a good school you'll (8) **enhance/receive/learn** tuition from experienced professors and (9) **obtain/do/make** practical experience that will really (10) **enhance/obtain/gain** your CV. In your shoes, I wouldn't hesitate for one moment!

3 Look again at the list you made in 1. Are any of the ideas in the letter to Sonia the same as yours? Which phrases would you add to your list?

4 With a partner, decide which collocations in 2 relate to professional rather than personal experience. Use them to write sentences about yourselves that you could use in a job interview.

Funding

5 Read the extract below about how to pay for studies. Choose a verb from the box to complete each gap.

obtain   finance   borrow   support   win   subsidize   arrange

If you're not lucky enough to be married to a millionaire or to have parents with very deep pockets, you may be wondering how to (1) _____ the next step in your education. Customs vary from country to country; one of the most popular solutions is to (2) _____ a student loan, sometimes interest-free or tax-deductible, that is only repayable when you are in full-time work. Many students who are unable to (3) _____ money from friends or family prefer to (4) _____ themselves by working part-time, and some are able to (5) _____ grants from local government or to (6) _____ scholarships from their universities. If you're already in work, try persuading your employer to (7) _____ your studies – in some countries companies are bound by law to contribute towards further education.

Discussion

6 What are the advantages and disadvantages of the methods of financing your education mentioned in the article? Which ones would you use?

7 Work with a partner. You are going to read about a businesswoman named Jacky. Ask questions to exchange information and complete the description of her education. Student A should turn to page 110. Student B should turn to page 112.

8 Talk about your education. Was it different from your parents' education? What sort of education would you like your own children to have?

Action verbs

9 Complete the CV with appropriate action verbs from the boxes. Then use them to write sentences for your own CV.

contacted
recruited
exceeded
met
presented
trained

2002–2004 Sales manager, Way2Go Travel, UK

1 _____ corporate clients by phone and 2 _____ incentive travel programmes to Boards of Directors
3 _____ and 4 _____ new sales reps
5 _____ sales targets for every month and 6 _____ annual objectives by twenty per cent

---

chaired
designed
managed
drew up
motivated
implemented

2004–2007 Sales and marketing manager, Hondo Holidays, Texas

7 _____ sales materials and 8 _____ innovative advertising campaigns
9 _____ and 10 _____ a team of 40 telesales operators
11 _____ a working party and 12 _____ proposals for a new e-commerce division

---

Career stages

10 Decide which verbs from the box can refer to people who …

1 are currently enjoying having no work
2 lost their jobs due to poor company performance
3 are making positive career moves
4 are leaving a job they were unhappy with
5 are making a geographical change
6 lost their job due to disciplinary problems

to be laid off   to quit   to be on assignment   to be promoted   to be suspended
to be resting   to be made redundant   to be transferred   to take a sabbatical
to give in your notice   to be dismissed   to join a company

Listening for gist

11 🎵 1:02 Listen to six speakers talking about career changes. Use expressions from 10 to describe each situation.

12 Work with a partner. Discuss the situations below.

What would you do if …
1 you were promoted to a job you knew was too difficult for you?
2 you were made redundant after 25 years' service?
3 you were unfairly dismissed for harassing an employee?
4 you gave in your notice the day before the firm announced a 33 per cent salary increase?
5 you were transferred to Alaska?
6 you were on sabbatical for a year?

Internet research

Search for the keywords *"action verbs for resumes cvs"*. Update your CV using dynamic action verbs and phrases.

Listening and discussion

13 🎵 1:03–1:05 Listen to three people talking about career choices. Make notes on the problems they face. Discuss what you would do and why. Then compare your answers with page 110.

1 | Building a career

Refresh your memory

Past simple
She worked in Paris last year

Past continuous
She was planning to resign at the time

Past perfect
She had already heard the news

Present simple
She works in London

Present continuous
She's travelling in Asia

Present perfect simple
She has travelled ten thousand miles.

Present perfect continuous
She has been visiting suppliers.

Zero conditional
If she meets her targets, she gets a bonus.

First conditional
If she gets the job, she'll move to Spain.

Second conditional
If she was/were President, everybody would resign.

will
Oil prices will continue to rise

going to
Some day I'm going to start my own business

Present continuous for future
I'm flying to New York tomorrow

▶ Grammar and practice pages 116–117

1.3 Grammar   Tense review

Test yourself

1 A businesswoman, Lindsey, is describing her career status, history and aspirations. In the first extract, identify and correct the six errors relating to verb tenses in her story. Change the verbs to the correct form of *past simple*, *past continuous* or *past perfect*.

> When I left school I wasn't sure what to do next. I was applying for a place at university, but while I had revised for my exams I already decided that I didn't feel ready for university. I had read a lot about East Africa, and one day when I watched a TV documentary about Ethiopia, I suddenly knew that that was where I was going. In fact it was while I had worked with an NGO in Ethiopia that I was becoming interested in business.

2 In the next extract, Lindsey explains her current projects. Complete the extract with the correct forms of the verbs in brackets. Use *present simple*, *present continuous*, *present perfect simple*, or *present perfect continuous*.

> I (1) _____ (just finish) my course at the Franklin School of Business and I (2) _____ (currently work) at JPC again while I (3) _____ (consider) various opportunities. As JPC's Finance Director (4) _____ (leave) the company unexpectedly, I (5) _____ (agree) to manage the finance department until a new appointment is made. For example, for the last three weeks I (6) _____ (design) a new audit procedure which I believe will significantly improve financial control. However, I (7) _____ (look) for a position in East Africa for some time now, and this one (8) _____ (seem) perfect for my profile.

3 In a job interview, Lindsey gave the following answers. Each answer is a conditional sentence. Choose the correct form of the verb to complete each sentence.

> 1 If I **get/am getting/got** the job, I **am trying/will try/tried** to make myself available as soon as possible, but I **am not/will be/wouldn't be** able to start immediately unless JPC **will agree/would agree/agreed** to let me go.
> 2 You see, if I **make/will make/made** a commitment, I **am doing/do/did** my best to respect it.
> 3 If by any chance the job **will be/would be/were** based in Kenya, I **am taking/would take/took** it anyway, even though I'd prefer to use my Amharic.

4 Lindsey is being asked about her objectives and mobility. Choose the correct future verb forms to complete the text: *will*, *going to*, or *present continuous*.

> In the short term, I hope (1) **I'll become / I'm becoming** a department manager quite quickly. I've learnt a lot about management on the MBA, and (2) **I'm going to put / I'm putting** the theory into practice as soon as I can. On the personal front, (3) **I'll get / I'm getting** married next June; over the next couple of years my fiancé (4) **will write / is going to write** TV and movie scripts, so (5) **he is going to be / he is being** totally mobile and happy to move as necessary.

10   *The* **Business**

Time markers

5 Decide which time markers from the box are usually associated with the present simple and which are associated with the present continuous.

> usually   currently   always   at present   at the moment   often

6 Decide which time markers from the box are usually associated with the past simple and which are associated with the present perfect.

> ever   in   never   ago   already   (not) yet   when   just   since   for   last

Internet research

Search for the keywords "*how to write accomplishment statements*". Make a list of key points to remember when describing your accomplishments in a resume or interview.

Listening

7 🌐 1:06 Every ten years, the Franklin School of Business organizes a reunion party. Listen to a conversation between two of its graduates, Fraser and Jess and answer the questions.

a   What is Fraser doing at the moment?
b   Where did Fraser work before?
c   Why did Fraser leave that job?
d   What has Fraser been doing recently?
e   What did Jess do after leaving the business school?
f   What is Jess doing at the moment?
g   What is Jess doing soon?
h   What does Fraser discover about Jess?

8 Write out your answers to 7 as complete sentences, taking care to use the right verb forms.

Role-play

9 With a partner, imagine you meet twenty years from now at a reunion party. Make polite conversation following the cues below.

what ... do?
what ... at the moment?
what ... after leaving college?

how long ... your most recent job?
what ... recently?
what ... next?

Balloon debate

'We have a very low drop out rate.'

10 Work in groups of three or four. You all work for the same private business school. Due to budget restrictions, there is not enough money to pay everybody's salary, so one person must be made redundant. Choose one of the positions below, then each present details of your past accomplishments, current projects and future objectives: the group must then decide who has made a good case for continuing and who has to drop out.

Marketing Manager

Accomplishments: created positive image and brand name
Projects: develop new markets and international contacts
Objectives: become one of top ten schools in the world

Personnel Manager

Accomplishments: fired boring professors, hired top consultants
Projects: implement performance-related incentives
Objectives: higher salaries and longer holidays for all staff

Head of Administration

Accomplishments: made school profitable after years of losses
Projects: get corporate sponsorship and govt. funding
Objectives: improve facilities and profitability

Director of Studies

Accomplishments: replaced old books with multimedia programs
Projects: develop revolutionary methods of learning
Objectives: 100 per cent success in exams with only 50 per cent study time

1 | Building a career

Listening and discussion

1 🎧 **1:07** Listen to eight interview questions. Which of these questions about personal choices are reasonable interview questions? Give reasons.

Listening

2 🎧 **1:08–1:09** Ruth and Anaïs applied for the same job with Banco Agricolo. Listen to two extracts from their interviews and complete these statements with Ruth or Anaïs.

1 _____ chose to study business because it pays more than languages.
2 _____ chose to study business to prepare for a career as an international manager.
3 _____ chose the Franklin School of Business mainly for the quality of its programmes.
4 _____ chose the Franklin School of Business mainly to be with her boyfriend.
5 _____ has not prepared or organized her ideas.
6 _____ presents well-prepared and well-organized ideas.
7 _____ gives vague and sometimes irrelevant reasons.
8 _____ gives appropriate, precise and well-structured reasons.

3 Put the expressions you have just heard in the appropriate group, as in the examples:

Introducing a point: *1, …*
Seeing both sides: *3, …*
Combining reasons: …
Adding ideas: *2, …*

1 *Firstly …*
2 *Besides,*
3 *On the whole …, however …*
4 *As regards* choosing business …
5 *It not only* prepared me to work …, *but it also* means that …
6 *In addition*, a business degree always gets attention …
7 *As far as* my choice of business school *is concerned,*
8 *It's true that* the big names …, *but on the other hand*, newer schools like Franklin …
9 *For one thing*, they have better facilities, *and for another*, they're less expensive.
10 *What's more*, their curricula are …

4 With a partner, use expressions for combining reasons and adding ideas to complete these answers to interview questions. What were the questions?

1 Mainly for the variety. I _____ get out of the office a lot, _____ I meet a lot of different people. _____ the salary was much better than anything else I was offered!
2 Well, it's very close to what's known as the 'Plastics Valley'. _____ to lots of jobs, there are very good communications. _____, it's one of the most beautiful areas in the country.
3 Several reasons really. _____, it really relaxes me after a hard week, and _____, it keeps me fit. You can't beat badminton for a good workout; and _____, it's a great way to meet people.

5 With a partner, use expressions for introducing a point and seeing both sides to explain the advantages and disadvantages of the following:

1   Living in your parents' home or moving away and sharing a flat with friends.
    Example
    Firstly, living with your parents is not always easy. On the whole it's cheaper to stay at home, but the experience of living away from home is richer. As regards sharing with friends, it's true that sometimes there will be personality clashes, but, on the other hand, it's good to know that there's always a friend around when you need help.
2   Studying something you dislike but are good at, and which pays well, or something you love doing, are perhaps not so good at, and which is badly paid.
3   Having a part-time job or borrowing money from the bank to pay for your studies, or working for two or three years before going to university.
4   Taking an interesting but badly-paid job in a small company in order to get more responsibility, or a boring but well-paid job in a large company with few career prospects.
5   Changing companies, cities and countries regularly to increase your experience and salary, or working all your life in the same town for the same company.

Role-play

6 Role-play the following job interviews. Student A should interview Student B for a job as manager of the world's biggest night-club in Ibiza, then Student B should interview Student A for a job as manager of the world's most famous circus. Follow instructions 1–4.

Internet research

Search for the keywords *"illegal interview questions"*. Make a list of questions you don't have to answer in an interview, and the best way to react if an interviewer does ask them. Are there 'illegal' questions which you find perfectly acceptable?

1   Meet in separate groups of As or Bs to decide what qualities, skills and experience you will be looking for in the ideal candidate. Prepare questions to test the candidate in each area.
2   Agree on a time limit, and meet a partner to hold the interviews. Each candidate should give reasons why they are the best person for the job.
3   After the interviews, meet again in your groups of As or Bs to decide which candidate will get the job.
4   Meet in your pairs of A and B to announce the result and give your partner reasons why they did or didn't get the job.

1.5 Writing Cover letters

Brainstorming

1 When applying for a job or a placement, you should always send a cover letter with your CV or resume. In small groups, divide the list below into *Dos* and *Don'ts* for writing dynamic cover letters. When you have finished, compare your ideas with the list on page 110.

> Start your letter 'Dear Sir or Madam'
>
> Write a formal introduction in the first paragraph.
>
> Ask directly for an interview.
>
> Write at least 400 words – the more information you give, the better.
>
> Use sophisticated language to make a good impression.
>
> Follow the AIDA model used in advertising – attention, interest, desire, action.

2 Use the action verbs from the box to complete this email cover letter.

broken	capture	developed	doubled	exceeded	modernized
obtained	optimize	present	trained		

Delete Reply Reply All Forward New Mailboxes Get Mail Q▾ From Search Mailbox

Dear Mr Crouch

Having (**1**) _____ objectives and (**2**) _____ sales records in all my previous positions, and recently (**3**) _____ my MBA in marketing at Warwick University, I feel I am an ideal candidate for the position of European Sales Manager at Starfield Nightclubs.

In my last job as senior sales representative for Roxy Entertainment Ltd., I (**4**) _____ new products for teenage customers, (**5**) _____ sales staff, and (**6**) _____ the membership management system. Over a two-year period, I more than (**7**) _____ average revenues per venue.

Nightclubs are a highly competitive sector of the entertainment industry, and I am certain I have the skills to (**8**) _____ market share and (**9**) _____ Starfield's profitability.

I would be happy to (**10**) _____ my ideas in more detail at interview, and I will call you early next week to arrange a meeting. If you have any questions, please feel free to contact me before then. Thank you for your time and consideration.

Yours sincerely,
Kiara Pointer

---

3 Decide the purpose of each paragraph in 2. Which paragaph is intended to

- request action?
- give details of the applicant's accomplishments?
- get the reader's attention?
- relate the applicant to the company, showing why the company should hire her?

4 Match sentence beginnings 1–10 with endings a–j to make typical dynamic sentences for cover letters.

1 My outgoing personality **makes** me
2 I recently **graduated**
3 I **served** as
4 I **attended** school
5 I **supported** myself
6 Jobs such as bartending **enhanced**
7 I have the skills to **embark on**
8 I **would like very much to**
9 I will **follow up** this letter with
10 I can **arrange a time**

a my formal education.
b to meet with you.
c a phone call.
d a strong candidate.
e a career in insurance brokering.
f talk with you.
g by working in radio advertising sales.
h from the University of Oregon.
i in Michigan, Arizona and Oregon.
j president of the debating society.

Brainstorming

5 In small groups, read the two job ads. For each position, list at least two qualities and two skills that the ideal candidate should have.

Development Officer for Executive Education

Based in Paris, you will promote the specialist training services of a top international business school to companies throughout Europe. You will generate and follow up leads, handle client appointments and presentations, prepare tenders and secure client commitment before handover to account managers.

Brand Manager EMEA

Based in London, but with extensive travel, you will be responsible for maintaining and developing a household name in video games. Liaising with head office in Japan, you will design and implement marketing campaigns for the Europe, Middle East and Africa region, and ensure that cost and profit objectives are met.

Writing

6 Divide into two teams, As and Bs. The As will apply for the position as Development Officer for Executive Education, and the Bs for the position as Brand Manager, EMEA. Follow the instructions below to write your letter.

1 With a partner from the same team, list real or imaginary examples of your experience, skills and accomplishments which you want to mention in your cover letter.
2 Plan the four paragraphs of your letter, using the examples you have listed.
3 Write a cover letter, remembering to use action verbs whenever possible.

7 In teams, A and B, exchange your cover letters. Read the other team's letters, and decide which candidates deserve to be short-listed for an interview. Announce your decision to the other group.

Internet research

Search for the keywords "what not to put on your resume". Compile a class list of the top ten errors.

1.6 Case study **Mangalia Business School**

Discussion

1 Decide which of the following features are more advantageous for an international business school.

history: more than 100 years old *or* modern new school
funding: public *or* private
students: 80% local and 20% foreign *or* 20% local and 80% foreign
faculty: business leaders *or* researchers
location: international metropolis *or* small seaside town
site: campus *or* city centre

Reading

2 Read the information about Mangalia Business School and list its strengths and weaknesses in terms of its ability to compete on a global market.

Mangalia Business School (MBS)

Founded in 1992, MBS is a private business school in southeast Romania with an excellent reputation for quality in Central and Eastern Europe. Situated on the Black Sea coast, close to the Romanian Business Centre, which hosts international conferences and seminars, Mangalia's climate and cultural heritage make it the ideal location for both summer schools and all-year study on a well-equipped seaside campus with comfortable accommodation for 300 students. The School offers internationally recognized undergraduate and masters degrees, as well as executive education tailored to the needs of individual companies. Faculty are recruited from Central Europe's most successful companies. Work placements are organized in Romania, Bulgaria, Hungary and Ukraine, providing invaluable experience of international business.

Courses

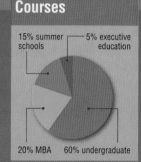

15% summer schools — 5% executive education
20% MBA   60% undergraduate

Listening

3 🌐 1:10 Listen to an extract from a presentation given by Radu Ionescu, the Dean of MBS, and answer the questions.

1 What alternatives is MBS facing due to globalization?
2 What does Radu Ionescu expect from his guests?
3 What has Ion Bumbescu offered, and what are his conditions?

Discussion

4 In small groups, hold a meeting to discuss the brief below and draw up proposals for MBS's five-year plan.

Students

12% Bulgarian
11% other European
2% non European
19% Hungarian
56% Romanian

Mangalia Business School

Brief for international consultants

1 Sponsorship
Should MBS accept Bumbescu's offer to sponsor the school? (see point 3)

2 Tuition fees
Until now fees have been average for business schools of this type. Should MBS maintain this policy, raise fees to a higher than average level, or reduce them to a lower than average level? (see point 3)

3 Development projects
MBS can afford to invest in the development projects below as follows:
At current (average) fee levels, one project only.
If Bumbescu's sponsorship is accepted, two projects.
If fees are increased, one additional project.
If fees are reduced, one project less.
The possible projects are as follows:
• strengthen faculty and increase research funding
• improve and extend facilities
• improve placement and career services
• develop international recruitment and exchange programmes
• your ideas ...

4 Promotion
Please consider the following, as well as your own ideas:
Who should MBS target: undergraduates, future MBAs, corporate clients?
Where should MBS look for its future clients: Romania, Central Europe, Western Europe, the US, the Far East, worldwide?
How should MBS promote itself: materials, media, events, incentives?

Listening

5 🌐 1:11 Listen to a radio news report. How does this news affect your proposals?

Presentation

6 Present your proposals. The class should vote for the best presentation.

2 | Information

Discussion

1 Look at the pictures and answer the questions below.

a   How is the office of the 1950s different from today's workplace?
b   What do you imagine the office of the future will be like?
c   Do you expect technology to make your life easier or harder?

Summarizing

2 Read the article opposite. Decide which statement a–c best summarizes the writer's overall argument.

a   Technology helps people save time.
b   Technology makes people work harder.
c   Technology is a waste of money.

3 Read paragraphs 1–4. Choose the correct summary a–d for each paragraph.

a   How several factors have combined to make the workplace more pressurized.
b   Poorly planned IT systems generate more not less work.
c   Managers see investment in information technologies as a productivity solution.
d   Working conditions have become uncomfortable in recent times.

4 Read paragraphs 5–7. Write a sentence to summarize each paragraph.

5 The article you have just read refers to 'pressure, tight deadlines, and non-stop work'. However, in a recent survey, American workers admitted to spending an average of nearly two hours in every eight-hour workday calling friends, surfing the Internet, or running personal errands. Who should you believe?

Listening

6 🔊 1:12 Listen to four people being interviewed about their attitudes to IT. Which are for and which are against IT?

7 Listen again. Match each speaker with these opinions. Do you agree with their opinions? Why? Why not?

a   IT exploits workers and damages health.
b   IT helps organize our lives better.
c   IT causes more problems than it solves.
d   IT can become an addiction.

Discussion

8 To what extent do you agree with these statements?

1   The computer is the most important invention in the history of civilization.
2   A computer makes it possible to do tasks which were completely unnecessary before.
3   To make mistakes is human, but to really mess things up you need a computer.

Internet research

Search for the keywords *"smart dust"* to learn about an emerging technology. Discuss possible applications, and how they might change our lives.

THE IT FALLACY

1 In recent years, three forces – downsizing, globalization, and the need for speed – have combined to change the work environment. What used to be a comfortably busy routine has become a non-stop workshop in which most people feel they can never stop to take a breather.

2 The result of downsizing is a mad dash to cram more work into fewer people. If six people are doing the work that ten used to do, and at the same time are expected to meet or exceed previous budget and productivity targets, something has to give. To this pressure-cooker environment in which everyone is supposed to 'do more with less', we can add the globalization trend that has swept through corporate boardrooms. To the extent that global competitors have a lower cost structure – which many do because their labour costs are so much lower – US and European firms have yet another reason to keep budgets and headcounts lower. The final ingredient in this mix is fierce competition, which has resulted in the pressure to do everything faster.

3 One way that corporate leaders justify the quest for efficiency and speed is to point to the multibillion-dollar investments that have been made in IT equipment and services. The new PCs and corporate networks are supposed to boost productivity and profits, and will, in fact, allow their companies to 'do more with less.'

4 This is true. But another truth has become buried under the technology sales pitches. Achieving those gains will happen only after a significant initial investment in training and 'system integration' to make sure that all the pieces connect well with each other. Pouring thousands of PCs and miles of cables into a corporation is a great way to waste money unless the systems and processes that technology is meant to automate are overhauled. Unfortunately, this has all become somewhat irrelevant. The expectation is that more technology means more speed and more output per employee – and when those results don't always magically occur, the only way to produce them is to require people to work longer hours.

5 Oddly, the same thing happens even when the technology delivers as promised. Consider the case of presentation software such as Microsoft's PowerPoint, which has become a standard office tool. Before PowerPoint, a graphics presentation would have to be created by a graphic artist. With PowerPoint and its software cousins, just about anyone can sit down at a PC and, without much training or practice, produce an on-screen presentation or a slick set of slides, handouts or transparencies that look fully professional.

6 On one hand, this software actually is a productivity tool – it takes only hours to do what might have taken days previously, and the result is just as good, if not better. But it doesn't stop there. Now everyone sees how easy it is to use these programs, they are used more and more. Thus, a senior manager who wouldn't have considered asking an analyst to spend a couple of days working up a slide presentation using Stone Age technology, doesn't hesitate to direct the same analyst to prepare that presentation using the desktop PC and PowerPoint. The goal is for this analyst to save time by using the software; the likely outcome is that he or she spends more time on presentations and has less time available for other aspects of the job.

7 If you're starting to think that instead of working on a plan to cope with pressure, tight deadlines, and non-stop work, it's time to polish up your resume and look elsewhere, I'm afraid I have some bad news. The grass really isn't much greener anywhere else – or at least, not a whole lot greener.

2.2 Vocabulary Information systems and communication

Discussion

1 'Information is too valuable to be left to IT departments. In today's business world, every manager should be a computer specialist.' To what extent do you agree?

Comparisons

2 Decide whether these phrases indicate a small or a large difference.

a bit more expensive   a whole lot more expensive   considerably more expensive
far more expensive   marginally more expensive   infinitely more expensive
slightly more expensive   somewhat more expensive

3 Use expressions from 2 and appropriate adjectives to compare

a) two computers you have used.
b) two ways you communicate with your business contacts or your friends.
c) two software applications you have used.
d) two ways you use the Internet.
e) two printers you have used.
f) two electronic devices you would like to own.

4 Explain the difference between each pair of computing terms.

1 a server and a PC
2 a laptop and a palmtop
3 a suite and an application
4 a patch and a plug-in

5 a virus and a bug
6 a crash and a hard-disk failure
7 the Internet and an intranet
8 a workgroup and a workstation

IT terms

5 George Skopelitis is in charge of IT user support at First Northeast Bank. He's having a very busy time at the moment. Choose the correct verbs to complete the email he sent to his boss.

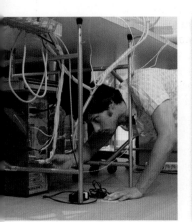

Delete Reply Reply All Forward New Mailboxes Get Mail   Search Mailbox

Maurice,
As you know, our IT resources are more and more stretched as we try to cope with an ageing system. We desperately need to (1) **advance/upgrade/promote** the operating system: software applications are (2) **crashing/ collapsing/falling** more and more frequently, and the server (3) **fell down/went down/dropped down** three times last week. There have also been several cases where important documents have been (4) **rubbed out/blanked/ deleted**. Of course I have (5) **inserted/installed/placed** patches and (6) **uploaded/downloaded/unzipped** new drivers wherever possible, but we can't go on like this. What's more, there's no time for new projects like (7) **setting up/fixing up/putting up** mobile Internet connections so that our sales teams can (8) **register/note/ enter** data on the system when they're on the road. We really need investment now!

6 Use the correct verbs from 5 to complete these sentences

1 Most PCs come complete with an office package, but sometimes you have to _____ it yourself.
2 On average, when a company's IT system _____ it takes ten days to fix everything.
3 IT users lack imagination. When asked to _____ a password, the most common choice is 'password'.
4 There are several programs which can rescue your data if you accidentally _____ files.
5 An incorrect memory address is the most common reason why PCs _____.
6 It only takes minutes to _____ a Webmail account that you can access from anywhere in the world.
7 One of the few remaining advantages of desktops is that it's easier to _____ components.
8 Research suggests that people who _____ illegal mp3s are also big spenders on legal music sites.

Listening

7 🔵 1:13 Listen to eight messages on George's voicemail. Match each speaker 1–8 with the problem they are experiencing a–h.

a) they can't install something
b) some computers need upgrading
c) they need to download a program
d) the whole system went down

e) they have to enter data quickly
f) their computer keeps crashing
g) a connection hasn't been set up
h) they deleted some files

Giving information

8 George has made notes on his messages, but his word processor has deleted the words in the box. Listen again and complete the notes with the missing words.

> back   in   informed   know   ring   loop   touch   an update

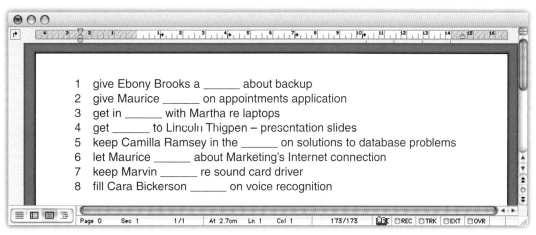

```
1   give Ebony Brooks a _____ about backup
2   give Maurice _____ on appointments application
3   get in _____ with Martha re laptops
4   get _____ to Lincoln Thigpen – presentation slides
5   keep Camilla Ramsey in the _____ on solutions to database problems
6   let Maurice _____ about Marketing's Internet connection
7   keep Marvin _____ re sound card driver
8   fill Cara Bickerson _____ on voice recognition
```

9 Replace the expressions in bold with expressions for giving information from 8.

1   Can I **give you an answer** later this morning? I'm in a meeting at the moment.
2   I'd appreciate it if you could **include me in the group of people you inform**.
3   We don't have a firm date for the meeting yet. We'll **tell you** as soon as we do.
4   While I'm away in the Far East, I'd like you to **give me regular progress reports** by email.
5   Before the meeting starts, can you just **give me some details** on what was said last time?
6   I just can't manage to **contact** her – I've tried everything: phone, fax, email, snail mail, even pigeon!
7   When you get back from your holiday, I'll **report** on what's been happening.
8   Could you **contact me by telephone** please? My email server's down at the moment.

Pairwork

10 With a partner, prioritize the tasks on George's 'to do' list for tomorrow – remember he's only supposed to work eight hours a day!

- CEO wants Web meeting available in all departments asap – need half a day.
- sound card drivers for Marvin (President's nephew!) – simple – half an hour?
- Cara re voice recognition – needs maybe an hour over lunch?
- CEO's assistant wants WiFi – but she only works at her desk! one hour or so.
- information from database vendors – a couple of hours; but probably no budget this year.
- abstract of presentation for New York conference – deadline is tomorrow! – one hour.
- fifteen new laptops needed – HP's special offer ends tomorrow – an hour or two?
- appointments application – two or three hours' work, but software update due in three weeks.
- Ebony Brooks re backup software – should take 30 minutes, but she's a slow learner!
- Marketing's Internet connection is down again – at least an hour and a half.

Internet **research**

Software, hardware, firmware, freeware, shareware, adware, spyware, malware, blogware ... . Use the *define:* function of your search engine to find definitions of these words (eg *define: malware*). How many more *-ware* words can you find?

2 | Information

Test yourself: comparing solutions

1 Complete the dialogues with words from the box.

as many	far more	half as	infinitely more	lot less	a lot
only half	fraction of	several times	twice as		

1. A: Cruxoe's software is really pricey; it's _____ expensive than Frydae's!
   B: Yes, but Frydae's applications don't have nearly _____ features.
2. C: My internet connection is 16 Mega – it's _____ faster than yours.
   D: Yes, mine is only 8 Mega; it's only _____ fast as yours.
3. E: Why don't you get a budget desktop? Just as fast, and _____ the price.
   F: Yes, it's true the big brands can be _____ expensive.
4. G: Why pay _____ as much for a laser printer when an inkjet will do the job?
   H: Well, maybe inkjets only cost a _____ the price, but it's the cartridges that really add up.
5. I: Why do you insist on buying PCs? They're a _____ reliable than Macs.
   J: Basically because there's _____ software available.

2 Use comparative or superlative forms of the words in the box to complete the quotations. You need to use some words more than once. Add *more*, *most*, *less*, or *least* where necessary.

bad	good	far	imaginative	honourable	useful	unlikely

1. There is only one thing in the world _____ than being talked about, and that is not being talked about. (Oscar Wilde)
2. Money is _____ than poverty, if only for financial reasons. (Woody Allen)
3. The man who goes _____ is generally the one who is willing to do and dare. The sure-thing boat never gets far from shore. (Dale Carnegie)
4. It has been said that democracy is the _____ form of government except all the others that have been tried. (Sir Winston Churchill)
5. Income tax returns are the _____ fiction being written today. (Herman Wouk)
6. You can go a long way with a smile. You can go a lot _____ with a smile and a gun. (Al Capone)
7. A life spent making mistakes is not only _____, but _____ than a life spent doing nothing. (George Bernard Shaw)
8. Nothing is impossible. Some things are just _____ than others. (Jonathan Winters)
9. The _____ ideas come as jokes. Make your thinking as funny as possible. (David Ogilvy)

Test yourself: getting help

3 Put the words in these requests in the correct order. The words in bold are already in the right place.

1. **How** computer do I on switch this?
2. **Will** off please printer that turn you?
3. **Can** you is me on/off switch tell the where?
4. **Do** you be in know meeting room the which will?
5. **Could** you tell attachment I me open should this what with?
6. **Would** you an sending mind email me just to address my test new?
7. **I** mind if you'd wonder my asking small a favour you?
8. **Do** you could know me think let you whether will not he attending or be?

Refresh your memory

Comparisons

half as	fast	
twice as	speedy	as
ten times as	rapid	

a lot	faster	
far	speedier	than
much	more rapid	

Superlatives

the fastest
the speediest
the most rapid

▶ **Grammar and practice** pages 118

Comparing outcomes

4 Complete the article using a comparative phrase suggested by the prompts. The first two gaps are done for you.

Since 1965, Moore's law has observed that computer chips become _twice as powerful_ (powerful x 2) every 24 months. A similar formula, Kryder's law, says that hard disk space is only _half as expensive_ (1/2 expensive) as it was two years ago. Gordon Moore says his law is (1) _____ (+ beautiful) he had first realized: contrary to Murphy's law – anything that can go wrong, will – Moore's law means everything gets (2) _____ (+ good + good).

However, the picture is not (3) _____ (= positive) it once seemed. Yet another law, Wirth's law, states that software gets slower (4) _____ (+ rapidly) hardware gets faster! Moore's law also means that new products must be developed (5) _____ (+ quick + quick). Any product which is launched just two or three months late will be 10–15 per cent (6) _____ (+ slow), (7) _____ (+ bulky) or (8) _____ (– generous) in storage capacity than the competition.

Moreover, physical barriers like temperature make it almost impossible to run PCs at speeds (9) _____ (+ high) 5 GHz . It now makes sense to use more memory space to accelerate disk access, since space is becoming (10) _____ (– expensive) than computer processing speed.

5 Match the two halves of these quotations:

1. The nicer I am,
2. The more you chase money,
3. The more I want to get something done,
4. I'm a great believer in luck, and I find the harder I work,

a the more I have of it. (Thomas Jefferson)
b the less I call it work. (Richard Bach)
c the more people think I'm lying. (Andy Warhol)
d the harder it is to catch it. (Mike Tatum)

6 With a partner, complete these sentences to make your own quotations.

The older I get, the ...
The more money you earn, the ...
The harder you work, the ...
The more I ..., the ...
The ...er the ..., the ...

Dealing with requests

7 Cross out the inappropriate response to these requests for help, as in the example.

1. Will you get me a cup of coffee, please?
   a No I won't.
   b Yes, if I can have one of your biscuits.
   c Sorry, I've got too much to carry.
2. Can you tell me how to switch this projector on?
   a Yes, I can.
   b No idea, I'm afraid.
   c I'm sorry, I never use it myself.
3. Could you possibly get me a sandwich when you go out to the post office?
   a Yes, with pleasure.
   b Sure, if you could answer the phone while I'm out.
   c Yes, I could possibly.
4. I wonder if you could spare the time to make a few photocopies for me?
   a Yes, I would.
   b I don't see why not.
   c I should think so.
5. Would you mind giving me a hand with this table? It's rather heavy.
   a No problem.
   b Yes.
   c Not at all.

Internet research

Search for the keywords *"Murphy's computer laws"*: hold a class opinion poll to find your three favourite laws.

Negotiating

8 Work with a partner to practise asking for help. Write a list of five things you need to do tomorrow, then negotiate to delegate the ones you don't want to do to your partner.

Discussion

1 Decide how far you agree with these statements about telephoning. Write *I agree, It depends,* or *I disagree.*

1 It's important to have a few moments of small talk before getting down to business.
2 You can never be too polite on the telephone.
3 It's much easier to say 'yes' than to say 'no'.
4 When you can't help someone, it's better to say 'no' directly than to make up excuses.
5 The caller decides when to end the call; the receiver should wait for the caller's signal.

2 Discuss your answers to 1 with a partner. Do you think it's different in other parts of the world?

Listening

3 🔊 1:14–1:17 Listen to four telephone conversations and answer the questions below.

a Which one is polite, informal, impolite or too polite?
b In which conversation are the speakers friends, acquaintances, colleagues from different departments or managers in a large company?

4 Listen again and answer the questions.

1 What does each caller want?
2 Why can't the other speakers help?
3 Which two conversations include some small talk? What do they talk about?

5 Complete these expressions from the recordings. Then listen again to check your answers.

Conversation 1
1 I _____ you to give me ...
2 I'd _____ to _____ you, but ...

Conversation 2
3 Have you got a _____ of minutes?
4 Do you _____ to know how to ...?
5 I _____ I could help you, but ...
6 Anyway, I won't _____ you any longer,

Conversation 3
7 I was wondering if I could ask you a _____ .
8 Do you think you could _____ send me ...?
9 Normally I'd be _____ to help, but ...
10 I mustn't _____ _____ any more of your time.

Conversation 4
11 Any _____ I could ...?
12 The _____ is, ...
13 Anyway, I'd better _____ _____ .

Internet research

Search for the keywords *conference call etiquette*, *video phone etiquette*, *cell phone etiquette*, and *voicemail etiquette* to find tips for using new phone technologies. In small groups, decide on your top three tips for each category.

6 The four categories below relate to stages in the conversations. Decide how the expressions in 5 are used and add them to the lists. The first two are done for you.

Checking the other person can speak now: …
Requesting help: *1*, …
Refusing help: *2*, …
Ending the call: …

7 Complete these dialogues with suitable expressions, then practise them with a partner.

Alex	
Billie	Oh, hello Alex. How's it going?
Alex	
Billie	No problem. I was just going to have a break anyway.
Alex	
Billie	Well, I'm sorry to disappoint you, but I don't know much about it actually.
Alex	
Billie	OK. But just let me know if there's anything I can do.
Alex	
Billie	OK, bye.

Chris	Hello, it's Chris here. I'm not disturbing you, am I?
Dee	
Chris	I'm just calling to ask if you'd mind doing me a favour, actually.
Dee	
Chris	Well, do you think I could possibly borrow your copy of Office 2007? I need to re-install it, and I can't find mine.
Dee	
Chris	Oh I see. Well, never mind, I thought I'd ask just in case. Anyway, I won't keep you from your work. Thanks.
Dee	

Erin	Hi. It's me. Sorry to bother you. You wouldn't happen to have the new IP address, would you?
Frankie	
Erin	Brilliant. Thanks a million.
Frankie	
Erin	OK then, I'll let you get back to work. Thanks a lot. Bye.

Role-play

8 With a partner, practise role-playing different telephone situations. Remember to use suitable formal/polite or direct/informal language, and to include small talk as appropriate. Student A should look at page 111, Student B should look at page 112.

2 | Information

Discussion

1 First Northeast Bank has realized that many members of staff just ignore memos. Think of some reasons why memos often get ignored.

Reading

2 Read the recommendations on memo style. Then answer the quiz that First Northeast sent to all their managers. Choose the option which best matches the style recommendations.

FIRST *Northeast Bank*

Writing memos

1 Personalize your memos: use *I*, *you*, *we* to make people feel directly concerned.
2 Use active rather than passive verbs for a more conversational, reader-friendly style.
3 Prefer verbs to nouns, and avoid jargon and technical terms; write sentences which 'your grandmother would understand.'
4 Make it clear and unambiguous what you want people to do and when.
5 Focus on the benefits to the reader, not on rigid rules or procedures.

Quiz

1 A memo is **a document that you send to people inside the company.**
   a method of documentary communication for internal use.
2 The objective of a memo is **to solicit decisions and policy or behavioural changes.**
   to get people to do something.
3 In the past, we wrote memos on paper: now **we often send them by email.**
   electronic transmission has been widely adopted.
4 To write a good memo you need **careful forethought, layout and revision.**
   to plan, organize and edit your ideas carefully.
5 A good memo **tells you clearly what you have to do and when you have to do it.**
   is one in which both the desired outcome and the target time frame are specified.
6 The purpose of this quiz is **to ensure that the principal rules of memo-writing are respected.**
   to help you write effective memos.

3 Read the suggested format for memos. The paragraphs in the memo below are not in the correct order. Number the paragraphs from 1–4.

Format for memos
1 Define the problem.
2 Tell the reader why they should feel concerned.
3 Say what result you want to get.
4 Say what you want the reader to do and when.

VAN DER HEYDEN B.V.

Subject: Unauthorized software

☐ I would like us all to carry out this check by 15 September latest. Please examine your laptop carefully, and delete any unauthorized software. If you need help, I will be available every afternoon between 1 and 5 p.m. Thank you for helping to protect our colleagues, our jobs and our company.

☐ If inspectors find unauthorized copyright material on our systems, individual users, management and the company itself can face heavy fines and even criminal prosecution. It is in everybody's interest to avoid this risk.

☐ As you probably know, the European Commission is stepping up its fight against software piracy, and we expect to see systematic inspections of medium-sized companies like ours in the next six months.

☐ This is the reason why I'm asking every employee in the company to check that there is no unauthorized software on their computer. This could include unlicensed copies of business software, shareware programmes downloaded from the Internet, and even mp3 music files.

4 Match the examples of officialese 1–10 with the more user-friendly versions a–j.

1	it is recognized	a)	difficulty
2	with a view to alleviating	b)	immediately
3	adjacent to	c)	there's not enough
4	it is imperative	d)	if there was
5	it is inadequate	e)	next to
6	staff are reminded	f)	please remember
7	area of concern	g)	we must
8	in the event of	h)	thank you for ...
9	forthwith	i)	to solve
10	... is appreciated	j)	we realize

Writing a memo

5 With a partner, rewrite this memo in a more user-friendly style.

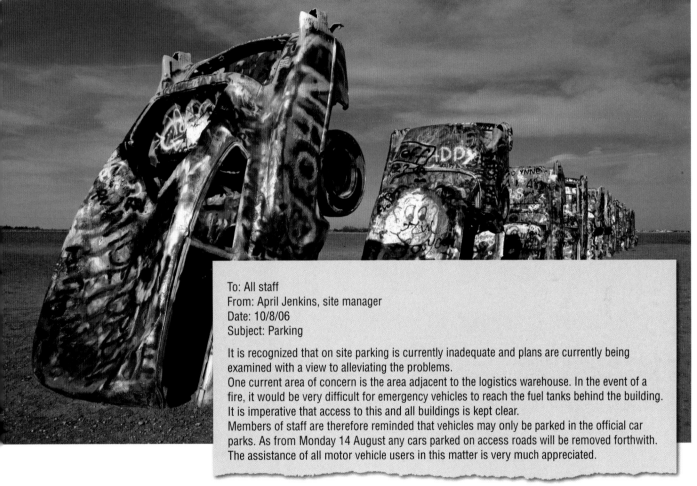

To: All staff
From: April Jenkins, site manager
Date: 10/8/06
Subject: Parking

It is recognized that on site parking is currently inadequate and plans are currently being examined with a view to alleviating the problems.
One current area of concern is the area adjacent to the logistics warehouse. In the event of a fire, it would be very difficult for emergency vehicles to reach the fuel tanks behind the building. It is imperative that access to this and all buildings is kept clear.
Members of staff are therefore reminded that vehicles may only be parked in the official car parks. As from Monday 14 August any cars parked on access roads will be removed forthwith. The assistance of all motor vehicle users in this matter is very much appreciated.

Listening and writing

6 🔊 1:18 Listen to a voicemail message from your manager and write the memo he refers to.

Writing

7 Work with a partner. Your top management have asked you to make a proposal for the company's three-day international IT conference. Think about these questions.

a Why is an IT conference important to an international company?
b What objectives do you think management want to achieve?
c What are the ingredients of a successful conference?

8 Write a memo proposing dates, a location, and a programme for the IT conference. You will also need to get approval for your budget. (Last year's budget was $700 per person.)

9 Read all the memos and vote for the best proposal.

2.6 Case study Meteor Bank

Discussion

1 When experienced staff leave a company, what are the consequences? Decide whether these possible results are *likely* or *unlikely*.

> more mistakes   younger, more dynamic teams   increased productivity
> improved customer service   better promotion prospects   more overtime
> higher training costs   higher salary costs   better morale

Reading

2 Read the newspaper clipping. What possible reasons can you think of to explain why experienced staff have been leaving Meteor's IT department?

Rising Star promises to make sparks fly

YOUNG Londoner Saul Finlay has been appointed IT Manager at Meteor Bank. Thanks to an aggressive commercial policy, the Nigerian bank is growing rapidly all over West Africa, especially through its subsidiaries in Ivory Coast, Ghana, and Cameroon. Together with the rising demand for electronic banking services, rapid growth is putting increasing pressure on the bank's IT department in Lagos. In an interview yesterday, Finlay promised to 'drag the IT department kicking and screaming into the twenty-first century.' When asked if ...

3 Read the memo and answer the questions:

Meteor Bank

To: Astrid Kuhn, Managing Director
From: Joseph Ikpeba, Operations Manager.
Subject: IT policy

Our system downtime problems are going from bad to worse (see attached figures) and we are beginning to lose corporate clients. The problem appears to be the result of exceptionally high staff turnover in the IT department. Half of our systems administrators are new graduates with less than one year's experience, and Saul Finley is recruiting again for the third time in six months.

I'm afraid I have to remind you that both downtime and staff turnover were very minor problems before Saul arrived in 2005. Saul's answer is that he needs investment in even more new hardware. However, I am not sure that this is the solution; I feel strongly that we should investigate further, not least because some staff have implied that the system failures might be deliberate.

Could I possibly ask you to speak to some of the people involved, and to hold an executive committee meeting as soon as possible to decide how to deal with these problems?

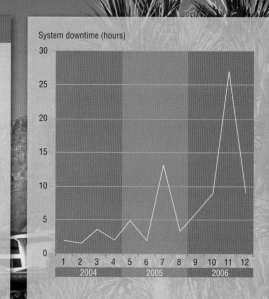

System downtime (hours)

IT Turnover	2004	2005	2006
Total IT staff	64	68	78
New hires	7 (11 %)	19 (28 %)	31 (40 %)
Retirements	4 (6.3 %)	5 (7.3 %)	6 (7.6 %)
Departures	3 (4.7 %)	10 (14.7 %)	15 (19.2 %)

1 Who wrote the memo and why?
2 What does he want?
3 What has changed at Meteor Bank since 2005?
4 What reasons can you suggest for the trends in the figures?

4 🔊 1:19–1:22 Astrid Kuhn decided to investigate. Listen to the reactions she received when she spoke to four members of staff, and complete the notes.

Tonye Ameobi   Vincent Bonvalet   Kehinde Ojukwu   Joseph Ikpeba

	Tonye Ameobi HR Manager, Lagos	Vincent Bonvalet IT manager, Ivory Coast	Kehinde Ojukwu Senior systems administrator, IT department, Lagos	Joseph Ikpeba Operations Manager
opinion of Saul				
mistakes				
successes				
solutions recommended				

Discussion

5 To what extent do you feel Saul Finley is to blame for Meteor's problems?

6 Work in groups of three or four. Student A turn to page 110. Student B turn to page 112. Student C turn to page 114.
If there is a fourth student, they should be the chairperson. Discuss the agenda below and draw up an action plan for Astrid Kuhn.

Executive Committee Meeting

1 How can we reduce staff turnover?
2 How can we reduce system downtime?
3 How should we react to accusations of malicious damage in the IT department?
4 Should we agree to S Finley's request for investment in IT equipment in Lagos, or invest in improving our IT network in our foreign subsidiaries?
5 Should we consider outsourcing IT?
6 How should we evaluate S Finley's performance, and what action is needed, if any?

Review 1

Building a career

1 Complete the text about going to University. Definitions are given in brackets to help you.

At high school you might take an ¹apt_____e test (test of your ability) and have a chance to go to university. How do you choose the university? Perhaps by the quality and reputation of the ²f_____ty (all the teachers); perhaps because you were persuaded by one of the ³al_____i (previous students); or perhaps by the sports and social ⁴f_____ies (rooms, equipment and services). Then, having chosen, you will be just one of many thousands of ⁵a_____nts (people who have formally asked for a place). Hopefully, you will be successful and you will ⁶sh_____ u_____ (phrasal verb: arrive in a place where people are expecting you) with everyone else on the first day.

2 Make expressions by matching the beginnings and endings of each phrase.

1 acquire skills which will serve you ...   ☐ a
2 boost future ...   ☐
3 don't miss out on ...   ☐
4 have checks and balances ...   ☐
5 go to enormous lengths ...   ☐
6 improve employability ...   ☐
7 interview and short-list ...   ☐
8 obtain practical experience that will ...   ☐
9 rate applicants on a scale ...   ☐
10 send a ...   ☐

a a lifetime
b a wonderful opportunity to gain knowledge
c candidates
d earnings
e by going to business school
f in a process
g of one to six
h mailshot
i to do something
j enhance your CV

3 Complete the sentences with the words below.

assignment	chair	dismissed	draw up	exceed
laid off	implement	meet	present	recruit
sabbatical	train			

1 After you _____ new sales reps you have to _____ them.
2 It's good if you can _____ your sales objectives, but it's even better if you can _____ them.
3 It's not enough just to _____ a few proposals on paper, you've actually got to _____ the plans.
4 When you become more experienced you might have to _____ working parties and even _____ new programmes to the Board.
5 If you lost your job because of the company's problems, you were _____ , but if you did something wrong then you were _____ .
6 If you are working in another geographical place, you are on _____ ; if you are not working because you want to study or write then you are on _____ .

4 In each sentence, put one verb into the past simple (*did*), one into the past continuous (*was/were doing*), and one into the past perfect (*had done*).

1 I _____ (find out) the other day that Pierre from the sales department has been dismissed. I _____ (wonder) why I _____ (not/see) him for a while.
2 I _____ (just/finish) working on the spreadsheet when the computer _____ (crash). I can't explain it – I _____ (not/do) anything unusual with the program.

5 Put each verb into the most likely form. You might need an auxiliary like *will* or *would*. Use contractions.

A: If I (1) _____ (see) Anita, I (2) _____ (tell) her about the job vacancy as well.
B: But Anita's on vacation, trekking in the Himalayas. If you (3) _____ (see) her, it (4) _____ (be) very surprising!
A: Anita? Trekking in the Himalayas? Now that really is surprising. If Anita (5) _____ (go) on vacation she usually (6) _____ (go) to the beach.

6 Fill in the missing letters in these linking words.

Introducing a point
1 As re_ _ _ _ds ... / As _ _ _ as ... is con_ _ _ _ed
Seeing both sides
2 On the wh_ _ _ _..., how_ _ _ _ ... / It's true that ..., but _ _ the o_ _ _ _ h_ _ _ ...
Combining reasons
3 Not o_ _ _ ..., but a_ _ _ ... / For o_ _ th_ _ _ ..., and for an_ _ _ _ _ ...
Adding ideas
4 Bes_ _ _ _, ... / In add_ _ _ _ _, ...

7 Use **one** expression from **each** of the categories in exercise 6 to complete this text. Remember that one expression might have two parts.

I've lived in the same town all my life. My family and friends are here, and it's calm and peaceful. (1) _____ , there's a good sense of community and I'm happy. But I am starting to wonder about my career. (2) _____ it's a small town and there aren't many interesting jobs, _____ I want to develop my language skills and work in an international environment. (3) _____ salary _____ , that's not so important right now – experience is more important. So I don't know what to do. (4) _____ I think the best thing is just to wait and see what jobs are available locally – _____ , if I see a really interesting job advertised in another area, then I'll apply for it and see what happens.

8 Put the action verbs in the box into the sentences from different cover letters.

broke	developed	doubled	enhanced	supported

1 I _____ previous sales records.
2 I more than _____ average revenues per nightclub.
3 I _____ a range of new products for teenage customers.
4 I _____ myself financially by working in radio advertising sales.
5 These part-time jobs _____ my formal education.

Review 2

1 Make expressions by matching each verb to a phrase a–f below.

1 Meet ☐   3 Make ☐   5 Waste ☐
2 Keep ☐   4 Boost ☐   6 Take ☐

a ... a multibillion-dollar investment in IT equipment and services
b ... or exceed budget and productivity targets
c ... only hours to do what might have taken days previously
d ... productivity and profits
e ... budgets and headcounts low because of global competitors
f ... money by investing in IT without at the same time overhauling the business processes it is meant to automate

2 Underline the correct words in **bold**.

1 Another word for a PDA (personal digital assistant) is a **laptop/palmtop**.
2 A short set of commands to correct a bug in a computer program is called a **patch/plug-in**.
3 If you get a better and more recent version of some software (or hardware), you **promote/upgrade** it.
4 A collection of PCs and servers all connected together on a local area network is called a **workgroup/workstation**.
5 If a server stops working for a time you say that it **went down/fell down**.
6 If you load and configure a new piece of software on your computer, you **insert/install** it.
7 To keep your computer programs up-to-date you have to frequently **download/offload** patches and new versions.
8 If you make some new technology ready for use (for the first time), you **set it up/fix it up**.

3 Match the beginnings and endings of the phrases.

a fill   in touch with someone
b get   someone an update
c get   someone in on something
d give   someone know about something
e give   back to someone about something
f let   someone a ring (= call)

4 Match each expression in exercise 3 to the best definition below. Be careful – some are very similar.

1 tell someone about things that have happened recently ☐
2 give someone the most recent information ☐
3 tell someone something ☐
4 speak or write to someone, especially after you have not spoken to them for a long time ☐
5 contact someone by telephone ☐
6 give someone an answer at a later time ☐

5 Correct the mistake in each sentence.

1 X's software is far more expensive as Y's.
2 Y's software doesn't have nearly as many features than X's.
3 My internet connection is lot faster than yours.
4 My internet connection is only halve as fast as yours.
5 Big brands can be double as dear.
6 Ink jet printers cost a fractal of the price of laser printers.
7 Why buy a PC? They're a lot fewer reliable than Macs.
8 There's infinity more software for PCs.
9 I think Yahoo is a worser search engine than Google.
10 Yes, but have you tried the Microsoft Live search engine? It really is the worsest.

6 Put the requests below in order, from 1 (the most informal and direct) to 6 (the most polite and indirect).

1 ☐   2 ☐   3 ☐   4 ☐   5 ☐   6 ☐

a Could you give me a hand?
b Give me a hand!
c Will you give me a hand, please?
d Do you think you could give me a hand?
e I wonder if you could just give me a hand for a moment?
f Would you mind giving me a hand?

(Note: your answer may not be the same as the in the Key, but it should be similar; it also depends on your voice)

7 Fill in the missing letters to make expressions used in telephoning.

1 I was w_ _ _ _ing if I could a_ _ you a fa_ _ _r?
2 Anyway, I won't k_ _ _ you any l_ _ _ _r.
3 I'm not dist_ _ _ing you, am I?
4 Is t_ _ _ _ any ch_ _ _ _ I could ...?
5 Do you ha_ _ _n to know if ...?
6 Have you g_ _ a co_ _ _ _e of minutes?
7 I mustn't t_ _ _ up any m_ _ _ of y_ _ _ t_ _ _.
8 Is this a g_ _ _ t_ _ _ to c_ _ _?

8 Match the expressions in exercise 7 to the uses below.

a) checking the other person can speak now ☐☐☐
b) requesting help ☐☐☐
c) ending the call ☐☐☐

9 Rewrite this memo using the more user-friendly language in the box.

> know   need   if there was   issue   please
> regularly   remember   thank you for

As you (1) are aware, government regulations state that fire drills have to be carried out (2) on a regular basis. This is a particular (3) area of concern for us following the minor incident in the factory last month. Clearly, (4) in the event of another fire we would have to pay significantly more for our insurance cover.

We are planning to have regular drills from now on. (5) I would be grateful if you could make sure that all staff in your section know exactly what procedures to follow when they hear the alarm. (6) You are reminded that these drills will be held at random times and without your previous knowledge.

If you (7) require any further information, please do not hesitate to contact me.

Your cooperation (8) is appreciated.

3 | Quality

3.1 About business   What quality means

Discussion

1 The list below gives factors that influence decisions to buy. Number each factor 1–7 depending on how important they are to you. (1 = most important; 7 = least important).

> price   design   value for money   quality
> modernity   durability   environmental friendliness

2 Compare your answers with another student. Describe how the order would change if you were buying the products in the pictures.

Scan reading

3 Read the article opposite. Match the headings a–h with the paragraphs numbered 1–7. There is one heading you do not need.

a) No survival without quality
b) Reliability is not enough
c) Quality and cost
d) Quality culture

e) Superficial quality
f) Quality in design
g) Closing the gap?
h) Quality for quality's sake

Reading for detail

4 Read the article again and decide if these statements are T (true) or F (false).

1 Western companies have caught up with the Japanese in terms of quality.
2 The Japanese expect things to work properly.
3 Producing reliable products guarantees a stong market position.
4 For a quality program to succeed, senior management do not need to understand the key concepts.
5 Quality analysis is a sensible way to solve any performance problems.
6 The iPod is not the only Apple product which has enchanting quality.

5 Find words or expressions in the text with the following meanings. The number of the paragraph is given.

a) something which suddenly becomes very popular (paragraph 1)
b) try hard to do something difficult (paragraph 1)
c) expect something to be there as normal (paragraph 2)
d) a variety of objects or things (paragraph 3)
e) mistakes you should avoid (paragraph 4)
f) things which are fashionable for a short time (paragraph 4)
g) to make something unsuccessul or unpleasant (paragraph 5)
h) something surprising or impressive (paragraph 6)

Listening

6 🔊 1:23 Industry analyst, Warwick Fender, is speaking about quality in the household electrical goods sector. What products do you think he will talk about? Listen and check your answer.

7 Listen again and answer the questions.

1 The white goods industry has been accused of designing products to last _____ .
2 Consumers today expect to _____ electrical goods more often.
3 Repairing products is expensive due to the cost of _____ and _____ .
4 Ethical consumers are reassured that it is increasingly possible to _____ products.

Discussion

8 Work in small groups. Look at the products in the pictures again. Do they have taken-for-granted quality or enchanting quality, or both? Are any of them designed with planned obsolescence in mind? Present a short summary of your group's ideas to the other groups.

Two kinds OF QUALITY

As I write this, I'm travelling on a plane. The executive sitting next to me has carefully unpacked his Bose headphones and iPod Nano. Both these products have associations with quality, a concept which can be misunderstood but which is of great importance to success in business. The Japanese actually have two words for quality, and an understanding of each is necessary to compete today.

1

Quality remains an elusive target for many Western companies, even though the craze for quality has been around for some twenty years. Yes, progress has been made. In 1980 the average car produced by Ford had twice as many product flaws as the average Japanese car. By 1986, the Japanese auto industry lead over Ford had shrunk from 100 per cent to about 20 per cent, as Ford made quality its number one priority. But since that impressive burst of progress, many companies have struggled to keep up on quality, even as the Japanese began building more of their products in the West with local workers.

2

The truth is, the Japanese have an unfair advantage. Japanese culture intrinsically values quality and appreciates the small details. In fact, the Japanese expression for quality is *atarimae hinshitsu*, which can be roughly translated as 'taken-for-granted quality'. What do the Japanese take for granted when it comes to quality? They take for granted that things should work as they are supposed to, and they even see an elegance to things working properly, whether it's cars, subway schedules, traditional flower arranging or the famous tea ceremony.

3

Japanese manufacturers became so obsessed with taken-for-granted quality that they created a stream of innovations that built on the concepts of Ed Deming,

the renowned quality-management consultant. Their innovations included lean manufacturing, just-in-time industry, and design for quality. In today's competitive markets, manufacturers need to make quick progress towards this kind of quality. If they don't, you can take for granted that they will go out of business. This is true even for small, entrepreneurial companies. The ability to create products and services that work is no longer a source of long-term competitive advantage. It has become just the price of admission to most markets. If the stuff your competitors make works better, your customers aren't going to be customers for long.

4

Though much improved, our quality record still isn't what it might be. Here are two traps I've seen a lot of companies fall into on the road to quality. One is, faking a commitment. There's no way around it. Whether you're adopting total quality management (TQM), or other quality schemes, these techniques require everyone in a company to learn how to think and work differently. Too many senior executives adopt the latest fads as they come and go, without taking the time to learn what these processes are and how they work. They leave the detail of quality to the folks below them: a sure way to have a quality program fail.

5

At the other extreme, some companies become so quality-process obsessed that quality-management techniques cease

to be a tool to improve the company's performance and instead become an end in themselves. Statistical analysis should be used for questions for which a company doesn't readily have an answer. Instead, organizations sometimes go through long analytical processes for problems that a little common sense could have solved. And nothing sours an organization on quality faster than meaningless work.

6

That brings us to the second of the two Japanese expressions for quality: *miryoku teki hinshitsu*, which means 'enchanting quality'. This kind of quality appeals not to customer expectations about reliability – that things should do what they're supposed to – but rather to a person's aesthetic sense of beauty and elegance. That's what I think Apple Computer got right with the iPod and its many offspring. The nano belonging to the man sitting next to me is a marvel, not just of miniaturization, but of rounded edges in a world of sharp corners.

7

And as I put on my own Bose headphones, I realize how much I appreciate being able to retreat to my Zen space amid the rumble of the aircraft engines, rattling serving carts, and chattering passengers. If these products didn't work properly when you turned them on, nobody would buy them. They would lack *atarimae hinshitsu*. But with the hungry competitors in most markets today, taken-for-granted quality by itself may not get the job done.

3 | Quality

Discussion

1 Work in small groups. Discuss which of these definitions best defines your idea of quality and why.

> Quality means delivering products or services to customers faster, better and cheaper.
> Quality is the correct application of procedures and standards.
> Quality means meeting the customer's needs and expectations.
> Quality means that goods are not defective or damaged.
> Quality is designing and producing reliable products that do what they're supposed to do.
> Quality is in the eye of the beholder.

Reading

2 Read the article which describes five stakeholders with different ideas of quality. Match each stakeholder with a definition above.

Quality is in the eye of the stakeholder

If a product or service lacks quality, most people would agree that it is substandard in some way. Perhaps the workmanship is shoddy, the packaging is flimsy, or the service unreliable. But defining quality from a business perspective is less simple.

- **The marketing manager**, who is responsible for evaluating consumer research, market conditions and competitor data, sees quality very much in terms of customer expectations and customer satisfaction.
- To **the design engineer**, who designs products or components to tight specifications and strict tolerances, quality has more to do with whether the design is fit for purpose and whether the product or part performs its intended function. Colour changes or deluxe models are secondary considerations.
- **The process engineer** employs lean manufacturing techniques to ensure that products are produced with the minimum waste of effort, money, time, space, and materials. So quality involves what the Japanese call *Kaizen* (continuous improvement), and doing things right first time (RFT).
- Internal or external **quality auditors** verify compliance with standards such as ISO 9001. Quality means that recorded procedures are in place, and being applied and respected.
- And finally, **the end-user**. Whether they want something cheap, heavy-duty, or disposable, they won't buy it in the first place if it is scratched, cracked, or flawed in any way!

Listening

3 🔊 1:24 Listen to three people talking about quality. Decide which type of stakeholder each speaker represents.

Wordbuilding

4 Use the correct form of the words in brackets to complete the sentences. Check your answer in the article in 2.

1 Internal _____ carry out checks every year to ensure ISO standards are maintained. (audit)
2 Exacting technical _____ mean that this machine will give many years service. (specify)
3 The components are machined to _____ of less than one millimetre. (tolerate)
4 Cheap copies of branded goods are often _____ . (standard)
5 They changed their provider because the service was _____ . (rely)
6 Adopting the RFT guidelines has led to an immediate _____ in product quality. (improve)
7 Our quality controllers make sure that we reach full _____ with ISO 9001. (comply)
8 Reports of strong customer _____ indicate that our production routines are effective. (satisfy)

Speaking

5 Work with a partner. Decide whether these adjectives refer to quality positively (+), negatively (–) or both (+/–). Use a dictionary to help you decide.

> tough   fragile   durable   reliable   shoddy   disposable   flawed   cracked
> poorly-designed   heavy-duty   flimsy   scratched

6 Tell you partner about a product you bought that you are either very pleased or very dissatisfied with. Use the adjectives to explain why.

Collocations

7 Match words 1–10 with a–j to form some common collocations in the field of quality standards.

1 best	a) requirements
2 customer	b) expectations
3 statutory	c) fault
4 design	d) improvement
5 continuous	e) practice
6 resource	f) objectives
7 industry	g) assurance
8 quality	h) specifications
9 measurable	i) management
10 technical	j) standard

8 Match the collocations in 7 with their meanings below.

1   how the materials, investment or labour to produce a product or a service are managed
2   a flaw in a product which is due to it being poorly designed
3   the qualities the end-user believes the product or service should have
4   what the Japanese call *Kaizen*, constantly improving the product and process
5   the precise guidelines which establish how the product should be built
6   the accepted norm in a particular field of business
7   defined targets established to measure improvements in quality
8   compulsory rules imposed by the government
9   the most suitable or efficient way of doing something
10   the system put in place to ensure that quality targets are met

Speaking

9 Work in small groups. You are the product development team responsible for developing one of the following products: a disposable plate, a dishwasher, a supermarket bag, a mobile phone, a car tyre, or your own idea. Choose a product and define what level of quality you want to achieve. Think about the following points.

- the quality of the final product for the user
- the quality of the materials you will use
- how long you intend the product to last
- whether you want to have a high or low profit margin
- whether you intend it to be an upmarket or a cheap product

10 Take turns to present your product concept to the other groups. Be prepared to answer questions and explain your strategy. Vote for the best product concept.

Internet research

Search for the keywords "W Edwards Deming". Who was he and what role did he play in the quality movement? Summarize your findings and report back to the class.

3.3 Grammar   Passive structures and *have something done*

Test yourself: passive structures, affirmatives and negatives

1 Complete the following conversation using the correct form of the verbs in brackets.

Sven	Hi, Juliana. What brings you to the coffee machine so early in the morning?
Juliana	Oh, hello Sven. Thought I'd grab a quick break. I wanted to make some copies, but the photocopier (1) _____ (service).
Sven	Again! It (2) _____ (service) every week! Last Tuesday, I had a ton of copies to make and it (3) _____ (repair). I know it (4) _____ already _____ (check) this week and I'm sure it (5) _____ (mend) again next week! What's the matter with it?
Juliana	Well, remember, when the old one (6) _____ (replace) they said it (7) _____ (use) properly: that people hadn't been following the instructions.
Sven	Yeah, I know. But, at least the old one didn't have to (8) _____ (dismantle) every week. And it was easy to use. This one's too complicated and we've had nothing but hassle with it since it (9) _____ (install)! The real problem is that we (10) _____ (train) to operate it, have we?
Juliana	You're right, Sven, but I've heard that some training (11) _____ (organize) at the moment. So, look on the bright side!
Sven	I guess so, Juliana. Anyway, let me get you a coffee.
Juliana	I'm afraid you can't. The machine's out of order! I was just going to check when it (12) _____ last _____ (service)!

Test yourself: passive questions

2 Write questions for the short answers. Use the prompts given.

Example
coffee machine/repair? – No, not yet.
Has the coffee machine been repaired?

1 photocopier/service/at the moment? – Yes it is.
2 it/repair/last Tuesday? – Yes, it was.
3 Do you think/it/mend by next week? – Most probably, yes.
4 When/the old one/replace? – Three months ago.
5 it/use/correctly? – No, it hadn't.
6 you/train/to operate it? – No, we haven't.
7 some training/organize/at the moment? – Yes, it is.
8 When/it/last/service? – Last month.

Test yourself: passive modals

3 Make these active sentences passive.

1 The maintenance people should fix it!
2 You could rewrite the procedure.
3 We must have made a mistake.
4 You might have informed me!
5 I can't have deleted it!

Test yourself: *to have something done*

4 Match the three sentences 1–3 with the appropriate explanation a–c.

1	I mended the car.	a)	Somebody mended the car.
2	The car was mended.	b)	I asked somebody to mend the car.
3	I had the car mended.	c)	I did the action myself.

Refresh your memory

Passive
be + past participle.
Will I be met at the airport?
They could have been delayed.
I've just been sacked (by the sales manager).
Passives can be less personal, perhaps to avoid blame.
Will the report be finished on time? instead of *Will you finish the report on time?*

have something done
Expresses an arrangement for a different person to do something for us.
I normally have my suit dry-cleaned every week.

▶ Grammar and practice pages 120–121

Listening

5 ♪ 1:25 Fuelflo manufactures fuel systems for civil and military aircraft. Recently, a customer, Airbridge, has complained of a problem with fuel pumps. Listen and match the company departments concerned with the problems.

Production   Sales   Stock   Logistics

1 _____ put the wrong fitting on the pumps.
2 _____ didn't give Production enough warning.
3 _____ sent two different parts together at the last minute.
4 _____ didn't spot the difference.
5 _____ decided to reduce stock movements.
6 _____ sent a delivery late.

6 Rewrite the notes above using the passive to make the comments sound less personal and less aggressive.

Example
1 The wrong fitting was put on the pumps.

7 At the end of the meeting, they made plans to solve the problem. Rewrite each of sentences 1–6 using the words given, and using the passive or *have something done*.

1 In future, we will arrange for the parts to be delivered separately.
   In future, we will have _____ .
2 We will ask Airbridge for earlier warnings of any changes.
   Airbridge will _____ .
3 Birgit will get someone to check the parts.
   Birgit will have _____ .
4 Somebody must brief the Stock Department.
   The Stock Department _____ .
5 We will give Airbridge a discount on their next order.
   Airbridge _____ .
6 An independent auditor will check the procedures.
   We will have _____ .

Role-play

8 Work with a partner. You both work for a company producing soft drinks. Recently, some consumers have complained of a strange taste in a small number of bottles and some have had to be recalled. It is summer time and your bottling plant is working round-the-clock to meet demand.

Student A is an internal quality auditor. Your job is to identify and solve the problem by asking tactful questions. Turn to page 111.
Student B is the Nightshift Supervisor. Try to avoid taking the blame, using the passive where necessary. Turn to page 112.

9 When you have identified the probable cause of contamination, work in small groups to define what corrective action should be taken. Compare your solution with another group.

Internet research

Search for the keywords "*bottle contamination recall*" to discover how some real contamination cases happened and the consequences for the companies involved. Report back to the class.

3 | Quality

Discussion

1 Work with a partner. Which factors do you think can make or break a presentation. Make a list of three 'make' factors and three 'break' factors, using the ideas below to help you.

> body language   visual aids   delivery   knowledge of the subject
> use of technical jargon   clear structure   length

Listening

2 🔘 1:26 Work with a partner. Listen to four brief extracts from presentations. Match each speaker with a presentation problem from the list below.

a Speed: too fast
b Inappropriate pauses
c Excessive jargon and acronyms
d Long sentences

e Incorrect vocabulary
f No checking to see if listeners are following
g Lack of signposting

3 Match the problems in 2 with solutions 1–7 below.

1 Using the correct word is important. Remember to use collocations and other common word combinations.
2 Keep sentences short. Your talk will be easier to follow and carry more impact.
3 Take time to check that your audience is following what you say.
4 Slow down. Pause. Give the audience time to think about what you are saying.
5 Learn and use key expressions to signal to your audience where you are in the talk.
6 Think about your listeners. Explain any jargon or acronyms they may not know.
7 Pauses in speech ... are like punctuation in writing. Use them ... to give more impact ... to what you are saying.

Predicting and listening

4 Work with a partner. Quality assurance engineer Marc Pinto is presenting the graph on the left. What do you think it represents? What do you expect he will say about it?

5 🔘 1:27 Listen to Marc's presentation and check whether your predictions were correct.

6 Listen again and decide how well Marc presents his information using the ideas in 2 and 3 to help you.

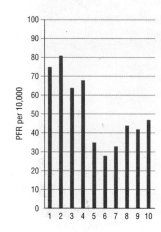

Signposting

7 Signposting presentations can help the listener. Listen to Marc's presentation again. Complete the signposting expressions which he uses.

Referring to graphics
This graph (1) _____ the ...
(2) _____ you can see, ...

Digressing
Just to digress a moment ...
By the (3) _____, ...

Restating/reformulating
In other (4) _____, ...
What I mean is ...

Emphasizing
And (5) _____, that's why ...
I must emphasize that ...

Checking understanding
Is that (6) _____ so far?
Does that make sense?

Ending one point
I think that (7) _____ ...
That's all I want to say about ...

Moving on
So, now let's turn to ...
Now, I'd like to (8) _____ at ...
Anyway, ...

Presentation

8 You are committee members of your company's sports and social club. You have allocated a budget of £450 to spend on one of the three items below. Work in three groups, A, B and C, to prepare a short presentation of your item to persuade the committee to buy it. Use the presentation outline to help you, and prepare one or two slides to illustrate your talk.

A Dishwasher

Water consumption	16 l/load
Energy rating	A
Energy consumption	1.1 kWh
Capacity	12 place settings
Noise rating	45 dB
Price	£334

B Washing machine

Water consumption	55 l/load
Energy rating	B
Energy consumption	1.3 kWh
Capacity	6 kg
Noise rating	52 dB
Price	£295

C Expresso coffee maker

Water consumption	0.4 l/4 cups
Energy rating	A
Energy consumption	1.25kWh
Capacity	4 cups/minute
Noise rating	N/A
Price	£423

Internet research

Search for the keywords "*presentation signposting*" and see how many other expressions you can find. Make a list of your five favourites and share them with the class.

Presentation outline:
Technical facts and figures
Advantages (and disadvantages?)
Why the product is a better choice than the other two
Conclusion

9 Take turns presenting your product. After each talk, give feedback on clarity and impact using the table on page 113. Decide which product to buy.

3 | Quality

Discussion

  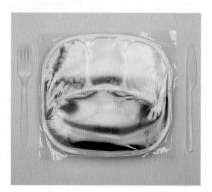

1 Look at the pictures. What sort of advice, instructions or warnings would you expect to find on the packaging of these products? Discuss your ideas with a partner.

2 Match these strange instructions 1–6 with the products a–f which they refer to.

1 Do not turn upside down
2 Warning: keep out of children
3 For indoor or outdoor use only
4 Wearing of this garment does not enable you to fly
5 Product will be hot after heating
6 Warning: may cause drowsiness

a) a child's Superman costume
b) a bread pudding
c) printed on the bottom of a tiramisu packet
d) a sleep aid
e) a kitchen knife
f) a string of Christmas lights

Reading

3 Decide whether the ten tips below for writing clear procedures are *Dos* or *Don'ts*.

Writing Clear Procedures – Dos and Don'ts

1 Use long sentences (15–20 words maximum)
2 Prefer active verbs
3 Be direct – use imperatives
4 Use long words
5 Use abbreviations or acronyms
6 Be consistent with terminology
7 Remember the reader – do not assume they know certain information
8 Put steps in the right sequence
9 Use headings and split information into chunks
10 Use 1, 2, 3, and not one, two, three or first, second, third

4 Read these assembly instructions for a bookcase. Which of the Dos and Don'ts do they break? Find examples and compare your answers with a partner.

Full assembly instructions for the assembly of a freestanding bookcase

Before attempting to assemble the FSB, the parts list should be checked to ascertain that all relevant items are included in the packet and that none are missing.
First of all, the specially designed wooden dowel pegs should be inserted in the appropriate holes drilled in the ends of the five shelves and the latter should be screwed to the side panels ensuring that the rounded shelf edges face the front of the unit.
Then the top and bottom panels should be fixed in place using the correct screws.
Before fitting the top and bottom panels, one must not forget to slide the back panel into position in the grooves provided to this effect at the rear of the side panels.
NB It is recommended that the unit be assembled in a horizontal position on an appropriate load-bearing surface, ie the floor.

Writing

5 Rewrite the assembly instructions to make them clear. Use the framework below and follow the advice in 3. Use one word in each gap.

Bookcase _____ instructions

1 _____ the packet contains all the _____ in the parts _____ .
2 _____ the bookcase flat on the _____ .
3 Begin by fitting wooden _____ in the four _____ in each _____ .
4 _____ the five shelves to the side _____ , with the rounded _____ towards the front.
5 _____ the back panel into place in the _____ at the rear of the side panels.
6 _____ the top and _____ panels and _____ them down.

Listening

6 🔊 1:28 Janice is assembling a TV stand she has just bought. She calls her friend Max. Listen to their conversation and answer the questions.

1 Why does she call Max?
2 What information does Max give her?
3 What does he promise to do in the end?

7 Listen again and write in the missing items on the parts list.

TV Stand – Parts List

1 _____ panel	1 cross _____
4 _____	4 _____
2 _____ panels	1 _____
8 _____	

8 Label the parts in the assembly diagram below.

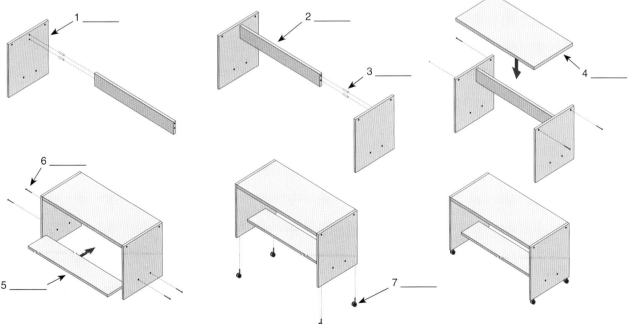

Writing a procedure

9 Work in small groups. Use the diagrams to write the assembly procedure for Janice. When you have finished, compare your instructions with the other groups. Decide which group has written the clearest instructions.

3 | Quality

Discussion

1 With a partner, decide whether the following facts about strawberries are true or false.

Strawberry FACTS

1. Strawberries are rich in Vitamin D and are low in fibre.
2. They contain no fat, cholesterol or salt.
3. Spain is the biggest producer of strawberries in the world.
4. The Romans cultivated strawberries as early as 200 BC.
5. Strawberries are members of the rose family.
6. They are unique, being the only fruit with seeds on the outside.
7. In medieval times, strawberries were regarded as an aphrodisiac, and a soup made of strawberries and sour cream was traditionally served to newly-weds.
8. The word strawberry comes from laying straw under the plants to protect the fruit.
9. Unlike many fruit, strawberries do not continue ripening after harvest.

Reading

2 Read the internal email from a supermarket chain with outlets in the Netherlands and Belgium, and the extract from a strawberry producers' brochure. Answer the questions.

1. What expectations would a consumer normally have about the quality of stawberries?
2. Why has the quality of incoming strawberries now become an issue?
3. Why do you think Schuurman and Zaluski may have different views on quality?
4. What do you think will be Suzanne's next course of action?

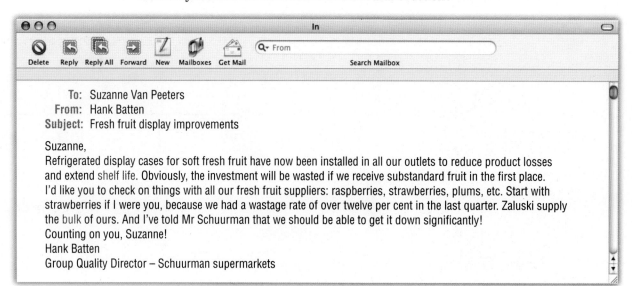

To: Suzanne Van Peeters
From: Hank Batten
Subject: Fresh fruit display improvements

Suzanne,
Refrigerated display cases for soft fresh fruit have now been installed in all our outlets to reduce product losses and extend shelf life. Obviously, the investment will be wasted if we receive substandard fruit in the first place.
I'd like you to check on things with all our fresh fruit suppliers: raspberries, strawberries, plums, etc. Start with strawberries if I were you, because we had a wastage rate of over twelve per cent in the last quarter. Zaluski supply the bulk of ours. And I've told Mr Schuurman that we should be able to get it down significantly!
Counting on you, Suzanne!
Hank Batten
Group Quality Director – Schuurman supermarkets

... The Zaluski cooperative, which represents nearly 50 small producers in the Pako area, has been packing and distributing strawberries for more than 40 years. Traditional farming techniques allied with the careful selection of appropriate strawberry varieties ensure that we produce Polish strawberries of unrivalled quality!

Listening

3 1:29 Listen to the telephone conversation between Suzanne Van Peeters, Schuurman's Quality Manager, and Piotr Sieberski, Managing Director of Zaluski Strawberries. What is the purpose of Suzanne's call?

Preparation

4 Read the information below and underline the main points Suzanne will need to raise during her audit meeting.

Key factors affecting strawberry quality and recommended best practice:

TEMPERATURE
- Less than a one-hour delay between harvest and the cooling of berries in the cooler is recommended. This means regular collection of picked fruit and frequent trips to the cooler
- Upon arrival at the cooler, fruit should be cooled to 0–1 °C before being placed in the storage room to await packing. Cold storage air temperatures should be monitored and records maintained.
- When shipping by road, trucks should be cooled to near 0 °C before loading. The refrigeration system must be checked on each load.
- The golden rule is *Don't break the cold chain*. Once strawberries have been cooled after picking, they should be kept cold until 30 minutes before eating!

PACKING
- Care should be taken to pack only sound fruit from harvesting trays to punnets. Decaying, damaged or shrivelled fruit should be removed.

HANDLING
- Strawberries are very fragile and bruise easily. Careful handling and sorting during harvest is needed.
- Training and supervision of harvesting teams is critical. Harvesters should be given an incentive to pick with care. Crew supervisors should monitor harvested trays to ensure that only sound fruit are being placed in them. Shallow trays should be used to prevent squashing (no more than 5 cm in depth).

RIPENESS
- Strawberries do not continue to ripen after harvest and will not increase in sugar content. Riper fruit tend to have a high sugar content and better flavour quality. Pick only ripe fruit, generally pink or red in colour.

CULTIVATION
- The use of heavy nitrogen fertilization has been associated with softer fruit and less flavour.

Listening

5 1:30 Listen to Suzanne's audit meeting with Piotr Sieberski and Klara Solak, the packing shed supervisor. Complete Suzanne's notes below.

Audit meeting – points to raise:

Harvesting procedures
No (1) _____ paid for quality fruit.
Pickers receive little (2) _____ .

Transport
Strawberries are placed in trays (3) _____ deep.
Transport to cooler takes (4) _____ hours.

Cooling process
Berries are cooled to (5) _____ .
They keep no (6) _____ of storage shed temperatures.

Packing procedures
Packers receive little (7) _____ .
No (8) _____ is paid for good packing.

Shipping
The (9) _____ on each truck is not always checked.

Cultivation
The use of nitrogen fertilizers will stop in (10) _____ years.

Presentation

6 Work in small groups. You are quality consultants to Schuurman supermarkets. Prepare a presentation of your recommendations for improvements to Zaluski's procedures to ensure top quality strawberries. Make your presentations and hold a class vote for the best one.

4.1 About business   The project team

Discussion

1 Work with a partner. Discuss the meaning of these statements. Choose the two which you think are closest to the truth. Explain your choice to another pair.

> **Project management and team-building quotes**
>
> Nothing is impossible for the person who doesn't have to do it.
>
> If you're six months late on a milestone due next week but nevertheless really believe you can make it, you're a project manager.
>
> There is no I in Teamwork.
>
> If you don't know where you're going, any road will take you there.
>
> Getting good players is easy. What's difficult is getting them to play together.

Listening

2 🔊 1:31 Listen to part of a project review meeting. What is being built? Which two stages of the project caused the delays? Choose from the list.

a Land purchase	e Excavation for foundations
b Project approval	f Dam construction
c Feasibility study	g Resettlement
d Geological survey	h River diversion

3 The Gantt chart below relates to the updated schedule. Listen again and complete the gaps with the correct project stages from 2.

	Project schedule			
	Year 1	Year 2	Year 3	Year 4
	J F M A M J J A S O N D	J F M A M J J A S O N D	J F M A M J J A S O N D	J F M A M J J A S O N D
Logistics	Feasibility study	Project approval (2) _____	Resettlement	
Engineering	(1) _____		(3) _____	Excavation (4) _____

Reading

4 Read the first three paragraphs of the article opposite. Answer these questions.

1 What examples of 'ineffective team-building activities' does the author mention?
2 Why do companies continue to run them?

5 Read the rest of the article. Match the four points of advice in a–d with gaps 1–4 in the text.

a Create an open and honest atmosphere.	c Have a common plan.
b Learn from the best leaders.	d Focus on a clear objective.

6 Which essential team building characteristic is missing in each situation a–d?

a We're going round in circles. It's like a ship without a captain!
b The project scope is too wide and unclear.
c I think we all know where we're going, but we have different views on how to get there.
d We all get on OK, but everyone's too politically correct.

Discussion

7 Work in small groups. Discuss these questions.

1 Have you ever played volleyball? What are the principles of the game?
2 Volleyball has often been called the ultimate team sport. Why is this and what lessons can be learned and applied to project management?
3 What similar lessons can be learned from other team sports or group activities? For example, playing in a band.

Internet research

Search for the keywords "*Gantt charts*" to discover more about them. How many different types of chart exist and how are they used in project management? Report back to the class.

Smells like team spirit

Weekend retreats and touchy-feely exercises may do more to create bad-feeling than build teams. Instead, take some lessons from a winning volleyball coach

It's time someone finally said it: most of what passes for team-building these days doesn't really build teams. So why do companies spend millions of dollars annually to make their employees go through ineffective team-building activities: walking around in blindfolds, navigating rope courses, and sitting crosslegged on the floor with paper and crayons illustrating their 'life paths'?

There are three reasons. While it's generally recognized that a great team will beat a mediocre team 99 times out of 100, little hard thinking goes on at most companies about how effective teams are actually built. Employees usually don't complain about silly team-building efforts, whether out of apathy or for fear of being labeled 'anti-team'. Finally, most team-building practitioners are well-meaning, sincere people whom no one wants to offend.

So if conventional team-building activities are largely ineffective, how do you build a great team? In 1978, I played a supporting role on a volleyball team that won the first National Championship in our university's history. That team was made up of people who weren't the most physically-gifted athletes in the world. But they merged into a force that was far greater than the sum of the players' individual abilities.

Nearly 30 years later, what I learned that season remains one of the most important lessons of my life. Great

teams – whether composed of athletes, businesspeople, fire fighters, military commandos, or what have you – teach us four key lessons:

1 _____ . One of the most memorable features of my 1978 team was the level of intensity which the players brought to every practice and game. The atmosphere was charged with an emotional commitment that caused members of the team to constantly push each other to give everything in service of the goal.

Far too often, a company thinks it has a team-building problem when what it really has is a goal problem. If you want to build a great team, make sure its members share a determined passion to accomplish something. How do you get that kind of commitment? By involving everyone in the development of the goal.

2 _____ . It's not enough to get a bunch of people together who care deeply about reaching a goal. They need to have a strategy for achieving it. The best team-building tool ever is a good strategy that everyone buys into. If you want to increase teamwork, don't focus on the team, focus the team on the task.

My team coach had a detailed strategy for winning that the players bought into completely. A part of the strategy was to overcome our physical shortcomings with a commitment to superior conditioning and training. So, for two months the team endured a schedule so demanding that it was the

talk of the campus.

3 _____ . Yes, trust and respect are key. But ironically, often the best way to increase levels of trust and respect on a team is to get them focused on the goal and the strategy. This gets people saying what they really think. When people say what they really think and are held accountable, trust and respect usually follow. Don't impose an atmosphere of false politeness.

There was plenty of conflict on the team and people sometimes lost their tempers. But on the court an atmosphere of respect always prevailed. All great business teams share that same quality.

4 _____ . There's no getting around it, great teams usually have great managers. My old team coach still coaches volleyball at that same university today. He has an unrivalled 426–162 win-loss record and has also coached a US team to a World Championship and an Olympic gold medal.

So, learn how to be a great coach. Aspiring business leaders would be a lot better off if they spent less time reading management literature, and more time around people like my old coach. The great college coaches may know more about team-building than anyone else in the world. After all, their leadership and team-building skills are measured in real time, in front of real crowds. And they start from scratch with a new team every year.

4 | Feedback

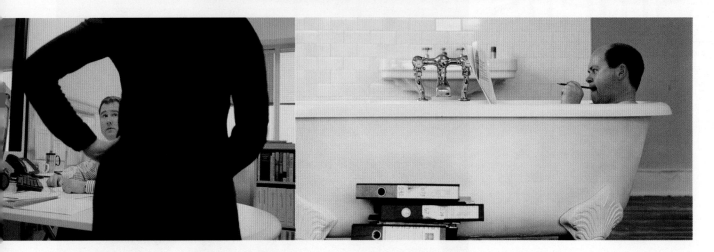

Discussion

1 Work with a partner. Match the nouns in the box with the descriptions a–e. Which character do you think would be most difficult to manage and why? Which description best describes you?

> The bully   The team player   The leader   The workaholic   The maverick

a This character does things their own way. They may be effective, but they're difficult to control.
b This person has a natural ability to encourage others and take a project through to success.
c This person doesn't know when to stop, and they often believe the office would collapse without them.
d This person imposes their personality on others, making other people feel bad in the workplace.
e This person has a natural ability to fit in. They make positive contributions and build good relationships.

2 Which character type in 1 would you associate with each adjective below?

> aggressive   anxious   charismatic   confident   cooperative   decisive
> easy-going   friendly   helpful   impatient   independent   individual   motivating
> obsessive   over-critical   single-minded   stressed   unpredictable

Listening

3 🔊 1:32 Listen to an HR manager and line manager talking about three different members of their team. Decide which of the labels in 1 best describes each person.

Anna _____   Bjorn _____   Katia _____

4 Listen again. Which adjectives do you hear that confirm your answer in 3?

Expressions

5 The expressions in **bold** all occurred in the recording. Match phrases 1–8 with the appropriate reply in a–h. Use a dictionary to help you if necessary.

1 Marion is in danger of **burning out**.
2 How are you **settling in**?
3 If we want to succeed, we must **pull together**.
4 He's always **passing the buck**!
5 She **gets on well** with everyone.
6 Don't **let me down**, will you?
7 Dave isn't **pulling his weight**!
8 You should learn to **take it easy**.

a Except Rob, but he doesn't like anyone!
b I wish I could, but things are just too hectic.
c I know! He asked me to do his report for him!
d No, you can rely on me!
e Perhaps we should run a team-building course?
f Yes. She's a workaholic. It's affecting her health.
g You're right, and that means more work for us!
h Fine, thanks, though I still don't know everyone.

Internet research

Search for the keywords *"project management tips"* and decide whether you would make a good or bad project manager. Prepare a one-minute talk to the class to explain your decision.

6 Match the people involved in a project in 1–5 with their definitions a–e.

1 Sponsor
2 Project manager
3 Project team members
4 End users
5 Key stakeholders

a The people who will benefit from the end results of the project on a day-to-day basis.
b The person or group of people who decided the project was needed in the first place.
c Anybody who might be affected by the project, whether positively or negatively.
d The person responsible for running the project and delivering on time and within budget.
e Staff chosen for the skills they can bring to the project, often from different departments.

7 Below are different people or groups involved in or affected by a motorway construction project. Match them with the five key players above.

a truck and car drivers
b the Ministry of Transport
c a senior engineer in a major civil engineering company
d a plant hire company, an environmental protection group, and villagers living near the proposed route
e a civil engineer, a surveyor, an environmental engineer and a transport consultant

Collocations

8 Complete the project management sentences using the correct form of verbs from the list which collocate with the nouns in **bold**. In some sentences, more than one verb is possible.

miss	reach	establish	achieve	meet	stick to	set	fix

1 Unless the team really pulls together, we'll never _____ **the deadline** on the Malaysian order.
2 The project has been difficult so far. However, once we _____ **the next milestone**, everything should get easier.
3 To make sense of our tasks, we need to _____ **a timeframe** within which we can all work.
4 Frank is such an unreasonable boss: he always _____ **our targets** for overseas sales too high.
5 Congratulations! We've _____ **our targets** for quality this year due to all your hard work.
6 We've been vague about the schedule for too long. It's time we _____ **a date** for definite and moved on.
7 In the end, I _____ **my deadline** for my accountancy project, but it didn't matter: everybody else was late too.
8 Sam's excellent at getting things done on time, but she finds it impossible to _____ **her budget**.

deadline

Speaking

9 Work in small groups. Take turns to describe your personality, your strengths and weaknesses, and what you would be good or bad at doing in a project.

4.3 Grammar   Regrets, speculation and habits

Test yourself: past modals

1 Two directors of a pharmaceutical company are discussing the reasons why a new software project is behind schedule. Correct the errors in **bold** with the correct form of the verb.

Rosanna	So, Bruce, where did we go wrong? We're two months behind schedule, Murray's just resigned and the end users are now saying the system will be unusable!
Bruce	Well, Rosanna, we (1) **should not choose** Murray as project manager in the first place. Mavericks like him just don't make good PMs. We (2) **can predict** he wasn't going to change if we hadn't been in such a rush. In retrospect, we (3) **should put** Isabelle in charge. She's no star but she (4) **will do** a steady job.
Rosanna	Yeah, I see what you mean, but it's easy to be wise after the event. She (5) **might be** a better choice in some ways, but (6) **will she listen** to the users? Their views (7) **ought to be taken** into account properly before we started the implementation phase. We (8) **must waste** at least one month asking them the wrong questions! If only we had got that right, we (9) **aren't** in the mess we are now!
Bruce	I just wish we had been given project approval a bit earlier. That way we (10) **can make** sure people bought into the project in the first place. Anyway, the question is, what are the lessons learned and where do we go from here?

Test yourself: third conditionals

2 Rosanna and Bruce are discussing the lessons learned. Rewrite the notes using the third conditional (*If* + past perfect, *would have* + past paticiple) as in the example.

Example
If we (put) Isabelle in charge, she (do) a steady job.
If we had put Isabelle in charge, she would have done a steady job.

1 If we (give) Murray a different role, he (not resign).
2 If we (not be) in such a rush, we (make) a better choice.
3 If the users (be) listened to, their views (be) taken into account.
4 We (not waste) one month if we (ask) the right questions in the first place.
5 If we (get) the project approval earlier, we (be able) to start correctly.
6 We (not have) all these problems if we (make) the right decisions!

Test yourself: *used to, be used to* and *get used to*

3 Complete these sentences using *used to, be used to* or *get used to* and the correct form of the verb.

1 We _____ (give) ourselves enough time, but these days it's just a mad rush!
2 Personally, I don't think I will ever _____ (work) like this.
3 You know, Murray has changed. He _____ (be) such a maverick.
4 You're right. He _____ (come) to me for advice, but now he does.
5 I remember when he joined us, he _____ (make) a lot of typos.
6 Yes, I remember! He _____ (use) a French-style AZERTY keyboard!
7 You can say that again! I _____ still not _____ (type) on an AZERTY after fifteen years!

Refresh your memory

Past modals
Use modal + *have* + past participle.
Sue would have done a better job.
For past regrets, use *should/ought to/could* + *have* + past participle.
For past speculation, use *may/might/could/must* + *have* + past particple.

Third conditional
Use *If* + past perfect in the condition. Use *would have* + past participle in the result.
If we had spent more on marketing, we would have sold more.

used to + infinitive
Past state or habit.
We used to work in a smaller office.
Familiarity with a strange or difficult situation.
be/get used to + verb-ing/noun/pronoun
I'm used to working until 7 p.m.

► Grammar and practice pages 122–123

Regrets

4 The photos show two people whose career paths have been very different. Which person regrets their decisions more?

GRANT Yeah, I remember Kim. I studied business administration at college with her: we had a great time. I took a job as a trainee accountant in London at the same firm as her. But I felt it just wasn't for me. I was earning good money, and they offered me a salary of £45,000 just to stay, but I said 'no'. Instead, I downshifted. I left to become a dairy farmer. When I look at the people I used to work with, we're really different now. They live in nice houses and drive expensive cars. But overall, I think I made the right choice. I'm really happy on my farm. I'm not at all stressed.

KIM I studied business administration at college, but I didn't really enjoy it. I always really wanted to be a vet, but I made the wrong study choices. In the end, I joined an accountancy firm. Now I'm a senior partner, which means I have a great salary. But I sometimes think there's something missing. My friend Grant, who joined the same time as me, left after a few years to start a farm. He asked me to help him set it up, but I said 'no'. I think it was the wrong choice. He says his job's not at all stressful, but mine is contant pressure.

5 Complete these sentences using an appropriate past modal form of the verb in brackets.

1 Grant _____ (have) a career as an accountant, but he left.
2 Grant _____ (earn) £45,000 or more, but he turned it down.
3 In the end, Grant doesn't think that he _____ (stay) at the accountancy firm.
4 Kim thinks she _____ (study) to become a vet, not an accountant.
5 Kim now thinks that she _____ (leave) the accountancy firm and started a business with Grant, but she said 'no'.
6 Kim _____ (live) a less stressful life on a farm.

6 Complete the sentences a–d with your own ideas based on the stories of Grant and Kim.

a If Grant had stayed at the accountancy firm _____
b If Kim had studied to become a vet, _____
c If Grant hadn't become a farmer, _____
d If Kim had helped Grant start his farm, _____

7 Read the list of activities in the list below. Which activities are part of Grant's past? Which activities are familiar parts of his life now?

> earn a lot of money   work with animals   work in London
> run my own business   have a slow pace of life   work under pressure

Internet research

Search for the keyword *downshifting* to discover more about this trend. Make notes on the different forms of downshifting and decide which you would adopt if you had the chance. Make a one-minute presentation of your choice to the class and vote on the best idea.

8 Write appropriate sentences about Grant using the ideas in 7. Use *used to* or *be used to* plus the correct form of the verb.

Discussion

9 Imagine you have recently quit a very well-paid business job to start a different life on a farm. Use the ideas in the box to imagine how you lived in the city and how you live now.

> Means of transport   Home   Food   Social life
> How you spend your money   Typical day   Holidays

10 Work in groups. Exchange memories of how you used to live. Say what you are finding it hard to get used to now.

4 | Feedback

Discussion

1 Decide how you would respond as a manager to each of these situations. Choose options from the list a–l.

1 A new employee has failed to complete an important project.
2 An experienced employee has failed to produce an important report.
3 A new employee has delighted customers with exceptional service.
4 An experienced employee has delighted customers with exceptional service.

a) fire the employee
b) supervise the employee more closely
c) scream and shout for twenty minutes
d) have a heart to heart talk to identify the causes
e) give them a final warning
f) do nothing

g) pay them a bonus
h) give them more autonomy
i) thank them for their hard work
j) give them a promotion
k) tell them not to overdo it
l) something else

Listening

2 ● 1:33–1:34 Listen to two interviews between Mrs Gomez, a store manager in the Philippines, and Rafael, a department supervisor. Answer the questions.

1 What was the objective of each interview?
2 What did Rafael do wrong or right?
3 How do you think Rafael feels at the end of each interview?

3 Read the two procedures for giving feedback below. Which contains advice relevant to the first interview in 2? Which is relevant to the second?

Recognizing merit

1 Make contact
  • Set the scene: describe the time, place and situation when performance was exceptional.
  • Refer to the work in question.
2 Give praise
  • Give a specific example of the facts or results you appreciate.
  • Point out the personal qualities which contributed to your employee's success.
3 Conclusion
  • Explain the positive consequences of the employee's behaviour for the company, the department, and for you yourself.
  • Keep the interview short and avoid discussing other subjects; one or two minutes are usually enough.

Constructive criticism

1 Make contact
  • Set the scene: describe the time, place, and situation when the problem occurred.
  • Describe the problems and the results – state facts, not opinions.
2 Diagnose the problem
  • Elicit the causes of the problem (behaviour, method, equipment, organization, etc).
  • Express your opinion.
  • Explain the consequences for the organization.
3 Commit to action
  • Offer suggestions which recognize the employee's good points but eliminate the faults.
  • Invite the employee to make comments.
4 Conclusion
  • Set new objectives, stating the methods to be used and a deadline.

4 Referring to the guide, explain why Mrs Gomez did not handle the interviews very well.

Search for the keywords *"how to manage difficult people"*. Draw up a list of your top ten tips.

5 The statements below are good examples of *Recognizing merit*. Decide which pieces of advice in 3 these statements relate to.

1 You came in to work when Maria was sick.
2 Thanks to you, everything went smoothly and we didn't lose any business.
3 I really appreciate your dedication to our customers, your solidarity with your colleagues, and the support you have shown me personally in dealing with the problem yourself.
4 You are hard-working and conscientious; these are qualities the company values highly.
5 Before you go, let me shake your hand. Well done Rafael, and thank you!

6 When giving constructive criticism, asking questions rather than making statements helps to reduce tension and establish a dialogue. Complete these questions to express Mrs Gomez's ideas more diplomatically.

1 I want to see you in my office, now.
_____ have a word with you in my office?
2 I don't know what the hell you think you're playing at, but I'm not having it!
_____ tell me exactly what happened with Mr Baitan on Friday?
3 I don't know what you did, but Mr Baitan was very upset.
_____ any ideas as to why Mr Baitan was quite so upset?
4 If this happens again, you're out!
_____ realize that this kind of problem can have serious consequences?
5 Now get back to work, and make sure you do better next time.
So what _____ we can do to make sure this situation doesn't happen again?
6 I think I've made myself clear.
So, before you go, _____ summarize what we have agreed?

7 🔊 1:35 Listen to another version of the first interview and check your answers.

8 Make these criticisms more constructive by reformulating these statements as questions. Use the words in brackets and the example to help you.

Example
You should've followed the company guidelines for dealing with complaints. (agree)
Do you agree that you should have followed the company guidelines for dealing with complaints?

1 We risk losing Mr Baitan's business if we don't find a solution. (realize)
2 You should ask for help next time you have a problem. (think)
3 You should have called me on my mobile. (think)
4 If you'd been more flexible, this wouldn't have happened. (agree)
5 You should've remembered that the customer is always right. (realize)

Role-play

9 You and your partner work in a large department store. Role-play four situations to practise giving constructive criticism and recognizing merit.

Student A should turn to page 113 for instructions.
Student B should turn to page 114 for instructions.

4 | Feedback

Discussion

1 The list below gives reasons for performance appraisals. Decide which benefit the employer most and which benefit the employee.

> reviewing progress   discussing rewards   setting achievable goals
> planning training   stating career objectives   encouraging communication
> identifying strengths and weaknesses

2 Work with a partner. Put the sections of a report in a logical order from 1–7.

Recommendations   Introduction   Conclusions   Procedure
Executive summary   Findings   Title

Analysis

3 Read the following report and number the paragraphs in the correct order 1–6.

Introduction of annual appraisal interviews

☐ Firstly, Webwide Consulting used a system of anonymous questionnaires to investigate employee attitudes. For instance, some questions related to company image and job satisfaction. In addition, **interviews were held** with all staff.

☐ The Management Committee decided to engage Webwide Consulting on 11 October to advise on the possible introduction of formal appraisal interviews. **This decision was taken** owing to dissatisfaction with the existing system. This report covers the method by which **information was gathered** and sets out a plan for adopting appraisal interviews.

☐ **A survey was carried out by external consultants** regarding the possible introduction of formal annual appraisal interviews. Their findings clearly show that most staff and managers are in favour. Consequently, *it is recommended* that a formal system be set up as soon as possible.

☐ **Three main areas of concern were revealed by the individual interviews**.
- Management are seen to lack interest in staff development.
- Employees get little feedback on whether hard work is recognized.
- Employees get no guidance on how to improve poor performance.

☐ 1 We should put in place a system of annual appraisal interviews within the next two months.
2 Each interview should be 45 minutes in length due to the tight schedule.

☐ In conclusion, the survey results clearly show that a more formal approach to appraisal interviews would reduce staff turnover, increase motivation, and foster team spirit.

4 Answer these questions about the report in 3.

1 Which headings from 2 match each of the paragraphs?
2 What other methods can be used to organize information in a report?

Linking words and phrases

5 Work in pairs. Match each word or expression in the box with the categories below. Find examples of similar expressions used in the report in 3.

moreover	due to	finally	to sum up	therefore	next	for example	overall

a) Sequencing
b) Giving examples
c) Adding
d) Expressing cause and result
e) Summarizing

6 Complete the sentences below with appropriate linking phrases.

1 We wanted the survey to be anonymous. _____, names did not appear on the questionnaire.
2 Firstly, staff completed questionnaires. _____, they were interviewed by consultants.
3 The questionnaire covered job satisfaction. _____, some questions touched on company image.
4 Interviews were limited to 30 minutes each _____ the very tight schedule.
5 _____, the results were positive but we agreed that there were lessons to learn.
6 Formal appraisal interviews will be introduced _____ dissatisfaction with the existing system.
7 There are several reasons for adopting appraisal interviews, _____ , they can motivate staff.

Report style

7 It is possible to write a report in an active or passive style. An active style is more direct. A passive style is more impersonal. Make the report in 3 more direct by changing the phrases in **bold** into active sentences.

Writing

8 Look at the email and the notes below. What does your boss want you to do?

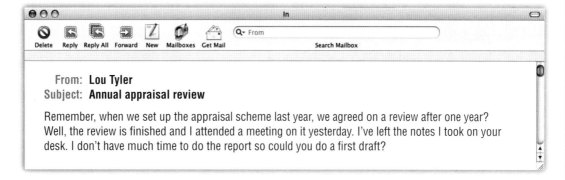

9 Write a short report for your boss using the company template below to help you.

Title
Introduction – explain the background to the report and why you are writing it.
Procedure – how was information gathered?
Findings –what information was gathered?
Conclusions – what conclusions can you draw?
Recommendations – what recommendations can you make?

4.6 Case study | Trident Overseas

Discussion

1 Imagine you are working on a different continent from your own in which the business culture is very different. Answer the questions below.

1 In your opinion, can the same business methods and ethical standards be applied all over the world? Should they be adapted to local culture?
2 What cultural differences might you find? Consider these categories.

recruitment   management style   productivity
time management   personal development

Reading

2 Trident is a British-based oil company which operates in Africa. Read the magazine article and the email from a sales manager. Answer the questions below.

1 What determines petrol prices?
2 Why is customer service important?
3 How do local managers often behave?
4 Who owns the stations?
5 Why has John Thorpe been out of the office?
6 What did he find out?

Trident put the service back in station

Drivers in Europe and America have become accustomed to buying petrol in deserted, fully automated petrol stations. In Africa, however, customers are greeted with a friendly smile and a polite welcome as they are directed to the appropriate pump. They can then sit back and watch uniformed forecourt staff fill the tank, top up the oil, and wash the windscreen.

With extreme driving conditions, few new cars, and little available income for engine repairs, oil sales are strategic and highly profitable. In many African countries petrol prices are government-regulated, so quality of service is the crucial factor in attracting customers who will buy oil as well as petrol. At Trident, staff training is a priority; management aim to ensure that customers keep coming back for friendly service and expert advice.

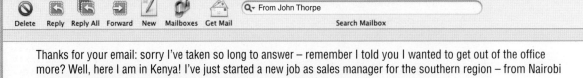

Delete   Reply   Reply All   Forward   New   Mailboxes   Get Mail   Search Mailbox

Q▾ From John Thorpe

Thanks for your email: sorry I've taken so long to answer – remember I told you I wanted to get out of the office more? Well, here I am in Kenya! I've just started a new job as sales manager for the southern region – from Nairobi to the Indian Ocean, down to Mombasa near the border with Tanzania.

Business in Africa can be very hierarchical; there are some really good managers, but for a lot of them, their idea of getting things done is to keep shouting until they get what they want. That's going to change! I have three district managers, who each have a team of sales reps who travel around the district meeting dealers. Some of the dealers own their service stations, so we have to handle them with kid gloves, or they'll just go over to the competition. More and more, we have what we call Young Dealers – employees who we train up to run the company-owned stations. So directly or indirectly there are three layers of management between me and the forecourt staff and mechanics – sometimes all shouting as loud as they can!

In fact there's been a lot of shouting in the Lamu district, and I've just come back to Nairobi from a three-day fact-finding trip. Their development project is way behind schedule, so I went down to have a word with the people in the field. It turns out it's quite a mess, and I could do with some help to sort it out, actually.

3 Complete the organizational chart for Trident in East Africa.

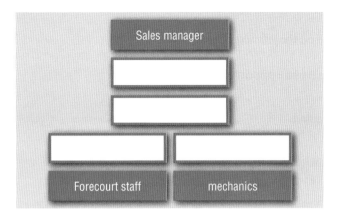

Internet research

Search for the keywords *"managing your manager"* to find tips on how to develop a better working relationship with your boss. What advice would you give the Kenyan Trident employees on managing their respective bosses?

Listening

4 John Thorpe spoke to three Trident employees on his fact-finding trip. Before you listen, read the notes and add the four names mentioned to the organizational chart.

5 🌐 1:36–1:38 Listen to extracts from the interviews and complete the notes.

Abeba, **Mechanic**

Says they are losing (1) _____ as a result of bad morale.

Mr Mbugua sacked some staff in order to hire his (2) _____ .

Mr Mbugua is Mr Wambugu's (3) _____ .

Mr Mbugua, **Young Dealer**

Would like Abeba to (4) _____ .

Has not checked whether Mrs Mohamed agrees with his (5) _____ policy .

Says that the company gives him no (6) _____ .

Mrs Mohamed, **Sales Rep**

Mr Wambugu gives her impossible (7) _____ , so she has no time to visit dealers.

Mr Mbugua treats (8) _____ employees very badly.

She tried to (9) _____ Mr Mbugua's appointment.

Believes that Mr Wambugu wants her to (10) _____ .

Discussion and role-play

6 John Thorpe has asked for your advice on handling the situation in the Lamu District. In small groups, discuss the problems and brainstorm possible solutions.

7 🌐 1:39 Listen to a voicemail message from Mr Wambugu. How does this affect your strategy?

8 With a partner from another group, role-play meetings with Abeba, Mr Mbugua, and Mr Wambugu to explain what action you have decided to take and, where appropriate, set new objectives.

Review 3

Quality

1 Make expressions by matching a verb on the left with the words the right.

1	struggle	something a number one priority
2	take	an end in itself
3	make	to keep up
4	fall into	something for granted
5	become	a person's aesthetic sense
6	appeal to	a trap
7	get	TQM or other quality schemes
8	adopt	the job done

2 Find an expression in exercise 1 that means:

a have difficulty in continuing to do something well ☐
b expect something to always happen in a particular way, and not think about any possible problems ☐
c develop into an activity you do for its own sake ☐

3 Fill in the missing letters in this text about different ideas of quality.

To the marketing manager, quality is about (1) m_ _ _ing the customer's needs and (2) ex_ _ _ _ _ _ions.
To the design engineer, who works with tight (3) spec_ _ _ _ations and strict (4) tol_ _ _ _ces, quality is about whether the design is (5) f_ _ for pur_ _ _e, and whether the product (6) perf_ _ms its intended functions.
To the process engineer, quality is about using (7) l_ _n manufacturing to ensure that there is minimum (8) w_ _ _e (of effort, money, time and materials).
To the quality auditor, quality means the correct application of (9) pro_ _ _ures, and (10) comp_ _ _ _ce with international (11) st_ _ _ _ _ds such as ISO 9001.
To the end-user, quality means that the goods are not (12) def_ _ _ive or (13) da_ _ged in any way. Any service that is provided has to be (14) rel_ _ _le.

4 Complete the sentences with the words in the box.

> faults   improvement   practice   requirements
> specifications   standard

1 If you have a system of continuous _____ you should be able to eliminate all design _____.
2 The process of 'benchmarking' is where best _____ is based on the industry _____.
3 Technical _____ in areas like safety are often based on statutory _____ imposed by the government.

5 Add one word each time, in the right place, to make a correct form of a passive.

1 that machine serviced regularly?
2 is it serviced at the moment?
3 has it serviced recently?
4 it serviced last month?
5 was it serviced during the lunch break yesterday when production stopped for an hour?
6 is it going to serviced next month?
7 it could been serviced last month.
8 it should have serviced last month.

6 Match a phrase in Box A with a phrase from Box B so that both phrases have approximately the same use in a presentation.

Box A
1 ☐ This graph shows the …
2 ☐ I think that covers …
3 ☐ In other words, …
4 ☐ Is that clear so far?
5 ☐ So, now let's turn to …
6 ☐ Just to digress a moment, …
7 ☐ Basically, …

Box B
a By the way, …
b Does that make sense?
c Now I'd like to look at …
d What I mean is …
e As you can see, …
f That's all I want to say about …
g I must emphasize that …

7 Now write the pairs of phrases from exercise 6 next to the most appropriate headings below.

Referring to graphics: __1e__
Digressing: _____
Restating/Reformulating: _____
Emphasizing: _____
Checking understanding: _____
Ending one point: _____
Moving on: _____

8 The assembly instructions below are too long or too complex. Change them according to the instructions.

1 The packet should be checked.
(*change passive to imperative*)
_____

2 Begin by fitting the specially designed wooden pegs in the four appropriate holes in the ends of each shelf.
(*delete two words together, then one more word*)
_____

3 Screw the five shelves to the side panels, with the rounded shelf edges towards the front of the unit.
(*delete one word, then three words together*)
_____

4 Before fitting the top and bottom panels, slide the back panel into place in the grooves provided at the rear of the side panels.
(*delete seven words together, then one more word*)
_____

5 The top and bottom panels should be fixed in place with the correct screws.
(*change passive to imperative*)
_____

Review 4

1 Fill in the missing letters in these sentences about team-building.

1 A to_ _ _y-f_ _ly exercise is one where people express themselves honestly and physically.
2 If a lot of h_ _d thinking goes on, then the thinking involves much effort.
3 A well-known saying states that 'The whole is g_ _ _ _er than the s_ _ of its parts.'
4 If you have enthusiasm and the determination to work hard at something, then you show c_ _ _ _ _ment.
5 If you acc_ _ _ _ish a goal, it is the same as saying that you a_ _ _ _ve it (succeed in doing it).
6 If you believe in an idea or a strategy, then you b_ _ i_ _ _ it (phrasal verb).
7 No one is perfect, but with effort we can ov_ _ _ _me our sh_ _ _ _ _mings.
8 If somebody is h_ _d acc_ _ _ _able for their thoughts and actions, then they have to explain them and be willing to be criticized.
9 Try to stay calm. Don't lose your t_ _ _ _r and get angry.
10 We have to go right back to the beginning and s_ _ _t from sc_ _ _ch.

2 Complete each description with the two most appropriate adjectives from the box.

> aggressive   charismatic   cooperative   helpful
> impatient   individual   motivating   obsessive
> stressed   unpredictable

1 A bully is _____ and _____.
2 A team player is _____ and _____.
3 A leader is _____ and _____.
4 A workaholic is _____ and _____.
5 A maverick is _____ and _____.

3 Match the expressions 1–8 to their meanings a–h.

1 burn out
2 settle in
3 pull together
4 pass the buck
5 get on/along well with
6 let someone down
7 pull your weight
8 take it easy

a work with other people to achieve something
b relax and not let things worry you
c make someone else deal with something that you should take responsibility for
d become familiar with a new job
e have a friendly relationship with someone
f do your share of the work
g disappoint someone, because you didn't do what you promised
h be unable to continue working because you have worked too hard

4 Match each verb with a noun. Several answers are possible, but the clues in brackets will guide you to one particular solution.

1 meet   a budget (= not change)
2 set   a date (= set/decide)
3 fix   a deadline (= finish at the right time)
4 miss   a deadline (= fail to reach)
5 achieve   a milestone (= arrive at)
6 stick to   a target (= decide/fix/establish)
7 establish   a target (= be successful after effort)
8 reach   a timeframe (= make it exist)

5 Complete the sentences using the correct form of the verbs in brackets. They are all past modals.

A: I regret what I did. I (1) _____ (should/do) things differently.
B: No, don't blame yourself. You (2) _____ (could/not/do) anything else. I (3) _____ (would/act) in exactly the same way if I had been in your shoes.
A: You're wrong. Things (4) _____ (might/be) very different if I hadn't been so stupid. I (5) _____ (ought/not/pay) attention to that terrible advice in the astrology section of my magazine.

6 Cover exercise 5 with a piece of paper. Now complete the sentences below using a third conditional form.

1 If I _____ (be) in your shoes, I _____ (act) in exactly the same way.
2 If I _____ (not/be) so stupid, things _____ (be) very different.

Before you check your answers, look at the modal verb you used in the second part of each sentence. Did you use *would* both times? What two other modals are possible and common here?

7 Reformulate these aggressive remarks as diplomatic questions. Use the words in brackets.

1 Come to my office right now! (can/word/you/my office)
   _____ ?
2 Why did it happen? (do/have/idea/why)
   _____ ?
3 It would have been a disaster! (do/realize/could/happened)
   _____ ?

8 Find a word or phrase in the email that matches these items: *consequently, due to, in conclusion, moreover*.

Because of increased raw materials costs, it will be necessary to increase the price of all our products in the next quarter. Therefore, we need an urgent meeting to decide on the exact amount and timing of the increases. In addition, we need to discuss how to present this price rise to our customers. There might also be a case for reducing costs by outsourcing some of our production to a low-cost country. Overall, there is a lot to discuss, so please keep your schedules free for a full-day meeting on Monday 31 August.

Do you think the use of the new words from the instructions makes the text more *formal* or more *informal*?

5 | Selling more

Discussion

1 Work with another student. Discuss these questions.

1 What marketing opportunities does the new technology in the photo offer?
2 Have you ever been targeted as a consumer using this advertising medium?
3 To what extent do you think that new advertising technologies should be regulated?

Skim reading

2 Read the text opposite quickly and find the answers to these questions.

1 How do viral web ads spread?
2 How has advertising changed as a result?
3 Has viral web advertising become easier or more difficult?

Inbox - Subscriptions - Favourites - Playlist - My Videos

▷ ▷ 〇 ━━━━━━━ ⚊⚊⚊⚊ ◁ share

Video Life
From: Snout 37
Comments: 53

Login to review video
★★★☆☆
653 ratings

Scan reading

3 Find what these figures from the article refer to.

1 $10,000
2 $250,000 to $500,000
3 five
4 500,000
5 $150 million
6 100 million

Reading for detail

4 Mark these statements T (true) or F (false).

1 Robinson proved that customers would spread advertisements if they were entertaining.
2 Companies have reallocated advertising budgets worth millions of dollars to the Net.
3 Individual video ads have more shock impact than they did in the past.
4 Video ads have to compete with increasing numbers of other online videos.
5 Video sharing sites believe that more ad content will attract users to their sites.
6 Most video viral ads appear on spots companies have paid for.

Listening

5 ◯ 2:01 Elaine and Marcus work for a tyre manufacturer. Listen and decide what they disagree about.

6 Listen again and complete these opinion statements.

1 Because they are entertaining, viral ads are easier to _____ than TV ads.
2 Virals are having _____ as they become more common.
3 Viral campaigns only reach a _____ of the population.
4 Humourous ads don't necessarily result in _____.
5 People _____ when they watch advertising by choice.

Internet research

Search for the keywords "*viral marketing videos*". Download some examples of video clips and hold a class vote for the best one.

Discussion

7 In small groups, explain why you agree or disagree with the opinions in 6.

8 Do you agree with the statement below? Describe viral or TV advertisements you like. How do they get your attention?

Like a James Bond film, a good ad has three essential ingredients: sex appeal, humour, and suspense.

9 Discuss how you would use sex appeal, humour, or suspense to promote these products.

| soda | holidays | jeans | chewing-gum | music | pizza | car tyres | printer cartridges |

Going viral

Six years ago, ad executive Ed Robinson carried out an experiment. He spent $10,000 to produce a humorous video about a man who meets an explosive end while inflating a child's raft. He attached his firm's Web address to the clip and emailed it to five friends. Then he waited.

By the end of the week, more than 60,000 people had seen the twelve-second video, Robinson says. The video had 'gone viral', passing from Robinson's friends to their own friends and from there, to blogs and sites across the Web. Within three months, Robinson's Web site received 500,000 hits.

For Robinson, the traffic was confirmation that the video and others like it could create a buzz and, in turn, make big bucks. 'I was trying to prove a point: If you entertain your audience, they will get it and the viral mechanism will make the audience come to watch you.'

Cashing in

Companies have gotten the message. Lured by the prospect of reaching millions of consumers without also spending millions of dollars for television air time or space in print media, companies have shifted more ad dollars to the Net. Video viral marketing – so named because it relies on computer users to spread commercials from person to person – has expanded from a negligible piece of the advertising pie to a $150 million industry, researchers estimate.

Victim of its own success

However, viral marketing has become a victim of its own success. As more ads and user-created videos go online, getting ads to go viral has become increasingly difficult. Whereas these ads were once relatively rare, they now have to compete with millions of other video clips. Companies need to spend more to give their message an edge. Today, Robinson's London company, The Viral Factory, charges $250,000 to $500,000 to create ads he guarantees will reach a wide audience.

Video sites

Not only do advertisers need to spend more to make the ads, but increasingly, they're having to pay to get them seen in the first place. Rather than waiting for new videos to drop into their mail boxes, users are now going to sites like *YouTube* for entertainment. Many of the hundred or so video sharing sites still don't charge for posting videos: they fear that too many ads will drive away audiences and stifle user-created content. After all, users go to these sites to see the videos most people find interesting, not ones some company paid to place. However, the largest and most popular sites, like *YouTube*, which shows about 100 million videos daily, already sell some spots, though they won't disclose advertising fees.

Going mainstream

It makes sense that video-sharing sites are wary of turning off users with too many ads. Neither the sites nor advertising companies want virals to become the new online spam. Still, with people spending more time on the Net, and many using video-friendly high-speed connections, it seems highly likely that viral video advertisements will become mainstream before long. And, as competition for online user attention increases, companies will be forced to do more to ensure their ads are watched. That in turn could encourage Web sites to charge more for spots. The bar has been raised.

Discussion

1 Explain what you think is meant by these quotations. Do you agree with them?

'Marketing is what you do when your product is no good' – Edwin Land, Inventor of Polaroid photography

'Business has only two functions – marketing and innovation' – Milan Kundera, Czech writer

'No great marketing decisions have ever been made on quantitative data' – John Sculley, former President of PepsiCo and CEO of Apple

2 Read the short text below and find the answers to these questions.

1   What are the four Ps?
2   What are the four Cs?
3   What is mix coherency?
4   What are mix dynamics?

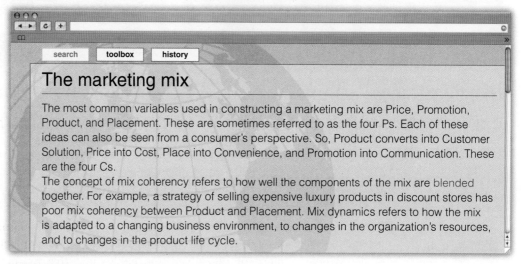

search   toolbox   history

The marketing mix

The most common variables used in constructing a marketing mix are Price, Promotion, Product, and Placement. These are sometimes referred to as the four Ps. Each of these ideas can also be seen from a consumer's perspective. So, Product converts into Customer Solution, Price into Cost, Place into Convenience, and Promotion into Communication. These are the four Cs.

The concept of mix coherency refers to how well the components of the mix are blended together. For example, a strategy of selling expensive luxury products in discount stores has poor mix coherency between Product and Placement. Mix dynamics refers to how the mix is adapted to a changing business environment, to changes in the organization's resources, and to changes in the product life cycle.

Discussion

3 Decide how successful the mix coherency and mix dynamics are in these examples. Use the four Ps or the four Cs to explain your answers.

1   An up market women's hairdressing franchise is opening salons in underground railway stations.
2   Accessories and spare parts for a popular portable cassette player are now only available by mail-order or Internet.
3   A distributor of T-shirts decorated with ecological symbols and slogans is advertising in women's fashion magazines.
4   An executive training company is promoting courses in business letter-writing on TV.
5   A video games company distributes discount coupons at football matches.

Listening

4 The marketing techniques below are part of the Promotion strand of the marketing mix. Match the marketing techniques 1–6 with their descriptions a–f.

1   undercover marketing
2   e-marketing
3   direct marketing
4   product placement
5   viral marketing
6   advertising

a) using electronic media like email or SMS to promote products
b) promoting products to target customers, for example, through addressed mail
c) persuading people to buy a product or service by announcing it on TV, radio, or in other media
d) marketing that spreads from consumer to consumer, often online
e) marketing in which customers do not realize they are being marketed to
f) putting products or references to products in media like films or video games

5 🌐 2:02 Listen to six examples of marketing techniques. Match them with the categories 1–6 in 4.

Internet research

Search for the keywords *"Maslow's marketing filter"*. Apply this technique to the ideas you developed in 8.

6 Complete the marketing collocations in sentences 1–10 with words from the box.

bring	declining	enter	flood	leader	niche	research	segmentation	share	study

1 The same product may interest teenagers in Europe and professionals in Africa: determining market _____ is about adapting the marketing mix to these different customer sub-groups.
2 Most companies are reluctant to invest in promoting a product if it faces a _____ market.
3 A custom-made product can be profitable if the company identifies and develops a small market segment or _____ market effectively.
4 Companies often try to capture market _____ by cutting prices or offering special deals.
5 Market _____ is needed in order to estimate the cost of doing business in a particular area.
6 The purpose of conducting a market _____ is to obtain information about customers' needs and how well they are met.
7 The company with the biggest sales in the sector is known as the market _____.
8 Manufacturers sometimes _____ the market with cheap products to 'buy' new customers.
9 Every great idea needs a manufacturer who is willing to invest in order to _____ it to market.
10 The quickest way for large retail chains to grow is to _____ new foreign markets.

Discussion

7 The following sales promotion techniques are often used to stimulate sales. Give examples of these techniques that you know. Use the list of products to help you.

1 BOGOF: buy one get one free
2 loss leaders: products sold at a low price to encourage sales of another product
3 tying: making sales of one product depend on the customer buying another
4 cashback: money returned after the customer has paid for something
5 bundling: selling several products together as one combined product

holidays	music	printer cartridges	soft drinks	software

8 Discuss solutions to these case studies. Explain how you would improve the marketing mix, what techniques you would use, and what sales promotion techniques would help.

Old Orchard

Old Orchard is a high quality apple juice made using organic fruit and traditional methods. It is sold at a premium price in restaurants and tea shops. Market share and profit margins are declining. How can Old Orchard update its image and diversify into new markets?

Crunchy Morning

Crunchy Morning make an exciting new range of breakfast cereals with unusual flavours, eg mint, grapefruit, strawberry and marmalade. How can Crunchy Morning capture market share on a saturated market?

That Touch Cosmetics

That Touch Cosmetics are well-known in Western Europe for their sensibly-priced skin care and beauty products for women. New management have ambitious objectives for growth. How can That Touch grow in what seems to be a mature market?

5 | Selling more

Refresh your memory

Question tags
Positive statement + negative tag
You're a frequent flyer, aren't you?

Negative statement + positive tag
You don't want to arrive exhausted, do you?

Use the same auxiliary or modal in the tag
You can't afford failure, can you?

If there's no modal, use *do*.
You need First Class service, don't you?

Negative questions
In contractions, put *n't* with the auxiliary
Don't you agree?

In the uncontracted, formal form, put *not* after the subject
Do your sales team not deserve the best?

▶ **Grammar and practice**
pages 124–125

Test yourself: question tags

1 Correct the question tags in these sentences.

1 A lot of people think branded goods are more expensive, aren't they?
2 But it's not just a matter of price, isn't it?
3 Brands guarantee style, design, and a certain level of quality, doesn't it?
4 An ordinary T-shirt won't last as long as a top brand, doesn't it?
5 Now, you wouldn't normally expect to see this kind of quality at these prices, do you?
6 Last week we sold 150 of these to a very well-known celebrity, haven't we, Mike?
7 She was going to give them to her friends at a very posh party she'd organized, hadn't she?
8 So ladies, get your T-shirt, as worn by Victoria – oops, shouldn't give the lady's name away, do I?

2 Choose the correct tag to complete each sentence.

1 So, you'd like to buy a second-hand car, …
   a isn't it?   b right?   c hadn't you?
2 Well, let's have a look at this little beauty, …
   a let us?   b do we?   c shall we?
3 Yes, does need a little work, …
   a doesn't she?   b doesn't?   c isn't it?
4 Somebody's broken the radio, …
   a hasn't she?   b haven't they?   c isn't it?
5 I'm going to have to get that fixed for you, …
   a haven't I?   b do I?   c aren't I?
6 Well, there's always room for negotiation,
   a isn't there?   b is there?   c isn't it?
7 Nobody'll ever say I'm not flexible, …
   a won't they?   b aren't I?   c will they?
8 So, just sign on the dotted line, …
   a do you?   b don't you?   c would you?

Test yourself: negative questions

3 Use words and phrases from the box to complete the salespeople's arguments.

Aren't you	Don't you	Don't you	Didn't they	Have you	Isn't
Wouldn't it	Wouldn't it				

1 *Wouldn't you* agree that spending your evenings doing chores is not much fun?
2 _____ be better if you could use that time to do something you enjoy?
3 _____ think a dishwasher could really improve your quality of life?
4 _____ concerned about your standard of living falling when you retire?
5 _____ help to know that, if something happened to you, your family would be secure?
6 _____ a few euros a week a very small price to pay for the peace of mind that a life insurance policy brings?
7 _____ never thought how nice it would be to get away from it all now and then?
8 _____ ever envy people who can jet off to their place in the sun?
9 _____ ever tell you what a good investment a timeshare can be?

Pronunciation

4 Read the two questions below. Which one asks for information? Which one suggests someone will agree?

a You don't happen to know how many you ordered last year, do you?
b You don't really want to run out of components, do you?

5 ♪ 2:03 Listen to someone asking the two questions. Pay close attention to the questions at the end. Which question has rising intonation ➚? Which question has falling intonation ➘?

6 ♪ 2:04 Questions with falling intonation are useful for persuading. Listen to eight questions from a training seminar about closing the sale. Decide whether each question is for getting information (I) or persuading (P).

1 _____   5 _____
2 _____   6 _____
3 _____   7 _____
4 _____   8 _____

7 Here are more questions from the sales seminar. Add suitable tags.

1 Just a question. You couldn't possibly give me a discount, _____?
2 It's out of the question. We couldn't possibly sell at a loss, _____?
3 So we agree that you'll try to get approval for the budget, _____?
4 You don't happen to know the date of the next finance meeting, _____?
5 You didn't by any chance send me an email yesterday, _____?
6 Still no news from your purchasing department; we started to discuss delivery dates, _____?
7 It's already week five, so clearly, there's no way we could deliver before March, _____?
8 I don't suppose you could agree to postpone delivery until May, _____?

8 With a partner, practise saying the questions in 7 with appropriate intonation. Invent suitable responses.

Listening and speaking

9 ♪ 2:05 Listen to attendees at the sales training seminar playing a game and complete the rules.

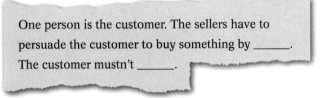

One person is the customer. The sellers have to persuade the customer to buy something by _____. The customer mustn't _____.

10 In small groups, play the game yourselves.

11 Make these sales arguments more persuasive by changing them to negative questions, as in the example.

Example
After a hard morning's work, your employees need a good, healthy lunch.
After a hard morning's work, don't your employees need a good, healthy lunch?

1 They deserve more than grabbing a hamburger or eating a sandwich at their desks.
2 They've earned the right to sit down to a proper meal in a restaurant.
3 There's a better way to keep them satisfied and motivated all afternoon.
4 You know that not being able to eat properly is one of the main reasons staff quit their jobs.
5 Your staff would appreciate receiving luncheon vouchers as part of their compensation.
6 You'd like to actually save money because luncheon vouchers are tax deductible.
7 It will be nice to do something positive for every employee.

12 Using question tags and negative questions, persuade a partner to buy one of the following.

a 1975 Volvo with 650,000 km on the clock
a collection of records of pre-war opera singers
a small 1960s house 50 metres from an oil refinery
a 4 metres x 3 metres painting of a tiger in the jungle
a 33-year-old racehorse
a camping holiday in Scotland in November

5 | Selling more

5.4 Speaking Dealing with objections

Discussion

1 Decide to what extent you agree with each statement. Choose from *I agree / It depends / I disagree*. Then compare your answers with a partner.

1 The customer is always right.
2 Selling a product, a service, or an idea all require the same skills.
3 You can't predict all possible objections before a negotiation.
4 An objection is a customer's invitation to be persuaded.
5 Customers will pay more to buy from people they like.
6 Never criticize the competition.
7 You can't get an agreement until all objections have been answered.

Listening

2 ⊙ 2:06–2:08 Listen to three conversations between sales representatives and their customers. Decide which salesperson makes each of the following mistakes.

a) criticizing the competition
b) giving in to pressure
c) overreacting and threatening the customers.

3 ⊙ 2:09–2:11 Read the descriptions of three common sales techniques. Listen to three improved versions of the exchanges in 2. Decide which of the techniques below each salesperson is using.

1 Use the 'feel, felt, found' formula.
   Tell the customer you know how they *feel*, but give an example of other customers who *felt* the same way but *found* they were wrong.
2 Redirect the objection to obtain more information.
   Use the objections as an opportunity to find out what the customer's position really is.
3 Welcome objections and try to establish agreement.
   Listen to the customer's objections and use persuasive questions to show understanding.

4 Listen again and complete the phrases the salespeople use.

Use the 'feel, felt, found' formula
I understand _____ _____ _____ . Like you, several customers _____ that this was more than they wanted to spend. However, they _____ _____ they were saving money.

Redirect the objection to obtain more information
So tell me, is the membership fee _____ _____ _____ you're not ready to sign up now?
So, if I could postpone your first payment to next year, _____ _____ _____ _____ to sign up today?

Welcome objections and try to establish agreement
I know exactly _____ _____ _____ . It's a big decision to make, _____ _____?
I _____ . We all want to get a product we can actually use, _____ _____?

5 Each salesperson ends with a question to confirm the customer's position. Listen and make a note of the question each salesperson uses.

Salesperson 1 _____   Salesperson 2 _____   Salesperson 3 _____

6 Match the objections and the answers used to redirect them.

1 Your price is too high.
2 We haven't budgeted for it.
3 I like your main competitor's products.
4 I don't have time to go to the gym.
5 I'll think about it.
6 I wouldn't use your product if it were free.
7 I only work with one supplier.
8 Your lead time is too long

a) You're probably wondering what's different about our service, aren't you?
b) Do you mean, why are our prices higher than the competition?
c) Can you find 30 minutes three times a week to look good on the beach?
d) You are asking yourself if it's worth finding the money, is that right?
e) Well, maybe we can test that theory! But of course you don't really mean that, do you?
f) Is the delivery date the only reason you're not ready to order?
g) If you like the deal I'm going to suggest, could you make a decision today?
h) Can I ask if there's a particular reason for only using them?

7 With a partner, write responses to each objection, starting each sentence with the words given. Then change partners and practise dealing with them.

1 We have a freeze on new investments. Call me back in six months' time.
Is the freeze the only _____?
2 Your competitor offered us the same service for twenty per cent less.
I'm glad you mentioned _____ .
But have you asked yourself _____?
3 I have doubts about your product's reliability and durability.
I understand how _____ .
A lot of our customers _____ .
But after they _____ .
4 I can't afford the insurance on a new car.
If I could show you how you _____?
5 I'm not sure that Head Office will be very pleased if we change our procedures.
You're probably asking yourself _____ .
Are you comfortable _____?
6 We need the parts now. We can't wait two weeks for delivery.
Do you mean that _____?

8 Work in small groups. You have started a company which organizes study trips for students and young business people to learn about business and culture in another part of the world. Brainstorm the following details about your study trip, as well as your own ideas.

destination   length of stay   type of organizations visited
travel and accommodation arrangements   social activities   cost

9 Predict at least five objections you expect your clients to raise. Think of answers to these objections and practice overcoming them.

10 Meet other groups and take turns trying to sell your study trip.

5.5 Writing Mailshots and sales letters

Discussion

1 Answer the questionnaire, then discuss your choices.

> ## A good mailshot should
>
> - be *as short as possible/neither too long nor too short/as long as necessary*.
> - put the most important point *at the beginning/in the middle/at the end*.
> - be written in *first person style (I)/second person style (you)/third person style (it)*.
> - focus on *features/benefits/costs*.
> - *always have a PS/never have a PS/have a PS and a PPS*.

Analysis

2 Read the sample mailshot below and choose a label for each paragraph:

> Action   Benefits   Credentials   PS   Hook   Promise

Dear Reader

New Business View multimedia magazine.

How do today's business leaders keep up to date without trawling through hundreds of pages of newspapers and magazines?

They rely on New Business View – the only digital multimedia magazine to bring you all the latest business news, trends and opinions on one handy, multi-format disk. Subscribe to NBV, and we guarantee you'll never need to buy another magazine!

Be the first to know about mergers and takeovers, marketing trends and management tools. Watch, listen and read, on DVD, in the car, or on your PC. NBV gives you a deeper understanding of the issues that matter, whoever you are, wherever you are and whenever you want. 'Better than an MBA' – NBV is your private briefing from the world's best business specialists.

NBV is used by executives in leading companies, large, medium and small, all over the world. Over half of America's top business schools recommend it as part of their programmes.

You too can enjoy a better view of the world of business. Subscribe now for twelve months or more, and receive three issues totally free of charge. Just fill in the attached form, or subscribe online at www.newbusinessview.com.

Sincerely Yours,

Jim Bradley

PS Reply within fifteen days, and get free access to NBV's new daily podcast!

3 Decide which paragraphs these tips on writing mail shots and sales letters refer to.

1. Don't forget to make it clear what you want – 'if you don't ask, you don't get!'
2. Give references which will persuade the reader that your product really delivers what it promises.
3. Tell the customer your USP – what only your product or service will deliver.
4. Provide additional motivation to act on the message.
5. Give readers details of the advantages they will enjoy.
6. You have less than five seconds to grab the reader's attention and make them want to read your message.

Internet research

Search for the keywords *"advance fee fraud"* to find out how dishonest writers persuade their victims to give them money.

4 Decide which part of a sales letter or mailshot you would put these sentences in.

1 Can you honestly say you would never prefer to stay in bed than to go to work?
2 I will call you early next week to arrange a demonstration of the software.
3 Over twenty per cent of Fortune 500 companies are already using our system.
4 Please feel free to call me for more information or to arrange an appointment.
5 There are only two kinds of company – market leaders and market followers. Which is yours?
6 This offer is available for a limited time only; call early to avoid disappointment!
7 Within six months you can expect a return on investment that no other consultancy can deliver.
8 Your company will enjoy significant gains in productivity, reliability and staff morale.

5 Sales letters and mailshots frequently build persuasive arguments by tripling: describing features and benefits in threes. Find and highlight four more examples of tripling in the letter in 2. What patterns of words are used in each group: verbs, nouns, adjectives, etc?

Examples
… all the latest *business news, trends* and *opinions*
Be the first to know about *mergers and takeovers*, *marketing trends* and *management tools*.

6 Use the tripling technique to build the arguments below. Add two more ideas to the sentences below.

1 The multimedia dictionary is ideal for students, _____ and _____ .
2 Regular sessions in your mini-gym will make you fitter, _____ and _____ .
3 Our office software helps you improve productivity, save _____ and increase _____ .
4 In this seminar you'll learn how to plan, _____ and _____ a presentation.
5 The new Porsche has improved handling, a redesigned _____ and _____ .
6 In less than an hour you'll be able to start using Homearchitect® software; in less than a day _____ and _____ .
7 The Norisko investment plan means you can save for a new house, _____ and _____ .
8 By the end of this CRM course, you'll have learnt how to handle difficult customers, how to _____ and _____ .

Writing

7 In small groups, write a mailshot for an electric bicycle, timeshare flats, a book club or a mail-order catalogue. Start by deciding the following features.

- who the target market is
- what the product's USPs are
- what its benefits are
- what its credentials are
- how you can grab the reader's attention
- what you want the reader to do
- what you can put in your PS

8 Write your mailshot. Remember to build persuasive arguments by tripling.

9 Give copies of your mailshot to other groups. Each group should choose the most persuasive mailshot (excluding their own). The group that makes the most 'sales' is the winner.

Discussion

1 The first hand-held mobile phone was marketed in 1983. It weighed half a kilogram and cost $3500. How have they changed since then? How will they continue to evolve?

Reading for implication

2 Read the introduction to the case, and answer questions 1–4 below.

'Min Su, have you any idea where Jung Jun is?' asked Thomas Ibanez, Seoul Deliveries' office manager.

'No, I'm sorry, I don't know,' replied Min Su, looking up from a bank of computer screens. 'He should have been back from a delivery an hour ago, but there's no sign of him.'

'Damn.' The Frenchman was frustrated. Running an efficient courier and delivery service was never easy in a city of ten million people and three million vehicles, but became especially difficult when drivers went missing. The old saying that 'time is money' was never truer than in the courier business.

'I suppose you've tried calling his mobile?' asked Ibanez.

'Yes, Mr Ibanez,' said Min Su, 'but he's on voice mail. Or more likely it's the battery. The drivers' mobiles are so old, the batteries are flat by the middle of the afternoon.'

'Alright, thanks, Min Su,' said Ibanez. 'Let me know as soon as you find out where he is. Oh, and listen, could you get in touch with Backchat Communications, and ask them to send us a proposal to renew our mobile phone fleet? They had an ad in the subway for phones with a geopositioning system – if we had those, we wouldn't have this problem. We desperately need to upgrade our technology.'

1 Why is Thomas concerned about Jung Ju?
2 Why do you think the saying 'time is money' is important in the courier business?
3 Jung Ju's mobile is on voice mail. How does Min Su explain this? What other explanations can you think of?
4 Thomas thinks geopositioning (GPS) may help. Why is this useful for a courier firm?

3 Read the advertisement, then answer the questions.

Backchat Communications – most popular mobile phone deals Monthly price plans and line rental

Basic	Smart	Hi-tech
400 minutes/month	800 minutes/month	1200 minutes/month
20,000 won/month*	40,000 won/month*	60,000 won/month*
Handset features: voice and text, built-in camera	Additional features: mp3 player, video games, Bluetooth	Additional features: email, PDA, FM radio, TV, geo-positioning system

* 12 months minimum Discounts negotiable for 18 and 24-month contracts.

1 Why are the Smart and Hi-tech plans more expensive than the Basic plan?
2 Why are Backchat prepared to negotiate discounts for longer contracts?
3 Which phone deal seems best for Seoul Deliveries' a) drivers? b) admin staff? c) managers?

Listening

4 ♪ 2:12 Listen to a conversation at Backchat between the Sales Manager, Harry Lim, and his assistant. Complete the notes.

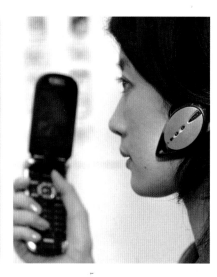

Customer:	Seoul Deliveries
Contact name:	(1)_____
Position:	(2)_____
Approx. number of units required:	(3)_____
User profiles and needs:	Admin staff – would like (4)_____ Managers – need (5)_____ Drivers – management want to motivate drivers with something (6)_____
Possible objections:	Drivers may object to (7)_____ (remind them about (8)_____) Managers may object to drivers (9)_____ and (10)_____ .

Internet research

Search for the keywords *"future of mobile phones"* to find out more about what we can expect in the future. Hold a class vote to decide on the most useful and the most useless applications.

Preparation

5 Divide into two groups, sellers with Backchat and buyers with Seoul Deliveries. Your goal is to negotiate the best possible deal. Discuss your strategy and what your main negotiating aims will be.

Negotiation

6 Work in small groups of two to four, with at least one buyer and one seller. Negotiate a deal. Write what you agree on the order form below.

Order form

Plan	Number of contracts	Period of contracts	Discount
Basic (20,000 won/month)	......	......	......
Plus (40,000 won/month)	......	......	......
Hi-tech (60,000 won/month)	......	......	......
Extras:	**number (paid)**	**number (free)**	
Spare battery	....	....	
Bluetooth headset	....	....	
Game and TV pack	....	....	

7 When you have finished your negotiation, calculate your score. Sellers go to page 113. Buyers go to page 115. Compare your score with other buyers/sellers to see who negotiated the best deal.

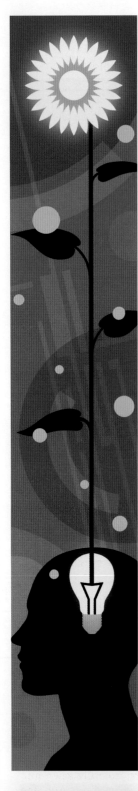

6.1 About business   Self-financing

Discussion

1 Decide which of the motivations below is most and least important when you start a business. Number the factors from 1–7 (1 = most important; 7 = least important).

☐ having total personal control
☐ the freedom of being your own boss
☐ making money quickly so that you can sell the business
☐ the satisfaction of providing quality goods and services
☐ the excitement of taking risks
☐ setting up a business for your children
☐ the ability to work at home

Reading

2 Read the title of the article opposite. What source of business funding do you think the author recommends?

3 Read the article and decide whether statements 1–7 below agree with the author's opinions. Write Yes (Y) if they agree with the author or No (N) if they disagree.

1 Venture capital is a good source of funding for new businesses.
2 Business schools give misleading advice on funding sources.
3 Investors always respond promptly to funding applications.
4 The process of obtaining funding will proceed at a fast pace.
5 Entrepreneurs who get funding rarely keep total control.
6 Venture capitalists have few good ideas to choose from.
7 Self-funding your own business ideas is too difficult to be practical.

4 Read the article again and match the headings below to paragraphs 1–6. One heading is not needed.

a Prepare for the worst
b Start small
c Choose partners carefully
d Consult widely
e Watch every penny
f Keep your integrity
g Identify markets

Listening

5 2:13 Listen to Alex Vecchia, a Californian business angel. How do his views differ from the writer of the article?

6 Listen again and complete the notes summarizing what Alex says potential investors will be looking for.

The team
must prove its honesty, determination and 1 _____
needs market knowledge and business 2 _____

The business
3 _____ financial forecasts
must show a high 4 _____ potential

The deal
must have a realistic business 5 _____
everything must be ready for the 6 _____ process

Discussion

7 Work in small groups. Your group has just won €500,000 on the Euro lottery. Discuss which company to invest in. Present your choice to the class and explain why.

Breezewatt – produces mini wind turbines which can generate 50 per cent of the electricity needs of the average home.

NewClear – produces high precision, high value components for nuclear power stations.

Fluban – has developed a vaccine against bird flu which has proved very promising in clinical trials.

Internet research

Search for the keywords *"bootstrapping business"* to find out more about do-it-yourself financing. Can you find any examples of successful companies that bootstrapped at the beginning?

THE ART OF DOING IT
yourself

WHAT advice would I give to new entrepreneurs who need funding? Forget about your business plan and buy a lottery ticket – your chances are better. My point is that when you need venture funding no one will give you any money until you already have a marketable product. In other words, funding comes just when you don't need it.

A myth spread by business schools is that the way to start a venture is to create a great business plan, perfect your pitch, and then present this to investors, starting with venture capitalists. If that doesn't work, you knock on the door of angel investors.

But ask any entrepreneur who has called on venture capitalists and they will probably tell you that it is almost impossible to even get calls returned. If venture capitalists do respond and you are invited to present your idea, the process will drag on for many months while you borrow more and survive on hope. If you do hit the jackpot, you are required to let the investors make many of the business decisions in exchange for an investment.

To be fair, most business plans don't deserve funding. Venture capitalists receive hundreds of plans every week, and few are worth the paper they are printed on. Everyone jumps on the same new trend, or the ideas are so far out that they have no chance of success. And great ideas aren't enough: it takes experienced management, excellent execution, and a receptive market. It's hard for even the best venture capitalists to identify the potential successes.

So what should an entrepreneur do? What all new entrepreneurs should understand is that, even if you have a realistic business plan for a great idea that can change the world, you need to develop it yourself until you can prove it. Focus on validating your idea and building it up. Raise money to get started by begging and borrowing from family and friends. And be prepared to dip into your savings and credit cards, obtain second mortgages, and perhaps look for consulting work or customer advances. There is no single recipe for developing your business idea yourself, but there are some essential ingredients. Here are some pointers:

1

Share your ideas with those who have done it before. You can learn a lot from the experiences of seasoned entrepreneurs, and they are much more approachable than you think. If you can't find anyone who is excited about your idea, the chances are it isn't worth being excited about. This may be time to reflect deeply and come up with another.

2

Speak to anyone who can help you understand your target customers. If you can sell your concept, some customers may help you fund it or agree to be a test site or a valuable reference. Customers don't usually know what they want, but they always know what they don't need. Make sure that there is a real need for your product.

3

Your idea may be grand and have the potential to change the world, but you are only going to do this one step at a time. Look for simple solutions, test them and learn from the feedback. If you're starting a restaurant, work for someone else first. If you're creating a software product, learn by doing some consulting assignments or create some utilities. You don't have to start with the ultimate product.

4

Focus on revenue and profitability from the start. Find creative ways to earn cash by selling tactical products, prepaid licenses or royalties. Pay employees partially in stock. Look for access to free hardware or premises. And sweep the floors yourself. In short, use any method to avoid costs.

5

It's going to take longer than you think. There will likely be product problems, unhappy customers, employee turnover, and lots of financial challenges. You may even fail a number of times before you achieve your goals. By learning from each success and failure alike, you increase the odds that you eventually make it.

6

Never forget the importance of business ethics and your own values. Ethics need to be carefully sewn into the fabric of any start-up. And the only way to reach long-term success is by achieving outstanding customer satisfaction.

With a lot of luck and hard work you may build a successful company that markets products customers really want. It is very likely that by this stage, you receive the phone calls from venture capitalists. This is the time to think of exit strategies and decide if you want to own a small piece of a big pie or a large piece of a small pie.

6.2 Vocabulary Funding a start-up

Discussion

1 Work in small groups. You are financial advisors to start-ups and small companies. What sources of funding would you recommend in these situations?

① **BUSYBODIES** is a temping agency providing clerical help to other companies. It needs a new photocopier/printer but it does not have the cash available to buy it.

② **FIXA** is a start-up providing home help for all sorts of everyday tasks or problems: gardening, household repairs, cleaning, ironing, etc. It needs £8,000 to cover start-up costs.

③ **DON BEAL** is an inventor. He has patented a new type of car engine which is 50 per cent more efficient than existing engines. He needs money to produce a prototype but wants to keep control of his business.

④ **ASC** is a small engineering company that has temporary cash-flow problems. It needs £1,500 to pay for raw materials. They are expecting to be paid £5000 in outstanding bills in the next two weeks.

2 Read the advice leaflet below about business funding. Match each type of funding with the correct description 1–6.

bank loan   equity finance   friends and family   grants   leasing   overdraft   self-funding

1 _____
Drawing on personal savings and credit cards can cover start-up costs without having to wait for other people's decisions.
The downside is that using credit cards can be expensive in the long-term.

2 _____
Regular repayments can make it easier to budget.
On the other hand, repayment schemes can cause cash flow problems. You may also need to provide security, such as business assets, or a guarantor.

3 _____
This can be a very flexible option for short-term or day-to-day requirements.
The disadvantage is that they usually bear a higher interest rate than other loans.

4 _____
They might be willing to provide an interest-free loan or not require security.
On the other hand, funding from this source can put strain on your relationships.

5 _____
You get your funding, while the investor only realizes their investment when the business is doing well. You also get their expertise.
On the downside, it's hard to raise this finance, and your own influence and share of the profits will be smaller.

6 _____
These appear to be a source of cheap financing. However, there is often strong competition, and you may be required to provide matching funds. You may also need to prove a wider benefit to the community.

7 _____
You can spread the cost of acquiring assets, and maintenance may be covered.
But it's more expensive than if you buy outright, and you don't own the assets until the end of the agreement.

3 Look again at your answers in 1. Would you change any of your recommendations?

4 Find words or phrases in the leaflet with the following meanings.

1 the amount of money you pay back each month
2 money coming into and out of your business
3 an item you agree to give if you fail to pay
4 a person who takes responsibility if you fail to pay
5 debt which you pay back without any additional charge
6 money you provide alongside government funding
7 the cost of keeping something working

Scan reading

5 Read the seven steps in an application procedure. Put the steps in order 1–7.

Seventh Heaven Angel Investors Group

The seven steps to heaven

a Screening meeting. If they didn't *turn* you *down* at Step 2, our review committee will invite you to a screening meeting. Be prepared to make a ten-minute pitch and answer any questions that *come up*.

b Self-assessment. Before *putting forward* your business plan for our consideration, you must *work out* if angel capital – and specifically capital from our group – is right for your company.

c Due diligence. If your presentation is successful, interested investors will *check out* the statements made in your business plan, presentation, and financial projections. They will go over your team's background and track record in detail.

d Funding. When all parties are happy with the terms and language contained in the term sheet, the deal can *go through*.

e Online application. Once you have decided to submit a plan, complete our application online. This is designed to identify the most important details about your business so that our internal review committee can *weed out* the non-starters.

f Term sheet. On successful completion of the due diligence process, interested angel group members will *draw up* a term sheet that *sets out* the structure of the investment deal, including type of equity and board of directors representation.

g Presentation to membership. If you *get through* the screening meeting, you will be invited to make a 30-minute presentation to our full membership, the goal being to convince members that your proposal is worth investigating in detail.

6 Use the phrasal verbs in 5 to complete the sentences.

1 Only two per cent of business plans _____ the complete funding process.
2 Problems often _____ in the early stages.
3 Business angels may _____ proposals for no apparent reason.
4 Angels always _____ an entrepreneur's background thoroughly.
5 It's worth getting a lawyer to _____ any contracts rather than trying to write them yourself.
6 The term sheet _____ all the conditions of the deal.
7 A lot of hard work is necessary before the deal finally _____ .
8 In your pitch, you should _____ clear and convincing arguments.
9 Get help if you can't _____ how much finding to apply for.
10 The screening meeting allows investors to _____ poor applications at an early stage.

Listening

7 🔊 2:14 Listen to four entrepreneurs explaining why their proposals were turned down. Decide which reason from the list below each person mentions.

lack of skills in the management team	no track record or proof of concept
financial forecasts based on assumptions	too complex
inadequate financial returns	not scalable: no growth potential
lack of trust	lack of market awareness
no clear exit route	

Discussion and presentation

8 Work in small groups. You work for a corporate finance firm bringing together investors and entrepreneurs. Using relevant phrases and vocabulary from the previous exercises, draw up a list of *Dos* and *Don'ts* for start-ups looking for funding.

9 Work with a partner from a different group. Present and compare your lists.

Internet research

Search for the key words *"business angels"* to find out more about their role in financing start-ups.

6 | New business

Test yourself: Future simple or future continuous

1 Complete the sentences using the future simple (*will do*) or future continuous (*will be doing*).

1 Don't call me at 2.30 because I _____ (talk) to the accountant.
2 I _____ (call) you tomorrow if I have time.
3 That was Dave on the phone. He _____ (not come) to the conference.
4 Good luck with the presentation. We _____ (think) of you.
5 Would you like a lift? I _____ (go) past your hotel on my way home.
6 I'll be seeing Dan tomorrow, so I _____ (tell) him then.
7 Where _____ you _____ (be) on Friday afternoon?
8 What do you think you _____ (do) a year from now?

Test yourself: Future continuous

2 Use the future continuous to make these questions about people's plans more polite.

Example
Are you coming with me tomorrow?
Will you be coming with me tomorrow?

1 Are you going to see Axel this week?
2 Are you eating with us this evening?
3 Is your boss coming to the meeting?
4 Will you stay in the office at lunchtime?
5 Are you going to phone the office?
6 Are you going to fly to Moscow?

Test yourself: Future perfect or future perfect continuous

3 Complete these sentences using the future perfect or future perfect continuous.

1 I _____ (not finish) the report by Friday.
2 He's going to get a medal because _____ (work) here for twenty years in June.
3 Pablo will be furious. When the plane gets in, he _____ (wait) for more than three hours!
4 Our next wedding anniversary is silver, so we _____ (be) married for 25 years.
5 She'll be exhausted when she arrives from Tokyo. She _____ (travel) for fourteen hours non-stop.

4 Complete the following conversation using the correct form of the verbs in brackets.

Cleo: August 19! Imagine, Tony. By this time next year we (1) _____ (float) the company and we (2) _____ (sit) by the Red Sea, sunbathing!

Tony: I don't believe it, Cleo. We (3) _____ (not go) public by then. We (4) _____ still _____ (try) to get the marketing right! Remember, Rome wasn't built in a day. And this coming Christmas is only our third anniversary – we (5) _____ (work) together for exactly three years. Anyway, stop dreaming! Now, when (6) _____ you _____ (see) that design consultant of yours next, Jules whatsisname?

Cleo: Well, I (7) _____ (not meet) him until next Thursday at the earliest. He's on a Nile cruise at the moment so he (8) _____ (not get) any further with the designs. And I doubt whether his employees (9) _____ (finish) anything before he gets back to the office. His staff hate him. He's a real dictator! And he certainly (10) _____ (not think) about us with all those pyramids to visit.

Tony: Talking of pyramids, I wonder if we shouldn't have just stuck with them instead of launching into this milk spa venture … ?

5 Sustain is company in the UK offering environmentally sustainable solutions to the building industry. Read Sustain's company history and complete sentences 1–6 below.

Sustain – COMPANY HISTORY

YEAR 1 started trading
opened warehouse in Staines
John Gregor named a managing director
YEAR 2 opened offices in Richmond
bought Housesmart, an interior design company
YEAR 3 began selling solar panels
started exporting products to Europe
YEAR 4 started receiving government grants for sustainable development

By the time Sustain reaches its fifth anniversary,

1 It _____ for _____ years. (trade)
2 John Gregor _____ managing director for _____ years. (be)
3 It _____ solar panels for _____ years. (sell)
4 It _____ offices in Richmond for _____ years. (have)
5 It _____ government grants for _____ years. (receive)
6 It _____ Housesmart for _____ years. (own)

6 Sustain is holding a party next week to celebrate its fifth anniversary. Read the invitation to the party. Complete the sentences about the guests' activities.

1 At 7.15, _____   3 At 10.00, _____
2 At 8.00, _____   4 At midnight, _____

7 Read the dialogue between the event planner and John Gregor. Complete the dialogue with the questions she asked using the future continuous.

Sue   Mr Gregor, I was wondering whether I could just ask you a few questions so that we can get all the planning right.
John   No problem. What would you like to know?
Sue   Firstly, what time (1) _____?
John   Personally, not until 7.30. I'll miss the cocktails unfortunately.
Sue   And (2) _____ a parking space?
John   No, I won't. I'm coming by train.
Sue   Fine. And how many awards (3) _____ ?
John   Three. Half an hour should actually be long enough.
Sue   Fine. Just a few practical things. (4) _____ the vegetarian option?
John   No, not for me, thanks.
Sue   OK. And finally, (5) _____ fancy dress?
John   Certainly not. Black tie. But I think some of the younger staff may enjoy dressing up.

Sustain

Fifth anniversary ball

Start 7 p.m. 5 November
Huntingdon Hotel*

Bring a guest
Black tie or fancy dress

7.00–7.30 Cocktails on the lawn
7.30–9.30 Three course dinner (vegetarian options available)
9.30–10.30 John Gregor gives company awards
10.30–11.30 Jazz band
11.30–2.00 Disco

*Hotel parking must be booked in advance if needed

Discussion

8 Work in groups. Sustain would like to expand, but will require a bank loan to do so. You have been asked to make a business plan for years 6–10. Complete the table with your own ideas. Say what you will be doing in each year, and what you will have achieved by your tenth anniversary.

Plan	
Year 6	
Year 7	
Year 8	
Year 9	
Year 10	

Internet research

Search for the key words *"environmentally sustainable solutions"* to find out more about changes in the construction business .

9 Present your business plans to the rest of the class. Vote to decide who has the best plans.

6.4 Speaking | Taking questions in presentations

Discussion

1 Work in small groups. The question and answer session is an important but unpredictable part of most presentations. Decide whether you agree or disagree with the following statements.

> If there are no questions, it means that you've made a really good presentation.
> It's better to answer questions during the presentation rather than waiting till the end.
> There's only one type of question: awkward!
> The question and answer session is an opportunity, not a threat.
> When answering a question, keep it brief.
> Never admit that you don't know the answer to a question. Bluff if necessary!

Listening

2 ◐ 2:15 Juliette Duncan, a presentations specialist, is giving a seminar on *Perfect Presentations*. Listen to the first part of her talk. What four pieces of advice does she give for fielding questions?

1 _____
2 _____
3 _____
4 _____

3 ◐ 2:16 Listen to the second part of Juliette's seminar. She mentions five types of question. Complete the list.

Five types of question

1 Useful 2 _____ 3 _____ 4 _____ 5 _____

4 Match each question type in 3 with the advice in a–f. There is one piece of advice you do not need. Listen again to check your answers.

a Make sure the question is irrelevant, be diplomatic and go on.
b You've already answered these questions in your talk. Remind the questioner and go on.
c Elicit questions by answering one of your own.
d They clarify what you're saying. Thank people for asking them.
e Ask somebody in the audience if they can answer the question.
f Don't bluff or lie. If you don't know the answer, offer to find out. If you don't want to answer, say so.

Commenting on questions

5 Read these comments on questions. Decide which of the five question-types in 3 they answer.

1 A question I'm often asked is: 'Where do you see the firm in five years?'
2 I'm afraid I don't have the figures with me. Can I get back to you on that?
3 I think I covered that in Part Two, but let me just recap.
4 To be honest, I think that raises a different issue.
5 I understand your position but I can assure you we've done our homework.
6 I'm glad you raised that point.
7 So, in other words you're asking ...
8 That's a very good question.

Speaking

6 Imagine your partner has given a talk about a company. Write five questions about the company using the prompts below.

a last year's profit figures
b when the company was founded
c the reasons for their successes
d who invented the company logo
e what colour they prefer

7 Work in pairs. One of you is the presenter and the other is the questioner. The questioner starts by saying that they have no questions, so that the presenter has to start the session. The questioner asks his or her questions from 6. When you have finished, swap roles.

Explaining and reformulating

8 A speaker is answering questions after a presentation about a new wind turbine. Put these expressions for explaining and reformulating in the correct gaps in the answer.

| That's why | so | It's quite simple | In other words | To be precise | To put it into perspective |

(1) _____, really. Our turbine is the most efficient on the market. (2) _____, twenty per cent more efficient than any of our competitors'. (3) _____ we're convinced that we'll meet our sales targets next year. (4) _____, we will sell more than 450,000 units in the European market in the next twelve months. (5) _____ that's twice as many units as this year, (6) _____ the future is rosy.

Presentation

9 Work in groups of three. Each member of the group should prepare a 60-second talk on one of the following topics.

your future career plans
the economy of your home town/country
a business idea you think will work
a subject of your own choice

10 When you have prepared your talk, tell your partners the subject so that they can prepare at least three questions each to ask you. When you are all ready, take turns delivering your talks and answering the questions using appropriate comments.

6.5 Writing **An executive summary**

Discussion

1 Look at the photos of four types of business. What do you think would be the risks and opportunities associated with investing in these types of business?

Scan reading

2 Read the executive summary from a business plan below. Answer these questions.

1 How is it different from other gardening businesses?
2 How will Greenman Gardening approach pricing?
3 Why is good service such an important part of this plan?
4 Which paragraph mentions the past and the future?

1 *Outline*
Greenman Gardening is a new medium-sized garden maintenance and design company located in the north of England. Greenman will be the first landscape gardening company in the country using tried and tested organic gardening techniques, in accordance with a detailed maintenance plan agreed with the customer.

2 _____
Greenman Gardening's emphasis will be on providing affordable organic garden maintenance services. Greenman will offer general maintenance, such as weeding and mowing, and small landscape projects such as walling, patios and other garden features.

3 _____
Greenman Gardening believes that the market can be segmented into two main groups. The first group Greenman Gardening will be targeting is young environmentally-aware homeowners. The second group is private home-owners who are either too busy or unable to ensure the upkeep of their garden on a regular basis.

4 _____
Greenman Gardening has assembled a strong management team. Paul Jacobs will be the general manager. Paul has eleven years' experience in the landscape gardening field. Karl Wenger will be responsible for the finance. Karl was a founder member of the Sustainable and Organic Horticulture Federation.

5 _____
1 By developing a reputation for personalized customer service and high-quality work, we will ensure that customers recommend us.
2 Landscape gardening can be seasonal, so temporary staff will be used in summer months to deal with increased demand.

6 _____
• Pre-tax income of £150,000 in Year 1.
• Pre-tax income of £220,000 in Year 2.

7 _____
Greenman Gardening is a quality landscape gardening service, listening to customers to ensure that their gardens are environmentally-friendly while reflecting their aspirations

3 An executive summary is often divided into sections. Match the seven common headings below a–g with the sections 1–7 in 2. The first one is done for you.

a Outline *1*
b Management team
c Mission
d Keys to success
e Core products and services
f Financial summary
g Target customers

Style

4 Answer these questions about the style of the executive summary.

1 Would you describe the summary as neutral or exaggerated? positive or cautious?
2 Is the summary written from a first or third person point of view?
3 Other than headings, what other techniques are used to organize information?
4 Which verb tense is used most often? Find and underline examples.

5 Using the ideas in 4, make small changes to sentences 1–5 to make them more appropriate to an executive summary. Decide which part of the summary they should belong to.

1 Greenman Gardening may increase turnover by 20–25 per cent in Year 2.
2 Sharon Roma will be the very best marketing manager for Greenman Gardening.
3 We will spend £20,000 on advertising in the first six months.
4 Greenman Gardening's competitive advantage is based on three factors: price, efficiency, and innovation.
5 Greenman Gardening are thinking of building an interactive website for customers to view landscape options.

Writing

6 Bowie's is a new business planning to open in an area called Shawton. It needs outside investment, but needs to put together a business plan. Read the information below and answer these questions.

1 What sort of business is it?
2 What arc its main products and services?
3 Who are its customers?
4 Why might it succeed or fail?
5 Who will run the business?
6 How much money do they hope to make?

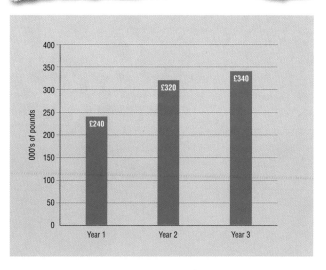

BOWIE'S CLOTHING COMPANY

MALE AND FEMALE STYLES

**T-shirts
Jackets
Jeans**

Personal fashion advisors available.
Open 9 a.m.–7 p.m.
Location: 7, Milson Road, Shawton

Kerry Clarke, shop manager: ten years' experience in retail.

Sam Marques, financial manager: part-owns two other successful retail businesses.

ABOUT SHAWTON

SHAWTON is a popular new place to live and work, especially for twenty and thirty-somethings in creative professions, like design and recording. Locals play hard and work hard, but like to look good. There's definitely competition to keep up with the latest fashions. If the area continues to grow in popularity, more retail outlets and other services will be needed to meet demand.

7 Using your answer in 6, write an executive summary for Bowie's business plan. Organize your summary using headings and express the main points appropriately.

6 | New business

Discussion

1 Answer the quiz below about starting a business.

Are you capable of minding your own business?

Could you start your own enterprise? Sure, you may have spotted a gap in the market, and even devised a cunning business plan for filling it. But do you personally have what it takes to turn a commercial idea into a profitable reality? Take our test to find out. **Answer Yes or No**.

1 Are you ready for a complete change?
2 Are you up for learning hard and fast?
3 Are you willing to take advice from others?
4 Can you stay self-motivated, even when faced with disappointment and difficulty?
5 Can you be emotionally resilient?
6 Are you able to think laterally?
7 Are you able to build up good working relationships?
8 Can you manage your time?
9 Can you work under stress?
10 Are you good at financial management?

2 Compare your answers with a partner. Say which areas would be your strongest and weakest points.

Reading

3 Kate Shapiro and Luis Hernandez are friends and former co-workers, living in Montreal, Canada. Read Kate's email to Luis and answer the questions.

1 Why was Luis depressed?
2 What does the winner of the fast pitch competition receive?
3 Why does Kate want to meet in a restaurant?

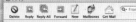

From: **Kate**
To: **Luis**
Re: **Let's go for it!**
Attachment: **Executive summary template**

Hi Luis,
Hope you got home alright last night. After our meeting with the bank yesterday, you looked really down! We'll just have to accept it as part of the learning curve and look for the 50K elsewhere.
Anyway, I'm still really excited about our Kaluma restaurant idea. And I'm still upbeat about the fast pitch competition next week. Just the fact we've been accepted for it means we're in with a chance! I know they don't offer direct funding even if you win, but there are always angels or venture capitalists in the audience who may be interested in the idea if the pitch is a good one. So, let's go for it!
I've been doing a ton of research on the net and I'm attaching an executive summary template which could help us get our pitch ready. Can we meet up Thursday to go over it? I thought we could eat at that new ethnic place in Cherry Street, you know, sort of get our minds focused in a real restaurant environment.
Drop me a line and let me know what you think.
Kate

4 What information can you already fill in on the executive summary template?

Listening

5 2:17 Two days later, Kate and Luis meet at the restaurant. Listen to their conversation and make notes to complete the rest of the template.

Preparation

6 Work in threes. Play the roles of Kate, Luis and Mario. Read the extract from the rules and, using the infomation on the template, prepare your pitch for the competition.

> 1 Pitches must be a maximum of 60 seconds, including any self-introductions and remarks. The microphone will be cut off automatically at the end of the 60 seconds, whether the pitch has finished or not!
>
> 2 Scoring is on a 1–10 scale (1 = lowest; 10 = highest) for each of the following criteria: interest, clarity, persuasion, and response to questions. The winner has the highest combined score.
>
> 3 Each pitch will be followed by a three-minute question and answer session.

Listening

7 2:18 Pitch coach, Darren Larkins, interrupts your preparation session to give you some last minute tips on making the perfect pitch. Listen to his advice and adjust your pitch if necessary.

Presentation

8 Each team has one minute to make their pitch, followed by a three-minute question and answer session. Other teams ask questions and act as judges. Use the scorecard to keep a note of the points you give but do not reveal them.

Internet research

Search for the keywords "angel fast pitch competition". How many fast pitch competitions can you find? Watch or listen to some of the winning pitches and choose the best one. Report back to the class.

Fast Pitch Scorecard					
Team	1	2	3	4	5
Interest					
Clarity					
Persuasion					
Response to questions					
TOTAL					

9 When every team has made their pitch, add up the points. The team with the highest total is the winner.

Review 5

Selling more

1 The words in **bold** are all in the wrong sentences. Move them so that the sentences make sense.

1 Ed Robinson emailed a video **mainstream** to some friends.
2 The friends posted the clip to **hits** and sites across the web.
3 Within three months, Robinson's web site received 500,000 **content**.
4 All this traffic was confirmation that video clips could create **virals**.
5 Companies have shifted more ad **blogs** to the Net.
6 But as more ads go online it is difficult for companies to give their advertising **interest** an edge.
7 Also, there is a danger that too many commercial ads will stop the development of user-created **dollars**.
8 Even Yahoo and Google still have few paid **message**.
9 Neither the sites, nor the advertising companies, want '**clip**' to become the new online spam.
10 But viral video ads are sure to become **ads** before long.

2 Complete the text with the words in the box.

coherency	convenience	cycle	environment
marketing	mix	place	price	product	promotion

The marketing mix is often defined as being 'the four Ps'. But seen from the customer's point of view, these should perhaps be the 'four Cs'. So (1) _____ becomes customer solution, (2) _____ becomes cost, (3) _____ becomes communication, and (4) _____ (distribution) becomes (5) _____.
This basic (6) _____ can be expanded to include sub-mixes. For example, the promotion variable can be further broken down into advertising, sales promotion, personal selling, publicity, direct (7) _____ and e-marketing.
The elements of the mix have to blend together, and this is called (8) _____. Further, the mix has to be adapted to a changing business (9) _____, to changes in the organization's resources, and to changes in the product life (10) _____.

3 Complete the text with the phrases in the box.

face a declining market	market leader
flood the market	market research
bring the product to market	market share
market segmentation	niche market

Start with some serious study – do some (1) _____ . Then you might discover how the market is divided up: the (2) _____ . If you have an innovative but specialized product, don't worry, there will be a (3) _____ for it somewhere. Once you've found a manufacturer, it's time to (4) _____ . Your aim initially will be to capture (5) _____ . To do this, you might have to (6) _____ with a large number of cheap products – even below cost. But if your product is a good one, and your competitors weak, then hopefully you will soon become the (7) _____ . However, here is a word of warning. Consumer tastes change very quickly and unless you continue to innovate you will soon (8) _____ .

4 Fill in the question tags at the end of each sentence.

1 Sales are up again this quarter, *aren't they* ?
2 It's not just because of our new advertising campaign, _____?
3 Profit margins look good as well, _____?
4 The new line of products won't be available until April, _____?
5 She's told Mike about the delay, _____?
6 Let's break for coffee now, _____?

5 Change the statements to negative questions to make them more persuasive.

1 It's time that you looked at some alternatives.
   Isn't it time that you looked at some alternatives?
2 You've been looking for a competitive edge.

3 Your customers ask for more functionality.

4 They would appreciate this model.

6 Look at the statement in italics made by a customer. Replies 1–5 below show how a salesman could deal with this objection. Fill in the missing letters.

Customer: 'The price is very high'

1 If I could po_ _ _ _ne your first payment until next year, would you be r_ _ _y to s_ _ _ up today?
2 I'm g_ _ _ you me_ _ _ _ _ _ _ that. You're probably wo_ _ _ _ _ _g why the price is higher than our competitors.
3 I understand how you fe_ _. A lot of our customers f_ _t that this was m_ _ _ th_ _ they wanted to sp_ _ _. But after using the product they fo_ _d that the be_ _ _ _ _s through increased productivity really justified the investment.
4 Is the price the o_ _ _re_ _ _ _ you're not re_ _ _ to sign up now?
5 Yes, I know ex_ _ _ _y what you m_ _ _. It's a big decision to make. But have you as_ _ _ yo_ _ _ _ _ _ why the price is set at that kind of level?

7 Match the sentences in exercise 6 to the uses below.

a) Welcoming the objection □ □
b) Finding out the customer's position □ □
c) Use 'feel, felt, found' □

8 Match the paragraphs typical of a mail shot to their descriptions below.

1 Hook □   3 Credentials □   5 Action □
2 Promise □   4 Benefits □   6 PS □

a saying what will happen if you use the product
b saying how you will get an advantage in your life
c finishing with a final reason to buy or act quickly
d saying what the reader should do next
e giving examples of existing users to establish credibility
f getting people interested in the product

9 Two of the paragraph types 1–6 in exercise 8 are not in the same order as the example in 5.5.2. They have been reversed. Try to guess which two, then look back to check.

Review 6

1 Fill in the missing letters in this article about starting a new business.

It's difficult to (1) r_ _ _e finance for a new business. (2) St_ _ -_ _ costs are usually high and (3) ven_ _ _e ca_ _ _ _ _ _ _ts may not even (4) r_ _ _rn your c_ _ _s. The process of looking for funds may (5) d_ _g _n for many months, and in the worst-case scenario you might even have to obtain a second 6) m_ _ _ _ge on your house. The best advice is to focus on (7) rev_ _ue and (8) pro_ _ _ _bility right from the start, and always look for ways to raise cash – perhaps through customer (9) ad_ _ _ces.

Learn from your failures, and you will increase the (10) o_ _s you eventually make it. But it's going to be difficult, and you will need determination and commitment to succeed. The bottom line is, you need to achieve (11) out_ _ _ _ _ing customer satisfaction if you want (12) l_ _ _-t_ _ _ success.

After the difficult early years you may get to the point where you can (13) p_ _ch your idea to a venture capitalist. Remember that they are looking for a business with a high (14) gr_ _ _ _ po_ _ _ _ial, and will want to carry out a full (15) d_ _ dil_ _ _ _ce process, including looking at your (16) au_ _ _ed accounts. They also need an (17) e_ _t s_ _ _ _ _gy that allows them to take profits on their investment after the business has been running for a while. But, with luck, you will (18) h_ _ the j_ _ _pot and obtain funding.

2 Complete each sentence with a form of a phrasal verb in the box. The clues in brackets will help you.

check out	get through	set out	come up
go through	turn down	draw up	put forward
work out			

1 When the new health and safety laws _____ we'll have to change the way the factory operates. (be officially approved and accepted)
2 They rejected all the proposals we _____. (suggest an idea so that people can discuss it and make a decision)
3 In her report she _____ her plans for reorganizing the department. (explains in a clear and detailed way)
4 It's a very confusing situation. I can't _____ what to do. (solve a problem by considering the facts; AmE: 'figure out')
5 Our brainstorming meetings usually generate a lot of ideas for new products, but only a few _____. (reach a good enough standard to pass to the next stage)
6 Something important _____ in the meeting this morning. I need to tell you about it. (was mentioned or suggested)
7 We agreed the deal in principle, now our lawyers have to _____ the contract. (prepare and write)
8 We should _____ his story carefully – I don't know whether we can trust him. (make sure that something is true or correct)
9 We were very reasonable during the negotiations, but they _____ our final offer. (refused)

3 Complete each sentence using the most likely form of the verb in brackets: either *will* or the future continuous (*will be doing*). Use contractions.

1 When I retire, I _____ (travel) around the world.
2 I won't be in the office on Monday – I _____ (travel) between Frankfurt and Berlin.
3 Is this seat free? No? Don't worry, I _____ (sit) over there.
4 This time next week I _____ (sit) under a palm tree drinking pina coladas.

4 Complete each sentence using the most likely form of the verb in brackets: either the future continuous (*will be doing*) or the future perfect (*will have done*). Use contractions.

1 By the time he retires, he _____ (work) here for over thirty years.
2 I don't think Markus will join us in the pub – he _____ (work) until late trying to finish the report.
3 By six o'clock we _____ (interview) more than a dozen candidates.
4 You won't be able to reach me on my mobile this afternoon – I _____ (interview) candidates for the new sales job.

5 Cover the box at the bottom of the page with a piece of paper.

The phrases below can be used when answering questions after a presentation. Try to remember the missing words, then take away the paper and use the words in the box.

1 I'm _____ I don't have the _____ with me. Can I _____ _____ to you on that?
2 I think I covered that in Part Two, but just let me _____.
3 To be _____, I think that raises a difficult _____.
4 I understand your position, but I can _____ you that we have done our _____.
5 _____ me explain. It's quite _____, really.
6 Our turbine is the most efficient on the market. To _____ _____, it's twenty per cent more efficient than any of our competitors'.
7 We will sell more than 450,000 units in the next twelve months. To _____ it into _____, that's twice as many units as this year.

afraid	assure	back	be	figures	get
homework	honest	issue	let	perspective	
precise	put	recap	simple		

7 | Financial control

Discussion

1 Work with a partner. Match the beginnings of these accountant jokes with their endings.

1　How many accountants does it take to change a light bulb?
2　Why do accountants get excited on Saturdays?
3　Why did the auditor cross the road?
4　There are just three types of accountants.

a　How much money do you have?
b　Those who can count and those who can't.
c　They can wear casual clothes to work.
d　Because he looked in the file and that's what they did last year.

2 What image does each joke give of accountants? What reasons can you think of for the image accountants have?

Listening

3 🌐 2:19 Listen to a careers consultant talking about changing perceptions of accountancy. Answer the questions below.

1　What three reasons does the consultant give for accountancy's traditional image?
2　What three reasons does the consultant give for accountancy's image improving?

Reading

4 Read the title, the first paragraph and the last paragraph of the article on the opposite page. Answer the questions below.

a　Do you think the 'Future accountant' T-shirt really exists?
b　Why does the author think it might be ironic?
c　Is the author positive or negative about accountancy in general?

5 Read the whole text. According to the author, which three personal characteristics do forensic accountants require?

6 For each question 1–4, choose the correct option a–d.

1　According to current perception, the accountancy profession
　　a　contains more attractive members.
　　b　is better paid than in the past.
　　c　has too many job applicants.
　　d　seems less boring than before.
2　The difference between forensic accountants and most other accountancy professionals is that their work always
　　a　involves attendance at major crime scenes.
　　b　relates to information used in legal procedings.
　　c　requires greater technical knowledge.
　　d　ensures that financial criminals get convicted.
3　Al Capone was finally sent to prison because
　　a　he was involved in a variety of crimes.
　　b　his financial affairs were exposed.
　　c　the Supreme Court convicted him.
　　d　his criminal gang betrayed him.
4　In the future, forensic accountants will
　　a　show how terrorist crimes get funding.
　　b　change attitudes to white-collar crime.
　　c　replace fingerprint experts on crime teams.
　　d　reduce levels of support for terrorism.

Internet research

Search for the key words *"extreme accounting"*. What does this involve? What do you think this idea is intended to achieve?

Discussion

7 Work in small groups. Discuss your opinions of the following questions.

a　How far are you convinced that accountancy's image is improving?
b　To what extent do you think accountancy is a good career choice? Why?
c　Is technology likely to make accountancy easier or more difficult in the future? Why?

WHY IT'S SEXY TO BE A
future
accountant

I RECENTLY SAW a student on a university campus wearing a T-shirt with the phrase 'Future accountant'. Given the profession's traditional image problem, it must have been ironic, mustn't it?

Perhaps not. There are signs that accountancy is putting its traditional image problem behind it. Increasing numbers of graduates are applying to join the profession, motivated not just by the prospect of high salaries but also by a change in perception. Ironically, it is partly its association with the twenty-first century's biggest financial scandals of Enron and WorldCom that has made accountancy become, well, sexier.

At the forefront of this image makeover is the specialism of forensic accounting, with its suggestion of crime scene investigators and technicians in white coats. In reality, a forensic accountant's work is chiefly concerned with any investigation of financial data which will eventually be used in some form of litigation. Some of them work for law enforcement agencies gathering evidence to support fraud and bribery charges. Others are expert witnesses who testify on either side in financial dispute cases.

While it might not always be CSI Miami, forensic accountants do need to develop some special skills which relate to their roles as investigators. For instance, a forensic accountant's work

can make them crucial figures in high-profile criminal cases like Enron, so a confident manner in court can be helpful. In addition, a systematic and analytical mind is essential. For example, in a fraud case, they may need to search financial records thoroughly, looking for patterns of similarities and coincidences that might indicate a cover-up. Imagination – not a characteristic traditionally associated with accounting – is also part of their skill set, as they dig deeper and try to get into the mind of suspected fraudsters.

Although the term forensic accounting is relatively recent, the importance of accountants in legal matters has a long history. The most famous case in which forensic accountancy has provided the pivotal evidence was in the conviction of the notorious Chicago gangster Al Capone. While Capone's criminal activities had included protection rackets and murder, he was finally convicted on the apparently lesser charge of tax evasion. Elmer Irey, an official at the US Inland Revenue Service, believed that Capone's conviction could be obtained on the basis of a Supreme Court ruling that the income from organized criminal activity was also subject to taxation. A team of investigators spent several years gathering evidence on Capone's net worth and expenditure, sometimes

working undercover as members of his criminal gang. They ultimately succeeded in assembling the documentary evidence needed to convict him.

Many believe that future demand for forensic accountancy services will only get bigger. Stories of scams and frauds emerge daily in the media, and, against the background of Enron and WorldCom, the problem of white-collar crime is being taken increasingly seriously by policy-makers. The US Sarbanes-Oxley Act is just one example of this change in attitude.

But it's not just in the area of white-collar crime that forensic accountants will find future employment. Terrorists require money for their activities but need to conceal their sources of funding to avoid capture. The role of the forensic accountant will be to reveal the money trail from terrorist suspects back to their sponsors. Their importance has recently led one senior British politician to liken forensic accountants to the fingerprint experts of previous generations.

The future looks bright for accountancy, and there are enough exciting roles in the profession to ensure that its image is not quite what it once was. So, in case you run into someone wearing a 'Future accountant' T-shirt, think before you congratulate them on their irony. They might just be serious.

7.2 Vocabulary Financial documents and regulation

Discussion

1 Work in pairs. Discuss the following questions.

1 How do you keep track of your personal finances? Do you keep accounts, use a computer programme to track your income and expenditure, or simply look at your bank statement?
2 Do you know today whether you are in credit or in debt?

Financial documents

2 Match the three main accounting documents 1–3 with the best description a–c.

1 profit and loss account
2 balance sheet
3 cash flow statement

a to indicate inflow and outflow of money over a specific period, in particular to make sure it does not run out
b to show managers whether a business made or lost money over a specific period
c to provide a snapshot of a business's value at a particular point in time, showing what it has and what it owes

3 Match the three main types of accounting document to the simplified examples below. Why are some numbers listed in brackets?

a _____

2008	
Cash receipts (a)	
Cash sales	€175,000
Loans	€40,000
Total cash receipts	€215,000
Cash payments (b)	
Rent	€102,000
Admin	€85,000
Total cash payments	€187,000
Net cash flow	€28,000

b _____

2008	
Net sales (c)	250,000
Cost of sales	(80,000)
Gross profit	170,000
Selling, general, and administrative expenses	(65,000)
Operating profit (d)	105,000
Other income	20,000
Earnings before taxes	125,000
Taxes	(25,000)
Net income	100,000

c _____

April 1 2008	
Assets	
Current assets (e)	
Cash	€75,000
Accounts receivable	€150,000
Total current assets	€225,000
Fixed assets (f)	
Land	€150,000
Total fixed assets	€150,000
Total assets	€375,000
Liabilities (g)	
Current liabilities	
Taxes payable	€100,000
Payroll	€125,000
Total current liabilities	€225,000
Long-term liabilities	
Loans repayable	€50,000
Total long-term liabilities	€50,000
Total liabilities	€275,000
Net assets (h)	€100,000
Owners' equity (i)	€100,000

4 Complete the sentences below with terms from the accounting documents labelled a–f.

1 A business's _____ are the sums that it will have to pay at some time in the future, such as loan repayments or taxes.
2 All funds going out of a business in a specific period are known as _____ .
3 The amount of profit after general running costs are deducted is known as _____ .
4 Businesses often have money in the bank or money owed to them, known as _____ .
5 The total income from all of a business's normal trading activity is known as _____ .
6 All money coming into a business in a specific period is known as _____ .
7 Some things that a business owns cannot be turned easily into cash: these things are its _____ .
8 The difference between what a business owns and what it owes are its _____ which are equal to the _____ .

Internet research

Search for the keywords *"financial statements beginners guide"* to find further information about the main financial statements. Which site presents the statements most clearly? Compare your findings and vote for the best site.

5 Match each of the accounting categories 1–6 with the examples a–f.

1 depreciation
2 plant and machinery
3 raw materials
4 accounts payable
5 payroll
6 extraordinary income

a Cherubs pre-school nursery employs five carers who get paid weekly.
b Focal photography shop owes €3,000 to its suppliers.
c Speedier deliveries owns six vans. Last year, the resale value of each van fell by 20 per cent.
d Jonson manufacturing has just raised €1.6 million from the sale of part of its site.
e Stronglite engineering has a small factory with a range of heavy-duty metal-working tools.
f KJK Products spent €10,000 on plastic pellets for manufacturing.

6 Answer the following questions about the categories in 5.

1 Where on the cash flow statement would you put **raw materials** and **payroll**?
2 Where on the profit and loss account would you put **depreciation** and **extraordinary income**?
3 Where on the balance sheet would you put **plant and machinery** and **accounts payable**?

Enabling and preventing

7 Read the short articles by three business owners describing how financial documents have helped improve their business. Complete each article with the correct form of a verb from the lists.

SALLY TIMMERMAN I run a clothing business in Barcelona called Tangerine. The balance sheet is an invaluable document for me. Because it's a snapshot, I find it (1) _____ me to really think about whether my business is in the best shape. The profit and loss account is helpful, but the balance sheet (2) _____ me see what I actually owe in the short and long term. It has also (3) _____ me from developing bad habits: for instance, it has (4) _____ me pay my creditors sooner rather than later, so that the balance sheet looks better and improves our position with the bank.

> let   make   encourage   discourage

JAIME TRIER When we started up, I used a cash flow forecast as part of our application to the bank and it (5) _____ us get a start-up loan. Our bakery business, Kernel, has gone from strength to strength since then, but keeping an eye on cashflow has always been important to (6) _____ cash imbalances. If we got this wrong, it might even (7) _____ us to go out of business. I used to use a spreadsheet, but I've invested in some accounting software now which (8) _____ me to present the information in the form I need.

> force   allow   help   prevent

DANA SOARES I set up DS Engineering ten years ago, with the help of investment from a group of business angels. Obviously, they demand detailed reporting on our finances. And, whilst their rules of investment don't (9) _____ certain practices in the way some accounting regulations do, they're understandably quite strict: they certainly wouldn't (10) _____ us to take any unnecessary risks. The profit and loss account (11) _____ the investors to see that we are making a profit and (12) _____ us to make better decisions on what to do next.

> prohibit   compel   permit   enable

8 Work in pairs. Use the verbs in 7 to write short explanations of what the following business documents are used to *enable, help, prevent*, etc.

health and safety guidelines   an annual report
a business plan   a meeting agenda

7.3 Grammar   Cause and effect, ability, articles

Test yourself: Cause and effect

1 Choose the most likely verb phrase to complete each sentence.

1   Our record profits **stemmed from/led to** an excellent sales campaign last year.
2   Rising consumer demand **resulted in/resulted from** an increase in interest rates.
3   A high number of unpaid invoices **originated in/gave rise to** cashflow difficulties.
4   Improvements in accounting software have **led to/developed from** faster and more accurate reporting.
5   Protests by shareholders **brought about/stemmed from** a change in the board.
6   Last year's losses **led to/arose from** market changes outside our control.

Test yourself: Describing ability

2 Complete the sentences with the correct form of the verb in brackets and another verb. You may need to use the negative.

1   Due to a severe shortage of money, the firm _____ (can) their suppliers last month.
2   Owing to a great effort in March, the sales team _____ (manage) all previous records.
3   The accountants _____ (be able to) the receipts, thanks to a poor filing system.
4   As a result of our competitors' problems, we _____ (succeed) our market share this year.
5   Gary _____ (manage) a loan, owing to a convincing business plan.
6   Due to low investment in R&D, the firm _____ (fail) any new products.
7   Firms _____ (can) less before a minimum wage was introduced.
8   Thanks to careful planning, we _____ (be able to) the deadline on this order.

Test yourself: Articles

3 Decide whether each sentence is correct or incorrect. If it is incorrect, correct it by adding, deleting, or changing the articles *a/an* or *the*.

1   Sue gave me a useful information about the new regulations.
2   Harry's a real technophobe: he just hates the computers!
3   The company were criticized for aiming products at the young.
4   To become accountant, Geri spent three years studying.
5   They bought a new machinery to help them meet the order.
6   Personnel are finding it difficult to find candidates with the intelligence.
7   Tina felt she didn't have the confidence to succeed in France.
8   Luke resigned after he was accused of an unethical behaviour.
9   When completing your expense form, remember to claim for the entertaining.
10 The CFO asked me to do a research to establish why our losses had increased.

4 Explain the difference in meaning between these expressions.

1   a   Jerry opened a restaurant in 1990 and he's still in business.
    b   Jerry opened a restaurant in 1990 and he's still in the business.
2   a   Toni couldn't attend the meeting since she was at college.
    b   Toni couldn't attend the meeting since she was at the college.
3   a   Stefan avoided talking about his private life in company.
    b   Stefan avoided talking about his private life in the company.

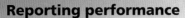

Reporting performance

5 *Fantastik* is a manufacturer of air-conditioning equipment. Read the targets for a set of key indicators and the firm's actual performance. Which targets did the company meet?

	Target	Actual
Unit sales	40,000	42,000
Value of sales	€1 million	€0.98 million
Repeat business	+ 5%	+ 5%
Admin costs	– 2%	– 3%
Raw materials (plastic)	– 4%	– 2%
Payroll	€250,000	€235,000
Operating profit	€220,000	€255,000

6 Complete the sentences using verbs for describing ability and your own words.

1 *Fantastik* hoped to sell 40,000 units, and *managed to sell 42,000*.
2 *Fantastik* planned net sales of €1 million. In fact, they only _____ .
3 *Fantastik* planned to increase repeat business by five per cent, and they _____ .
4 *Fantastik* set a target to reduce admin costs by two per cent. They _____ .
5 *Fantastik* hoped to reduce raw material costs by four per cent, but _____ .
6 *Fantastik* planned _____
7 *Fantastik* hoped _____

Explaining performance

7 Read the short articles. Make notes on factors which might explain each of *Fantastik*'s results.

HOTTEST ON RECORD

Yesterday, temperatures topped 38 °C for the fourth time in July. This means that we are having the hottest July since records began. Several offices have sent staff home after complaints about staff feeling ill at work. It's not all bad though: sellers of refrigerated products and air-conditioning …

Cost relief for businesses

After several years of spiralling costs, there are signs that businesses in Western Europe are finding it cheaper to operate. Labour costs have dropped slightly due to the availability of migrant workers from new European states. However, the picture for manufacturers is mixed: the price of oil is high. Consequently, petroleum-derived products are expensive, with knock-on effects on …

Exchange rate misery for exporters

Unfavourable exchange rates have meant that exporters have struggled to remain competitive, say industry analysts. 'We've also seen a big increase in unpaid bills', said one manufacturer yesterday …

8 Write a short paragraph about *Fantastik*'s performance. Use a variety of verbs from exercise 1 for describing cause and effect.

Example
Hot temperatures *resulted in* some sickness among staff. This *brought about* complaints and …

9 Complete the extract below from the CFO's speech to staff with *a/an*, *the* or no article.

Since I became (1)_____ accountant, I can't remember (2)_____ better year for (3)_____ air-conditioning business. We received (4)_____ information early in (5)_____ summer that (6)_____ hot weather was coming, and we increased (7)_____ production accordingly. Some people have found (8)_____ weather uncomfortable, notably (9)_____ elderly and (10)_____ very young. Many people have ended up in (11)_____ hospital. But (12)_____ demand for (13)_____ air-conditioning products has risen well in (14)_____ commercial sector, our main market. Congratulations to (15)_____ sales team, who had (16)_____ intelligence to sell effectively, and did (17)_____ great work all round. And I've got (18)_____ good news for you: all staff will receive (19)_____ bonus of €500 with (20)_____ next month's salary.

Speaking

10 Think of situations in which you

- managed to do something unexpected
- succeeded in meeting an important target
- failed to complete an important task
- weren't able to achieve what you had intended

11 Work with a partner. Tell your partner about the experiences in 10, explaining the events that led up to this and what effects the situation brought about.

Internet research

Search for the keywords *causes of business failure*. Find a story involving a strange chain of events and tell the class about it.

7.4 Speaking Communicating in meetings

Discussion

1 Work with a partner. Read the descriptions about how people behave in meetings and decide where you would put your culture on the scales. Compare your ideas with your partner.

In meetings, people generally:

are clear	are unclear
admit they don't understand	never admit ignorance
stick to the agenda	don't stick to the agenda
summarize decisions clearly	don't summarize decisions
are direct and sometimes rude	are indirect and never rude
often interrupt	rarely interrupt

Listening

2 🔊 2:20 The American group, Mahler, has recently acquired the French packaging company Polystok. Listen to the meeting between Alice, Mahler's CFO, and two Polystok employees, Serge and David. Answer the questions.

1   How successful do you think the meeting is?
2   How much do you think David and Serge understand?
3   How could the meeting have been more effective?

3 🔊 2:21 Now, listen to a second version of the same conversation. Why is the meeting more productive?

Analysis

4 Listen again and complete the expressions below.

Asking for clarification
Could you be (1)_____?

Clarifying
What I (2)_____ is …

Checking you understand
So, what you're (3)_____ is …

Checking other people understand
Do you (4)_____ what I _____?

Summarizing
Can we (5)_____ what we've decided?

5 Add each phrase below to the categories in 4.

a   In other words, …
b   What exactly do you mean by …?
c   I'm not sure I follow you.
d   To recap, …
e   Let me start again.
f   So you mean …
g   Does that make sense?
h   Before we close, let me just summarize the main points.
i   Am I being clear?
j   If I understand correctly …
k   Shall I go over the main points we agreed?
l   To sum up, …

Speaking

6 Read the four situations below. Decide what action you would recommend in each situation. Make short notes on your ideas.

a Levels of executive pay have been rising in your industry. This makes recruitment difficult for your firm. How should you respond?

b Your new CEO wants to introduce more American business practices. Some staff are resistant. What advice would you give the CEO?

c Your country's education system doesn't produce the graduates you need. How could you improve the standard of job applicants?

d Your firm has been criticized for employing too few women. How could you change this situation?

7 Work with a partner. Hold short meetings on the issues in 6. Follow the structure provided below. Take turns being A and B.

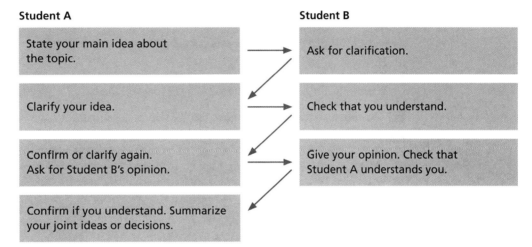

Student A

State your main idea about the topic.

Clarify your idea.

Confirm or clarify again. Ask for Student B's opinion.

Confirm if you understand. Summarize your joint ideas or decisions.

Student B

Ask for clarification.

Check that you understand.

Give your opinion. Check that Student A understands you.

Roleplay

8 Work in groups of three. Take the roles of Alice, Serge and David and read the appropriate role card: Alice (page 111), Serge (page 112) and David (page 114). Hold a meeting to discuss the points on the agenda and remember to clarify your position if necessary.

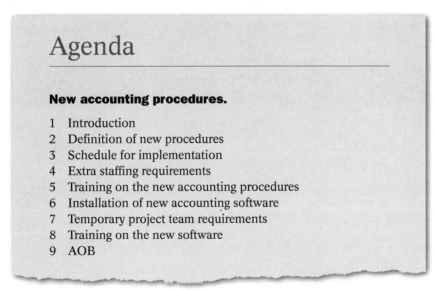

Agenda

New accounting procedures.

1 Introduction
2 Definition of new procedures
3 Schedule for implementation
4 Extra staffing requirements
5 Training on the new accounting procedures
6 Installation of new accounting software
7 Temporary project team requirements
8 Training on the new software
9 AOB

7.5 Writing Minutes

Discussion

1 Work with a partner. Read about the meeting situations 1–4 and answer questions a–c.

1 Hyperion Advertising office staff are meeting in a café to discuss their Christmas lunch.
2 Wells Engineering have just completed a major construction project. They are holding a one-off project review meeting today.
3 Living Colours is a printing company. The finance department are holding their fortnightly update meeting.
4 At Bitstore Electronics, two senior executives are meeting this afternoon to discuss which of four interviewees they will appoint as sales manager.

a How formal will each meeting be?
b What is the purpose of each meeting? What items do you think will be on the agenda?
c Which meetings require minutes? Why? How will the minutes be different?

2 Quickly read the minutes below. Decide which meeting from 1 they relate to.

Meeting minutes

Date: 11 June Time: 15.30
1 _____ : Room 344
2 _____ : Enzo Falconi (EF)
3 _____ : Alice Keller (AK), Francois Weber (FW), Dylan Sanders (DS)

4 _____	5 _____	6 _____
1 New staff	EF <u>announced</u> the appointment of Sally Collins as head of accounts payable.	
2 Office layout	FW expressed concern about the open-plan arrangement. We identified two main problems: telephone noise and lack of meeting rooms. AK proposed screens or full partitions. We agreed that EF (will investigate) the price of screens and FW will get quotations on full partitions.	EF and FW 25 June
3 Expenses claims	DS requested that all staff complete expense claim forms on time. We accepted that the form could be simpler. DS will prepare a new form by next meeting.	DS 25 June
4 Appraisals	We decided that the current appraisal system is not working, and we concluded that six-monthly appraisals would be better. AK to look into the practicalities of this.	AK 30 June

7 _____ : 25 June 13.00

3 Complete spaces 1–7 in the minutes with these labels.

Item   Action   Next meeting   Venue   Attendees   Discussion   Chair

4 Answer these questions about the minutes in 2.

1 What do you notice about how names are presented?
2 What is the purpose of the Action column?
3 Which verbs in the minutes tell you what happened? The first one is underlined.
4 Which verbs in the minutes tell you what actions are planned? The first one is circled.

Internet research

Search for the words *writing clear minutes* and draw up a list of ten tips for good minute writing. Compile a class top ten.

Summarizing discussion

5 Summarize these extracts from the meeting using appropriate verbs from the box. The first one is done as an example.

> congratulate   discuss   explain   reject   suggest   confirm

1 AK: Basically, there are two options: either we install screens or full partitions. Of course, screens would be cheaper, but, on the other hand, full partitions would probably be much more effective ...
   We discussed the pros and cons of screens or full partitions.
2 EF: So, to summarize, we all agree then that we don't want to keep the existing open-plan arrangement, OK?
3 EF: Well done, Sally. You've really done a great job in accounts receivable.
4 DS: The reasons why the current appraisal system is not working are that the interviews take too long and they only happen once a year.
5 DS: I've spoken to all the department heads and I can assure you that they all think the current expense claim form is too complicated.
6 FW: Why don't we get three quotations for screens and three for partitions?

Making action plans

6 Match the decisions 1–6 with the action plans a–f, using an appropriate action verb from the box. The first one is done as an example.

> chase up   contact   arrange   draw up   organize   evaluate

1 EF suggested celebrating Sally's promotion. He will *organize* – c
2 We decided to consult department heads on the new appraisal scheme. EF will
3 AK proposed getting examples of screens and partitions so she will
4 It was agreed that external advice on running appraisal interviews would be useful. FW will
5 We concluded that a more detailed cost breakdown was necesssary. DS to
6 It was noted that only one quotation has been received to date. DS to

a a visit to the suppliers' showroom.
b the other two suppliers.
c an after-work drink in the local pub for the accounts department.
d the best proposals and report back at the next meeting.
e a specialized management consultancy.
f a draft questionnaire before our next meeting.

Listening

7 2:22–2:24 Three months later, the Living Colours finance team are holding another meeting. Look at the three main items on the agenda below. What issues do you think the participants might raise regarding each point? Listen to three extracts from the meeting and check if your ideas were mentioned.

> **Meeting agenda** – Finance Department efficiency drive
> Date: 16 September
> Time: 14.30–16.00
> Venue: Room 346
>
> 1 Minutes of last meeting
> 2 Chasing up late payers
> 3 Covering for absent colleagues
> 4 Reducing office waste
> 5 AOB

Note-taking

8 Listen to the three extracts again. Make meeting notes on what they decided for items 2–4.

Writing

9 Use the notes you made in 8 to write the minutes of the meeting. Use the same format as the meeting minutes in 2 opposite.

7.6 Case study   Car-Glazer

Discussion

1 Work in small groups. Answer these questions about the activities in the list.

1 Are these actions honest or dishonest, or is there a grey area in between?
2 For which actions should employers warn, reprimand or dismiss people. For which should they do nothing?
- making personal photocopies at work
- using the company phone to make private calls
- embezzling money from the company
- going to the dentist during working hours
- throwing a 'sickie'
- surfing the net during office hours
- borrowing money from the petty cash

Reading

2 Read the three documents below and answer the questions.

1 What business is Car-Glazer in and what services do they offer?
2 What does Emily Wyatt do and how long has she been working for the Czech subsidiary of Car-Glazer International plc? Write her name on the organigram.
3 Who introduced Emily to Car-Glazer?
4 What problem is Car-Glazer facing with some of its technicians?

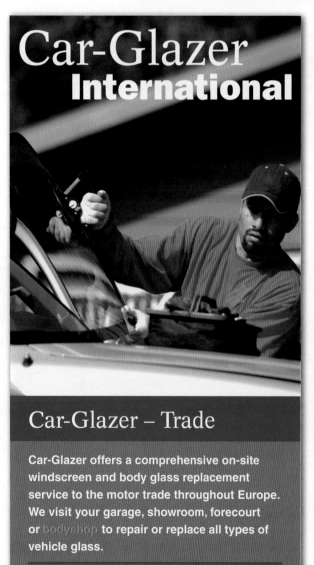

Car-Glazer International

Car-Glazer – Trade

Car-Glazer offers a comprehensive on-site windscreen and body glass replacement service to the motor trade throughout Europe. We visit your garage, showroom, forecourt or bodyshop to repair or replace all types of vehicle glass.

Chief Accountant

Reporting directly to the Director of Car-Glazer, Czech Republic.

Managing all aspects of the accounting function (accounts receivable and payable, budget, cash-flow, tax).

Establishing and maintaining accounting practices to ensure accurate and reliable data for business operations.

Hired Emily Wyatt 20 Feb 2008 (Referred to us by Filip Novak – they met at business school)

Memo

Date: 8 October 2008
To: All technicians

We are receiving a growing number of claims from garages for damage to vehicles in the course of glass replacement: paint chips, minor dents and scratches, broken mirrors, etc.
Please ensure that you work carefully and follow company procedures, as such claims cost us (and indirectly, you) money!
Counting on all of you to see a reduction in claims.
Andy Webb CEO Car-Glazer plc

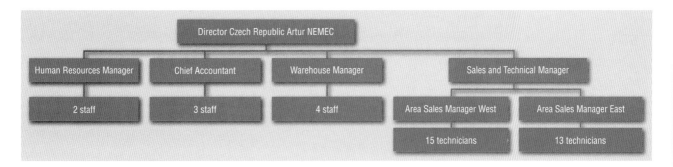

Analysis

3 Emily Wyatt arrives at work one morning to find this email waiting for her. Read the email and answer the questions.

1 What does Robert do in Car-Glazer? Write his name on the organigram.
2 What reasons could Nina Kovar have for being evasive?
3 What reasons could Garage Miler have for invoicing two separate bills and why might the technicians have caused more damage than usual?

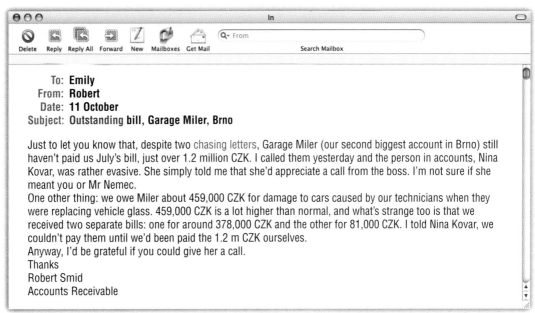

To: **Emily**
From: **Robert**
Date: **11 October**
Subject: **Outstanding bill, Garage Miler, Brno**

Just to let you know that, despite two chasing letters, Garage Miler (our second biggest account in Brno) still haven't paid us July's bill, just over 1.2 million CZK. I called them yesterday and the person in accounts, Nina Kovar, was rather evasive. She simply told me that she'd appreciate a call from the boss. I'm not sure if she meant you or Mr Nemec.
One other thing: we owe Miler about 459,000 CZK for damage to cars caused by our technicians when they were replacing vehicle glass. 459,000 CZK is a lot higher than normal, and what's strange too is that we received two separate bills: one for around 378,000 CZK and the other for 81,000 CZK. I told Nina Kovar, we couldn't pay them until we'd been paid the 1.2 m CZK ourselves.
Anyway, I'd be grateful if you could give her a call.
Thanks
Robert Smid
Accounts Receivable

Listening

4 2:25 Emily calls Nina Kovar. Listen to the conversation and answer the questions.

1 Who does Emily speak to in the end?
2 Who is Filip Novak? Write his name on the organigram.
3 What company car does Filip drive?
4 What car did Filip have repaired?
5 Why hasn't Garage Miler paid the outstanding bill?
6 In Emily's position, what would you do?

Discussion

5 Hold a meeting to decide what action Car-Glazer should take regarding Filip Novak. Consider the following courses of action:

- reprimand
- official warning
- temporary suspension
- dismissal
- other

Internet research

Search for the key words *"famous whistle blowers"*. What are whistle-blowers in the business world and what scandals have been brought to light by them?

Listening

6 2:26 During the meeting, Artur Nemec takes a call and announces some good news. Listen to what he has to say. How does this affect your decision?

8.1 About business   Fair trade or free trade

Discussion

1 Answer these questions.

1 What sort of products are traded under the label 'fair trade'?
2 When you buy a cup of coffee, what is 'a fair price'?
3 If you spent your holidays working on a coffee farm, how would you define 'a fair wage' and 'fair working conditions'?
4 If you owned a café, how would you define 'a fair profit' on a cup of coffee?

Predicting

2 Read the title of the article opposite and predict which of these points are expressed by the writer. Then read the article to check your predictions.

1 Fair trade products make rich consumers feel guilty.
2 Free trade would help the poorest farmers more than fair trade.
3 Fair trade products are low quality.
4 Fair trade farmers are encouraged to modernize their production methods.
5 Big coffee chains force farmers to reduce their prices.

Reading for detail

3 Read the article again and answer these questions.

1 What must be paid to get fair trade certification?
2 Why might western consumers be attracted to fair trade goods?
3 Which consequence of fair trade has led Mexican producers to expand production?
4 Why do richer producers benefit most from fair trade?
5 Which processes of agricultural development has fair trade discouraged?
6 How have consumer attitudes to coffee changed?
7 Which producers have improved income without help from fair trade?

4 Find phrases in the article that imply these strong opinions:

1 fair trade supporters know very little about economics (paragraph 1)
2 fixing fair trade prices unfairly deprives the poorest farmers of a way to make a living (paragraph 2)
3 fair trade supporters are naive to think they can solve all the problems of the developing world (paragraph 3)
4 fair trade supporters are out of touch with the realities of modern agriculture (paragraph 4)
5 fair trade prevents producers from increasing efficiency and revenue (paragraph 4)
6 coffee chains, unlike fair trade campaigners, benefit poor producers (paragraph 6)

Listening

5 🔊 2:27 Listen to a radio phone-in about the article. What two benefits of fair trade does the speaker argue for?

Discussion

6 Work in small groups. Discuss how far you think each of the statements below is true.

- Free trade rewards efficiency; fair trade rewards bad habits.
- Fair trade is the best protection some workers have against exploitation.
- Fair trade is just a fashion among rich western consumers.
- Free trade only looks to the short-term; fair trade looks at the bigger picture.

Internet research

Search for the keywords *"fair trade vs free trade"*; what values do the two movements share?

WHY **fair trade**
IS A BAD DEAL

IN THE NAME of fair trade, we are encouraged to pay more for everything from cups of coffee and chocolate bars to cosmetics and cut flowers. For a product to be certified as fair trade, the importer selling it in the West must pay a minimum price to producers. A voluntary price support scheme is entirely compatible with free trade: there is no conflict between altruism and the market economy. But while filling the shopping trolley with fair trade goods may relieve the guilt of middle class consumers, its wider effects may not really be so positive. A combination of economic illiteracy and misguided good intentions has created a monster that threatens the prosperity of the poorest producers.

Poverty relief would be much better served by a free trade and not a fair trade agenda. Fair trade policies, whether government-enforced or applied through ethical consumer schemes, distort the market. Producers in some countries may choose to produce certain crops only because they can get an artificially high price under fair trade schemes. This kicks away the ladder from the poorest producers who have no choice but to stay in the market. Take the example of Mexico, which produces a quarter of fair trade coffee. Because of the incentive of fair trade, Mexican producers have decided to keep producing coffee, even expanding production. Without this incentive, Mexico could be producing other crops more efficiently. This distorting effect is unfair on poorer countries such as Ethiopia where producing other crops is not an option. As a result of fair trade policies, they are faced with greater competition.

Fair trade also punishes producers who are less good at quality – generally the poorest. Setting a minimum price for products encourages retailers to buy only from more affluent producers that can invest in higher quality. Poorer producers may be able to supply lower quality products more cheaply, but there is no incentive to buy these, because the retailers cannot call it fair trade. By simply pronouncing it 'unfair' to pay below a certain price, fair trade supporters seem to believe they can ignore market realities, wave a magic wand and make everything better. But fair trade is like all attempts to control prices: the poorest are cut out of the market.

Free markets and more open trade have lifted hundreds of millions of people out of poverty over the last quarter century. They work because they encourage producers to pursue higher living standards by becoming more productive through mechanization and modernization. By contrast, fair trade supports a romantic view of peasant farmers toiling in the fields day in day out, rather than helping producers buy machinery and move into processing and packaging of products. The Fairtrade Foundation, which promotes the scheme in the UK, admits it has no policy on mechanization. It has even been encouraging producers to become less efficient by growing other crops in between coffee plants. This limits producers' ability to mechanize, locking them into poverty.

In stark contrast, Starbucks has been running community projects to help producers construct coffee mills and climb up the economic ladder. Shops like Starbucks, Caffé Nero and Coffee Republic have encouraged consumers to appreciate coffee as a premium product. Consumers are dropping the cheap instant coffee they were drinking in the office in favour of capuccinos and lattes made with high-price arabica beans. Many producers, following this logic, are now commanding higher prices. This is not because of fair trade but because they are responding to the demands of the market.

Despite attacks from anti-globalization activists, the truth is that Starbucks has done more than anyone else in expanding markets and raising incomes for coffee producers in developing countries. It is the coffee chains that are the real superheroes of the coffee market, not fair trade campaigners.

Brainstorming

1 In what circumstances might you do the following? Think of as many reasons as possible.

sign a contract	negotiate a contract	break a contract	cancel a contract
draft a contract	award a contract	renege on a contract	take out a contract

2 Calisto Instruments have drawn up a contract to supply JZ Music with 500 tenor saxophones for the Christmas market. Read the extract from the contract, and find expressions which mean:

1	accepted	6	pay the bill
2	in this document	7	considered as
3	promises	8	for whatever reason
4	not later than	9	inform
5	later in this document	10	impossible to change

this agreement, made and entered into this fourth day of June by and between Calisto Instruments, the Seller, and JZ Music Ltd, the Buyer:

1. The seller hereby undertakes to transfer and deliver to the buyer on or before 1 November, the goods as specified hereinafter.
2. The buyer hereby undertakes to accept the goods and pay for them in accordance with the terms of the contract.
3. The buyer shall make payment within 30 days of reception of the goods.
4. Goods shall be deemed received by the buyer when received by him at the port of Southampton.
5. The risk of loss from any damage to the goods regardless of the cause thereof shall be on the seller until the goods have been accepted by the buyer.
6. The buyer shall have the right to examine the goods on arrival, and he must give notice to the seller of any claim for damages within seven business days after such delivery. The failure of the buyer to comply with these rules shall constitute irrevocable acceptance of the goods.

3 Use the expressions from 2 to complete this second extract from the contract.

9. The seller (1)_____ (2)_____ to provide maintenance and repair for one calendar year. The buyer shall be required to (3)_____ to the seller of any request for repair. On expiry of the warranty, an extension agreement may be (4)_____: the buyer shall (5)_____ of the annual fee before any repair work can be undertaken, (6)_____. Signature of the warranty extension shall constitute (7)_____ acceptance of the terms and conditions (8)_____ specified. Warranties not renewed (9)_____ 1 April shall be (10)_____ lapsed.

4 Choose the correct word to complete the paragraph about litigation.

A legally (1) **holding/binding/sticking** contract is one which can be (2) **obliged/inflicted/enforced** by the legal system. Many contracts include a (3) **penalty/punishment/price** clause which (4) **concerns/applies/effects** if deadlines are not met. A company which fails to respect its commitments can be (5) **charged/processed/sued** for (6) **violation/breach/breaking** of contract. However, in some cases the two (7) **participants/parties/factions** can avoid the expense of litigation by agreeing an out-of-court (8) **settlement/agreement/conclusion**. If the case (9) **moves/goes/takes** to court, the loser may be ordered to pay millions in (10) **payments/damages/expenses**.

Discussion

5 Calisto and JZ Music have now signed the contract. Discuss what will happen if

1. Calisto deliver on 1 December.
2. Calisto deliver 500 alto saxophones instead of 500 tenor saxophones.
3. Calisto send JZ Music an invoice on 1 September.
4. the saxophones are delivered to Portsmouth.
5. some of the saxophones are damaged during shipping.
6. JZ inform Calisto of the damage in January after the Christmas holidays.
7. JZ refuse to pay.
8. JZ forget to extend the warranty.

Listening

6 Can you explain or give examples of these types of unethical behaviour?

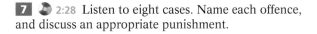

7 🔊 2:28 Listen to eight cases. Name each offence, and discuss an appropriate punishment.

Reading

8 Match the terms a–f below with the definitions 1–6.

a   accountability
b   regulatory bodies
c   borderline ethics
d   corporate governance
e   empowerment
f   best practice

1   deciding objectives, means and standards for a company
2   being required to justify one's actions to a higher authority
3   organizations which investigate irregularities, such as the Securities and Exchange Commission
4   a process that has been shown to give excellent results
5   paying workers the minimum wage allowed by the law, for example
6   encouraging workers to improve the way they do their own jobs

9 Complete the book review with the terms from 8.

IN her latest book, *Ethical Profits*, Hannah Shallanberger, who serves on the board of several corporations, argues that good (1)_____ is not incompatible with making profits. According to Shallanberger, values like honesty, fairness, transparency and (2)_____, when combined with commercial and manufacturing (3)_____, can help to make the world a better place.

Shallanberger blames Enron, WorldCom and other scandals first and foremost on spiralling executive pay. A world where six-figure salaries, stock options and golden retirements are a CEO's top priority encourages (4)_____ and leaves little space for global justice and social responsibility. Shallanberger advocates a third way. Companies which favour employee (5)_____, and which foster a sense of ownership and social responsibility throughout the organization, can not only obey the law, comply with and even exceed the requirements of (6)_____, but also give customers, employees, the environment, and shareholders a fair deal. This book is a must-read for anyone involved in business strategy.

Discussion

10 Complete the questionnaire, and then discuss your answers.

Ethical business or profit **first?**

1 Lying, cheating and bending the rules is
a) unacceptable.
b) OK as long as you don't get caught.
c) part and parcel of business.

2 A company should
a) respect the spirit of the law.
b) respect the letter of the law.
c) be morally beyond reproach.

3 The majority of corporate profits should go to
a) shareholders.
b) top management.
c) all company staff.

4 Honesty and responsibility is the best policy
a) always.
b) sometimes.
c) rarely.

5 Shallanberger's third way with 'ethical profits' is
a) the key to twenty-first century business.
b) a nice idea, but difficult to do.
c) hopelessly idealistic.

6 Making the world a better place is
a) a company's primary goal.
b) something companies can contribute to.
c) nothing to do with business.

8.3 Grammar   Obligation and permission, inversion

Test yourself: Obligation and permission

1 The statements below are answers to telephone enquiries about car hire. Choose the correct modal verbs to complete each comment.

1 You **mustn't/don't have to** drive more than 3000 km during the rental period.
2 You **are allowed to/must** follow our guidelines on how to use the vehicle at all times.
3 You **can't/don't have to** make any changes to the hire car under any circumstances.
4 You **must/can** put a child seat in if you want to, but it's your responsibility.
5 You **have to/can** bring your driving licence in order to collect the car.
6 You **must/don't have to** take out extra insurance, but it is recommended.

Test yourself: Obligation and permission in legal documents

2 The hire car company's Terms and Conditions are available online to download. Complete this extract from the document with the modal verbs.

| may   may not   shall   shall not |

On collection, the customer (1)_____ provide documentary evidence that he or she is legally entitled to drive. The customer (2)_____ use the vehicle strictly in accordance with these Terms and Conditions. The customer (3)_____ exceed a mileage of 3000 km during the rental period. The customer (4)_____ alter or modify the vehicle in any way. However, the customer (5)_____ install a child seat at his or her own risk. The customer (6)_____ request additional insurance at a cost of €20 per day.

Test yourself: Permission or possibility

3 The sentences below are taken from official documents. Decide whether *may* or *may not* indicate Permission or Possibility in each sentence.

1 The user may make one copy of the program to protect the original.
2 Misuse of the product may render the warranty null and void.
3 Untrained personnel may not operate this equipment without qualified supervision.
4 Operating procedures must be respected, or the product may not work.
5 Motorists may only use the emergency lane when authorized to do so by the police.
6 Photographs may not be taken without written consent.
7 Any amendment of this certificate may render it invalid.
8 Only staff may use this exit.

Test yourself: Inversion

4 Reorder the words in **bold** to complete these sentences.

1 Under no circumstances **child/used/shall/labour/be**.
2 Not until both parties agree **the court/will/the certificate/issue**.
3 Only once the contract has been signed **demolition/may/begin/work**.
4 On no account **held/the company/be/responsible/can/the damage/for**.
5 The goods **packaged/not/be/should/correctly/only** but also clearly labelled.
6 Should **not/payment/be received/seven/within/days**, a fine of €30 will become due.
7 On no account **the seal/broken/should/be**.
8 Under no circumstances **be/the use/will/pesticides/tolerated/of**.

Refresh your **memory**

Obligation
In most cases, we can use *must*, *mustn't*, *have to*, and *don't have to*. In very formal cases, you may encounter: *shall* and *shall not*.

Permission
In normal cases, we can use *can*, *can't* and *(not) be allowed to*. In very formal cases, you may encounter: *may* and *may not*.

Inversion
After certain negative phrases, subject and verb are inverted. *Not until all details were agreed did they sign the contract.*

▶ Grammar and practice pages 130–131

Internet research

Search for the keywords *"golden bull"* to find examples of 'legal-speak'. Note down the most amusing or the worst example and report back to the class.

Setting guidelines

5 Managers often give guidelines to new employees on how to conduct themselves on company business. Complete guidelines a–h using modals of obligation and permission.

a *You have to* obey the law and act ethically at all times.
b _____ use video or audio recording equipment on the company's premises.
c _____ use the Internet in an appropriate and responsible way.
d _____ disclose sensitive information about the company's products.
e _____ make negative claims about our competitor's products.
f _____ get permission to download software onto office computers.
g _____ accept small gifts from suppliers and other business partners.
h _____ buy or sell the company's shares in expectation of a major announcement.

6 Sentences 1–4 are taken from a formal employment contract. Rewrite these in less formal English.

1 Employees shall not make expense claims in excess of €20,000.
   Remember that you _____ than €20,000.
2 All employees shall maintain company property in good condition.
   If you work here, you _____ after company property.
3 The Employer may terminate the contract with a one-month notice period.
   As the employer, I _____ the contract with just a month's notice.
4 Employees may not use the telephones for personal use.
   I think I ought to warn you that you _____ or family.

Listening

7 2:29 Firms may also issue a code of practice to business partners as part of a contract. Listen to two managers discussing the terms of an outsourcing agreement in the Far East. Make notes on what they decide in these categories.

| Minimum age | Working hours | Breaks | Safety | Accommodation |

8 Work in pairs. Using your notes in 7, write formal guidelines for the suppliers in the Far East.

9 The clauses below were also included in the contract. Complete each sentence with a possible result.

1 Evidence of poor working conditions may *result in* …
2 Products not finished to agreed standards may …
3 Legal representatives appointed by us may …
4 Failure to use safety clothing may …

10 Rewrite these sentences from the contract, using inversion to make them more emphatic.

1 Unless you can implement the full terms of the contract, don't agree to it.
   Under no circumstances should …
2 We won't pay for the goods until the full shipment has been received.
   Not until the full shipment …
3 The goods will be considered received when they arrive at our warehouse.
   Only once the goods …
4 Health and safety must not be put at risk for any reason.
   On no account must …

Writing

11 Think of five rules relating to conduct in your school or job, for example. Then write the rules in the style of a formal employment contract.

Example
We mustn't use mobile phones during lessons/meetings.
Under no circumstances shall mobile phones be used during lessons/meetings.

8.4 Speaking Negotiating a compromise

Discussion

1 Discuss what compromise might be found in these situations. How satisfactory is the compromise for each party?

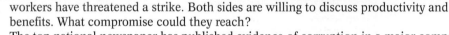

1   A bad atmosphere has developed between students and teachers in a language class. The students complain that they get too much homework. The teacher is disappointed by the lack of enthusiasm for speaking English. How could they reach an agreement?
2   Management at a car plant have offered a five per cent pay increase in response to workers' demands for ten per cent. The workers have threatened a strike. Both sides are willing to discuss productivity and benefits. What compromise could they reach?
3   The top national newspaper has published evidence of corruption in a major company. Unfortunately, the company is the newspaper's most important advertising customer. How can the two parties reach an agreement to maintain their business relationship?
4   A dairy producer sells most of its products to a major supermarket chain which has been making late payments. The supermarket claims the suppliers' products have fallen in quality. What could each side do to improve their relationship?

Listening

2 2:30 Leah works for an American fair-trade chocolate manufacturer, and Alfredo represents a workers' cooperative in Ecuador. Listen to a contract negotiation for cocoa beans and answer the questions.

1   What do they agree on these topics?
    • the fair-trade premium for top-grade cocoa beans?
    • prefinancing/advance payments?
    • growing the crop under shade trees?
    • children under fifteen?
2   What went wrong in the negotiation?

3 2:31 Listen to a second version of the negotiation, and answer question 1 above.

Why is this version of the negotiation more successful?

4 Listen to the second version of the negotiation again, and complete the missing verbs in these useful expressions.

Offering a compromise
I am ready to … , on the understanding that you …
I'm prepared to _____ you half way.
Shall we split the difference?

Accepting a compromise
That _____ fair.
I can _____ with that.

Accepting with conditions
We are _____ to agree to …, provided that …
I'd be _____ to …, unless …

Rejecting a compromise
I'm sorry, but I'm not sure that would work.
I think we'll have to _____ to disagree
I'm afraid you put me in a difficult position.

Internet research

Search for the keywords *corporate barter*. Make a list of benefits companies can derive from this type of trade.

Practice

5 With a partner, suggest more appropriate expressions for this negotiation, then practise the dialogue.

A I can pay ten per cent more, but you work Saturdays as well.
B No way! I coach my local swimming team on Saturday afternoons.
A How about 50–50? I pay five per cent more, and you work Saturday mornings.
B No. Not unless I can keep the company car at the weekend.
A Deal!

6 Work in pairs. Using the framework below, take turns being A and B to practise compromising in the following situations:

1 Student A wants to organize a two-day fair-trade conference in Berlin. B prefers a week in Hong Kong.
2 Student A wants to sell fair-trade chocolate in cheap 1 kg bars. B wants to sell it in expensive, individually-wrapped squares.
3 Student A is a coffee-grower and wants a five-year contract and a guaranteed minimum price. B is a manufacturer and wants a one-year contract and an index-linked price.
4 Student A wants to sell as many fair trade products as possible in their supermarkets at higher prices. B wants to sell the cheapest products at the lowest prices.

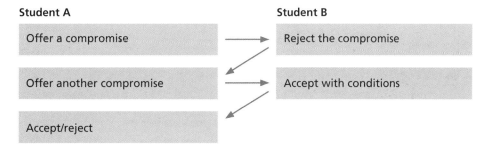

Student A

Offer a compromise

Offer another compromise

Accept/reject

Student B

Reject the compromise

Accept with conditions

Negotiation

7 Work in pairs. You represent small neighbouring countries in trade negotiations with each other. Student A should read the instructions and table below. Student B should look at page 115.

Student A

You have a surplus of some commodities and a shortage of others. Relations between your country and Student B's country are very friendly. Negotiate a deal with Student B to get the commodities you need.

	You have	You need	After negotiation, you have:
Coal	4 million tons	1 million tons	
Gas	2 billion cubic meters	5 billion cubic meters	
Oil	0	200 million barrels	
Wheat	3 million tons	1.5 million tons	
Coffee	0	2000 tons	
Tobacco	40,000 tons	25,000 tons	
Steel	8 million tons	6 million tons	
Gold	20 tons	20 tons	
Aluminium	200,000 tons	350,000 tons	
Chemicals	1 million tons	2 million tons	

8.5 Writing   Assertive writing

Discussion

1 Decide which of these adjectives complete the description of *assertiveness*.

Being assertive means being …

confident   rude   submissive   personal   polite
objective   aggressive   evasive   direct

Complaining assertively

2 Read this letter of complaint and answer these questions.

1 Which paragraph describes the customer's inconvenience?
2 Which paragraph describes factual details?
3 Which paragraph demands action?
4 Is the tone of the letter assertive or aggressive? Give reasons.

Dear Sir or Madam,

I am writing to **protest** about some problems we have experienced in relation to your products and customer service.

We purchased a printer from your online store two months ago. The invoice is attached. This product was immediately discovered to be **complete rubbish**. Due to an electrical problem, the printer makes a loud buzzing noise.

Despite **seemingly endless** emails and phone calls, we have been unable to obtain any assistance. What is **utterly intolerable** is the **total ignorance** displayed by your helpline staff. **Never in a million years** would this **excuse for** after-care service be acceptable from a high-street store.

We **want** you to resolve this situation to our satisfaction within seven days of receipt of this letter. Failure to reply by this **deadline** will result in the matter being referred to our legal department.

Yours faithfully,

E Lonamar

---

3 Replace each phrase in **bold** in the letter with a more appropriate phrase below.

especially frustrating   lack of interest   faulty   under no circumstances
expect   date   complain   level of   numerous

4 Rephrase these sentences to make them more assertive. Use the sentences starts and endings given.

1 It seems we can't print our annual report. I'm afraid that's especially annoying! (What is …)
2 I'm sorry but I don't think the printer delivers what your website promises. (In no way does …)
3 Unless you fix the printer before the end of the week, I'm afraid we'll have to consider suing you. (Failure … legal action)
4 People in the office find the constant buzzing noise annoying. (What people …)
5 Our Paris office needs a printer. I'm afraid I don't think it's very likely we'll recommend yours! (Under no …)
6 We might have to contact a consumers' association, as you don't seem to want to help us. (Unless …)

Responding assertively

5 Decide whether each expression implies that the speaker will give a *positive* or a *negative* response. Which 'negative phrase' suggests the speaker will negotiate?

in principle	as things stand	by and large	on the whole
unfortunately	to be honest	regrettably	

6 Choose the best expressions to complete this email.

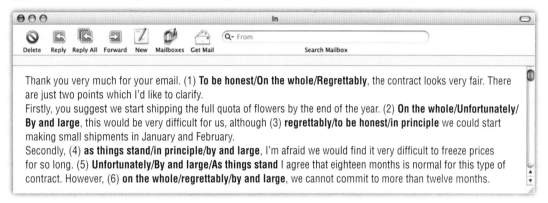

Thank you very much for your email. (1) **To be honest/On the whole/Regrettably**, the contract looks very fair. There are just two points which I'd like to clarify.

Firstly, you suggest we start shipping the full quota of flowers by the end of the year. (2) **On the whole/Unfortunately/ By and large**, this would be very difficult for us, although (3) **regrettably/to be honest/in principle** we could start making small shipments in January and February.

Secondly, (4) **as things stand/in principle/by and large**, I'm afraid we would find it very difficult to freeze prices for so long. (5) **Unfortunately/By and large/As things stand** I agree that eighteen months is normal for this type of contract. However, (6) **on the whole/regrettably/by and large**, we cannot commit to more than twelve months.

7 Using expressions from 5, write assertive one-line answers to these messages from your CEO.

1 We have a crisis. Can you fly to Canada tomorrow morning?
2 How would you feel about working two days a week from home?
3 I'd like you to get a couple of years' experience in the US before taking on more responsibility.
4 We need someone to manage the night shift. Do you think you can handle it?
5 We think you should do an MBA. What's your reaction?
6 Next year's sales conference is in Siberia. You'll be organizing it.

Writing

8 Divide into As and Bs. The As work for a fair trade clothing company in Bangladesh called Ganges Fashion. The Bs work for AQX Logistics, a global transport provider who handle Ganges' logistics operation in Europe.

1 Read your message below which you have received from your boss then discuss what to say.
2 Write a letter and deliver it to the other company.
3 Reply to the letter you receive.

Student A

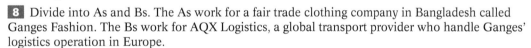

Hi
I'm furious with AQX Logistics. They promised us next day delivery of small packages, but they're often more than three days late. Their online tracking service never works because their system is down most of the time, and they've just put their prices up again! Unless they give us a better discount, we can't afford to work with them any more. Can you do me a favour and email them? If I do it, I'll just get angry. If they can't come up with a solution, tell them we'll get someone else. We've already warned them several times.
Thanks
Tareq

Student B

Message

FROM: Clyde Lang, Finance
TAKEN BY: Annette

Please write to Ganges Fashion. They've finally paid last quarter's invoices, but they've deducted the tax again. We've already explained they have to pay us first, then they can claim the tax back. And they're only supposed to have 30 days credit, not 90! If they don't pay the tax by the end of the month Clyde wants to suspend service.
NB Clyde was extremely angry, so he didn't want to write to them himself.

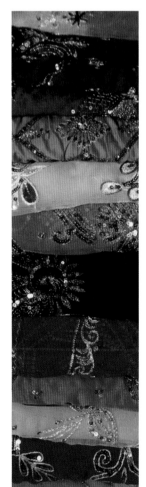

8.6 Case study Green Hills Coffee

Discussion

1 Explain these two quotations. Is there a place in business today for a 'gentlemen's agreement'?

An Englishman's word is his bond. – sixteenth century proverb
A verbal contract is not worth the paper it's written on! – Sam Goldwyn

Reading

2 Fiona Hills is President and CEO of Green Hills Coffee. Read the memo she received from her CFO and the attachment, and answer the questions.

1 What is the problem, and what are the risks for Green Hills?
2 What does the CFO want Fiona to do?
3 What special circumstances might affect Fiona's judgement?
4 Which clauses of the contract are concerned?

GREEN HILLS Coffee
THE TASTE OF QUALITY!

Re: Potential image problem

I heard yesterday that farmers in Guatemala are still employing child labour on coffee farms, although there are no contracts of course, so we can't prove it. I also discovered our biggest supplier is planting in virgin forest areas and using increasing amounts of pesticides – all clearly in breach of the terms of our contract (see attached). I know your father had a special relationship with the Cabrera family and used to turn a blind eye, but we have to sort this out quickly. There are other suppliers whose beans are just as good. We're already under pressure from fair trade brands – fair trade sales grew 40 per cent last year – we simply can't afford to be associated with these practices!

3.1 New planting in virgin forest areas is prohibited.

3.2 The supplier shall make continual reductions in the toxicity and use of agrochemicals.

3.3 Materials on the ICGA Prohibited Materials List may not be used.

4.1 All workers shall be employed under legally binding labour contracts.

4.2 Children below the age of fifteen may not be employed.

4.3 Working shall not jeopardize schooling or the social, moral or physical development of the young person.

Listening

3 2:32 Listen to a conversation at Granos Cabrera between Fabio Cabrera and his wife Magda and fill in their opinions.

	Fabio	Magda
Opinion of Gordon Hills		
Opinion of Fiona Hills		
Reasons for Granos Cabrera's problems		
Solutions to Granos Cabrera's problems		

4 Green Hills and Granos Cabrera have decided to send representatives to meet and negotiate on neutral territory in New York. Work in small groups, A and B, to prepare the negotiation. The As should consider Green Hills' options, and the Bs about Granos Cabrera's.

	Green Hills	Granos Cabrera
What we would like to obtain (maximum)		
What we must obtain (minimum)		
Possible strategies		
Our best alternative if no negotiated agreement is possible		

Reading

5 Read these two emails: who are they from and to, and how do they affect the situation?

… and we are planning an aggressive marketing campaign based on quality and price, which fair trade and organic brands will not be able to compete with. We know the quality of your beans, and we are prepared to offer 10–15 per cent more than your current distributor. In addition, we are prepared to help you increase your volume of production …

… our coffee is strictly organic and we are fair trade certified. Moreover, we are confident you will find our taste is smoother and richer than that of your present supplier, at a price which is only five per cent higher …

Internet research

Who buys fair trade foods? Search for the keywords *"green consumers"*. Draw up a customer profile for green, organic or fair trade products and services.

Negotiation

6 Hold meetings between Green Hills (As) and Granos Cabrera (Bs) to try to negotiate solutions.

Discussion

7 Compare the outcomes of the negotiations. Which strategies produced the best results?

Agenda

Child labour
New planting in virgin forest areas
Pesticides
Organic farming
Fair trade certification
Investment
Prices
AOB

Review 7

Financial control

1 Match the words and phrases in the box to their definitions below.

> bribery   fraudster   law enforcement agency
> litigation   protection racket   scam   tax evasion
> white-collar crime

1 use of the legal system to settle a disagreement _____ (informal equivalent: 'to go to court')
2 the use of illegal methods to pay less tax _____
3 the crime of giving money to someone so that they will help you by doing something dishonest _____
4 *informal* a dishonest plan, usually to get money _____
5 an illegal system in which criminals threaten to harm you or your property if you do not give them money _____
6 someone who obtains money from other people by tricking them _____
7 crime in which people who work in offices steal money from the company they work for _____
8 an organization such as the police that makes sure that people obey laws _____

2 Try to remember the words from financial statements to complete the gaps below. Some letters have been given to help you.

1 In the Income Statement, you start with the N_____ S_____s (income from trading activities), subtract the various costs and ex_____s , and you arrive at the O_____g P_____ (earnings from the trading activities of the business).
2 The basic equation in the Balance Sheet is: A_____ (things that the business owns) minus L_____s (things that the business owes) equals O_____s' E_____y .
3 In the old days, money owed to the company by its customers was referred to on the BS as 'debtors'; these days it is called acc_____ r_____ . Equally, money owed by the company to its suppliers was referred to as 'creditors', while these days it is called acc_____ p_____ .
4 A company's fi_____ a_____s are things that can't be turned easily into cash. They include pl_____ and m_____y (a factory and all its equipment), vehicles etc.
5 The items in the previous sentence lose value over time. This is referred to as d_____ .
6 A single word that means 'all the people that a company employs and the money that each of them earns' is p_____l .
7 An important item on the cash flow statement of a manufacturing company will be its payments for r_____ m_____s (physical inputs to the production process).
8 A company might have a one-time income from the sale of some land or the sale of a part of the business. This is referred to as ext_____y income.

3 Match an item from the first box with one from the second box.

> as a result   brought   due   led   on account
> owing   resulted   resulted   were caused

> about   by   from   from   in   of   of   to
> to   to

Now use the whole phrases to complete these sentences.

1 All the late payments by our suppliers *brought about* / _____ / _____ serious cashflow problems.
2 Serious cashflow problems _____ / _____ / _____ all the late payments by our suppliers.
3 _____ / _____ / _____ / _____ all the late payments by our suppliers, we had serious cashflow problems.

4 For each sentence, underline the one correct option in **bold**.

1 When I was younger I **could to / succeeded to / succeeded in / was able to** play tennis all afternoon without getting tired.
2 After five tries I finally **could / managed to / managed in / succeeded in** send the fax.
3 After five tries I finally **could / managed to / succeeded to / succeeded in** sending the fax.

5 Put a tick (✓) if the sentence is correct. Put a cross (✗) if it is not.

1 That's a very useful fact.
2 That's a very useful information.
3 That's very useful information.
4 Those are very useful facts.
5 Those are very useful informations.
6 In business, the facts are more useful than the theories.
7 In business, facts are more useful than theories.
8 I have the facts I was looking for.

6 Put the ten phrases into five matching pairs according to their function (how they are used).

1 Am I being clear?
2 Can we go over what we've decided?
3 Could you be more precise?
4 Do you see what I mean?
5 If I understand correctly ...
6 In other words, I ...
7 Shall I go over the main points we've agreed?
8 So, what you're saying is ...
9 What exactly do you mean by ... ?
10 What I mean is that I ...

Now write the phrase numbers above in the boxes below.

Asking for clarification ☐☐
Explaining your point more clearly ☐☐
Reformulating to check you understand ☐☐
Checking other people understand ☐☐
Summarizing ☐☐

Review 8

Fair trade

1 Make expressions about free trade and fair trade by matching each verb to a phrase a–h below.

1 relieve   a higher living standards
2 threaten   b a minimum price for products
3 pursue   c your guilt by buying fair trade goods
4 set   d the prosperity of the poorest farmers
5 ignore   e more productive through mechanization
6 lift   f people out of poverty
7 become   g market realities
8 climb up   h the economic ladder

2 The verbs 1–6 all collocate with *a contract*. Match each verb with its closest synonyms a–f.

1 sign   a discuss and finalize, draw up
2 negotiate   b produce a first version of
3 break   c enter into, accept
4 cancel   d give
5 draft   e end
6 award   f be in breach of, renege on, violate the terms of

3 Match each legal word (typical of a contract) 1–10 with its meaning a–j.

1 irrevocable   a settle the bill
2 give notice   b impossible to change
3 hereby   c promise
4 undertake   d in this document
5 make payment   e inform

6 deemed   f no longer effective
7 on or before   g for whatever reason
8 hereinafter   h considered as
9 lapsed   i later in this document
10 regardless of   j not later than
   the cause thereof

4 Use words from the left-hand column in exercise 3, in the correct form, to complete the sentences.

1 The seller _____ _____ to provide maintenance and repair for a period of one year.
2 The buyer shall be required to _____ _____ to the seller of any request for repair.
3 The buyer shall _____ _____ of the annual fee.
4 Signature of the contract shall constitute _____ acceptance of the terms and conditions _____ .
5 Warranties not renewed _____ _____ _____ 1 April shall be deemed _____ .

5 Complete each sentence with a pair of items from the box.

> goes to court / damages   legally binding / enforced
> parties / out-of-court settlement   penalty clause / applies
> sued / breach of contract

1 A _____ contract is one which can be _____ by the legal system.
2 Many contracts include a _____ which _____ if deadlines are not met.
3 A company which fails to respect its commitments can be _____ for _____ .

4 In some cases the two _____ can avoid the expense of litigation by agreeing to an _____ .
5 If the case _____ , the loser may be ordered to pay millions in _____ .

6 Make collocations by matching the phrases 1–6 with the words a–f.

1 commercial best   a bodies
2 money   b practice
3 requirements of regulatory c empowerment
4 good corporate   d trading
5 insider   e governance
6 employee   f laundering

7 Find a word from exercise 5 or exercise 6 which matches the definitions below. The words appear in the same order as above.

1 must be obeyed according to the law _____ (two words)
2 promises _____
3 be subject to a legal claim (in order that the other person can try to get money from you because you have harmed them) _____
4 people or group involved in a legal argument or legal agreement _____
5 process of taking a claim to a court of law _____ (*not* 'goes to court')
6 money that you pay to someone else as a punishment for harming them _____
7 putting money that has been obtained illegally into a legal business so that you can hide it _____
8 needs _____
9 the process of controlling and regulating an organization (formal) _____
10 giving someone more control over their life _____

8 Match a phrase 1–3 with a phrase a–c with the same meaning.

1 You mustn't do it.   a You have to do it.
2 You don't have to do it.   b Don't do it.
3 You shall do it.   c You may do it if you want.

9 Put the words in each sentence into the correct order.

1 I'm to meet half way you prepared.
2 Shall we difference the split?
3 I live that with can.
4 We are compromise to willing.
5 I'd do that to be reluctant.
6 I think to disagree to agree we'll have.

10 Look at the expressions in the box. Find five matching pairs (so that members of one pair have a similar meaning).

> as things stand   by and large   frankly   in principle
> on the whole   regrettably   the way things are now
> theoretically   to be honest   unfortunately

Additional material

1.2 Vocabulary: education and career
Discussion (page 8, exercise 7)

Student A

I wasn't a very motivated student when I was younger, so I _____ my exams in 1999 and had to retake them the following summer. I'd already decided I wanted to _____ then go to business school, so this time I _____ and _____ thoroughly; I passed easily. I spent a year abroad as an assistant in a secondary school and then went to business school – I'd already _____ and successfully _____ before resitting my exams.

In my second year as _____, I spent a semester as an intern at Hewlett Packard, which was very rewarding. In fact, I went straight into a job at HP after I graduated the following June. They encouraged me to do a _____ by correspondence – I just have to finish writing a dissertation. I need a break now, but I may take a sabbatical to study for an MBA in a few years' time.

1.2 Vocabulary: education and career
Listening and discussion (page 9, exercise 13)

Speaker 1

Bob's situation is similar to that faced by Steve Jobs, who quit Apple Computer in 1985. Jobs sold his shares and founded Next Computer. Although Next was never as successful as Jobs had hoped, in 1996 Apple bought the company, and Jobs became CEO the following year. Under his guidance, Apple brought out the iMac and the iPod; the rest, as they say, is history. Steve Jobs is now thought to be worth $4.4 billion.

Speaker 2

Lucy finds herself in a similar situation to Joanne Rowling, who wrote most of her first Harry Potter novel while she was unemployed or working part-time in Edinburgh cafés. After being rejected by twelve different publishers, Rowling's book was finally accepted - although her publisher advised her to get a part-time job as there wasn't much money in children's books. In February 2004, Forbes magazine estimated her fortune at £576 million (just over US$1 billion), making her the first person ever to become a $US billionaire by writing books.

Speaker 3

Mel's dilemma is similar to that faced by William Henry Gates III, now better known as the world's wealthiest individual, worth over $50 billion. In 1975 Gates dropped out of Harvard to pursue a career in software development with Paul Allen, his high school business partner; together they founded Micro-Soft, which was later to become Microsoft Corporation.

1.5 Writing: Cover letters
Brainstorming (page 14, exercise 1)

> **Dos**
> *Do ask directly for an interview.* Request an interview, and tell the employer when you will follow up to arrange it. It is imperative that you follow up.
> *Do follow the AIDA model used in advertising – attention, interest, desire, action.* Write cover letters that are unique and specific to you, but consider using four paragraphs: 1 get your reader's attention; 2 give details of your accomplishments; 3 relate yourself to the company, showing why the company should hire you; 4 request action.

> **Don'ts**
> *Don't start your letter 'Dear Sir or Madam'.* Address your letter to a named individual whenever possible.
> *Don't write a formal introduction in the first paragraph.* Use the first paragraph to grab the employer's attention.
> *Don't write at least 400 words – the more information you give, the better.* Never write more than one page. Each paragraph should have no more than three sentences.
> *Don't use sophisticated language to make a good impression.* Use simple language and uncomplicated sentence structure. Eliminate all unnecessary words.

2.6 Case Study: Meteor Bank
Discussion (page 29, exercise 6)

> **Student A**
>
> You represent the HR department at the meeting. You feel Saul Finley is the right man for the job and should be trusted to complete the work he has started. You believe high staff turnover is a good thing, because salary costs are falling and Saul is replacing older staff with new young technicians with more up-to-date skills. As the bank's IT expert, you think Saul should decide its IT policy. You recognize there are problems in the department, but you feel Saul is capable of dealing with them.

2.4 Speaking: Telephoning

Roleplay (page 25, exercise 8)

Student A

Call 1

You are new in a small law firm where the managing partner also deals with all computer problems. Your PC has broken down, so you call her/him for help. Your partner will start.

Call 2

You receive a call from a colleague you like a lot. You start by answering your phone.

Call 3

Your assistant has been on the phone with friends most of the morning. You have a lot to prepare for an important meeting tomorrow. Call your assistant to ask her/him to prepare a PowerPoint presentation for you. Your partner will start.

Call 4

You receive a call from your computer hardware supplier, who has recently sold you a large new computer system which isn't working very well. You are extremely busy preparing a business trip to Chicago next Tuesday, and you are not in a very good mood. You start by answering your phone.

Call 5

You work in Marketing in a large, very profitable manufacturing company. Your PC is three years old and very slow. Call your friend in the IT department to see if you can upgrade to a new machine. Your partner will start.

Call 6

You work in the HR department of an American factory. You have to be careful to respect legislation on employee rights and confidential personal information. You receive a call from the production supervisor. You start by answering your phone.

3.3 Grammar: Passive structures and *have something done*

Role-play (page 37, exercise 8)

Student A

Internal quality auditor
To comply with your company's ISO 9001 certification, the procedures below should be followed. Check that they are and ask any other questions you need to.

Quality audit – points to raise.

Compliance with ISO 9001:
- bottling lines to be checked before and during each shift
- any problems to be noted in the shift log
- at the end of each shift, the line supervisor should check if any problems have been reported and take any necessary action, eg ask the maintenance team to make repairs, change worn parts, etc
- all operators to receive quality training when they join the company

Other issues:
Quality tracking statistics show that the contaminated bottles were filled during the night shift on bottling line 3.

7.4 Speaking: Communicating in meetings

Role-play (page 91, exercise 8)

Alice

- Introduce the subject of the meeting: the change from yearly to monthly reporting, which will enable management to run the business better.
- You would like to see the new system in place in three months if possible but you are willing to compromise if Serge and David produce valid arguments.
- Mahler can provide training in US accounting procedures and on the new software that will have to be installed.
- Other extra costs will have to be paid for by Polystok.

1.2 Vocabulary: education and career
Discussion (page 8, exercise 7)

Student B

I wasn't a very motivated student when I was younger, so I had to _____ my exams in 2000 after I failed them the year before. I'd already decided that before _____ I wanted to take a gap year. I _____ easily because this time I completed all the coursework and revised thoroughly. I'd already applied and successfully attended an interview at a business school, so after resitting my exams I spent _____ as an assistant in a secondary school.

I spent a semester as _____ at Hewlett Packard in my second year as an undergraduate, which was very rewarding. In fact, after I _____ the following June I went straight into a job at HP. I'm now writing _____ for a Masters degree by correspondence which HP encouraged me to do. I may _____ to study for an MBA in a few years' time, but I need a break first.

2.4 Speaking: Telephoning
Roleplay (page 25, exercise 8)

Student B

Call 1
You are the managing partner of a small law firm. You are also the firm's computer expert, but you are very busy and fed up with receiving calls about trivial computer problems. You receive a call from one of your new employees. You start by answering your phone.

Call 2
You have been having problems with your email. You think you have fixed it, but you need to test it. Call a colleague and ask them to send you a test mail to your new address. Your partner will start.

Call 3
You've just spent most of the morning on the phone with your company's IT department, trying without success to get them to repair your computer – the only application which works properly is Word. You receive a call from your boss. You start by answering your phone.

Call 4
You work for a computer hardware vendor. You recently set up a large new system for your customer, and you would like to show it to one of your prospects. Call your customer to arrange a visit next week. Your partner will start.

Call 5
You work in the IT department in a large manufacturing company. You are working night and day to install new security systems on all the company's sites – all other investments have been cancelled. You receive a call from a friend in Marketing. You start by answering your phone.

Call 6
You are the production supervisor in an American factory. You think it would be good for morale to celebrate your operators' birthdays with a cake. Call HR to ask for a list of dates of birth for everybody in your department. Your partner will start.

2.6 Case study: Meteor Bank
Discussion (page 29, exercise 6)

Student B

You represent the foreign subsidiaries at the meeting. You think Saul Finley is ignoring the facts – fast growth in the subsidiaries, need for a less centralized IT system, discontent in his department – because he is building his own personal empire. You feel his record is very poor, and that he should be replaced as soon as possible.

3.3 Grammar: Passive structures and *have something done*
Role-play (page 37, exercise 8)

Student B

Nightshift supervisor
You are very busy at the moment. Two operators are off sick; three have received no training. You joined the company recently yourself and have had no time to read all the ISO 9001 procedures in detail. Last week, your Production manager sent you this email:

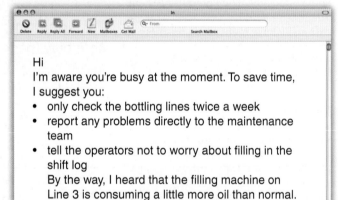

Hi
I'm aware you're busy at the moment. To save time, I suggest you:
- only check the bottling lines twice a week
- report any problems directly to the maintenance team
- tell the operators not to worry about filling in the shift log
  By the way, I heard that the filling machine on Line 3 is consuming a little more oil than normal. Have you noticed anything? I haven't told maintenance yet.

7.4 Speaking: Communicating in meetings
Role-play (page 91, exercise 8)

Serge

- You are not too happy about the proposed changes as they will mean a lot of extra work. However, you realize that you cannot oppose group policy, so you have decided to cooperate as long as things are done properly, and not in a rush.
- You think that a realistic time frame to install the new accounting software, to train accounting staff and to start monthly reporting, is from six to nine months.
- You would also like Mahler to provide training and to pay the extra staff you will have to employ. But you are willing to compromise.

4.4 Speaking: Coaching
Role-play (page 51, exercise 9)

Student A

Situation 1

Your job: Department Manager, Sports Department
While you were away on vacation, and unreachable, your mountain bike supplier phoned your assistant manager to say he couldn't supply the bikes you'd ordered for a big campaign starting the following week. Fortunately your assistant manager spent most of the weekend finding alternative suppliers and delivering bikes to the store, after negotiating even better terms than you had obtained from the original supplier. Show her/him just how pleased you are with what she/he did.

Situation 2

Your job: Manager, white goods department
Your boss, the General Manager, has asked to see you, probably to get/give feedback on the one-day training session you ran for sales assistants last month. You know she/he wasn't very happy about the cost, but was persuaded to go ahead. You are sure the training session was very beneficial – be prepared to justify the time and investment.

Situation 3

Your job: Manager, toy department
One of your sales assistants is a maverick. A brilliant communicator, she/he has a natural talent for selling and keeping customers happy. However, she/he is constantly late, sometimes spends several hours in the cafeteria, and rarely completes any paperwork. Tell her/him how you feel.

Situation 4

Your job: Administrative assistant, finance department
You are responsible for promoting the store's credit card. By encouraging your large circle of friends from university to sign up for the credit card, you have achieved excellent results. The Finance Manager has asked to see you - you expect she/he wants to congratulate you on your success.

3.4 Speaking: Delivering presentations
Presentation (page 39, exercise 9)

Use the table to give feedback on your colleagues' presentations.
1 = Poor, 2 = Acceptable, 3 = Good, 4 = Excellent

	1	2	3	4
Pauses				
Sentence length				
Signposting				
Speed				
Collocations				
Explanation of jargon				
Clarity				
Impact				

5.6 Case study: Backchat Communications
Negotiation (page 69, exercise 7)

Sellers

Follow the instructions below to calculate your score.

	Score
Give yourself 1 point for every Basic contract sold.	
Give yourself 2 points for every Plus contract sold.	
Give yourself 3 points for every Hi-tech contract sold	
Give yourself 1 point for every 18-month contract sold	
Give yourself 2 points for every 24-month contract sold	
Give yourself 1 point for every extra sold	
Deduct 1 point for every extra given free	
Deduct 1 point for every 5000 *won* discount given	
Total	

2.6 Case study: Meteor Bank
Discussion (page 29, exercise 6)

Student C

You represent the Operations Department at the meeting. You feel strongly that the current situation is unacceptable, and that the only way to resolve the problems is to outsource the department, even if it means cutting jobs, including Saul Finley's. This will immediately solve the problems of turnover, downtime, unrest in the IT department, and investment.

4.4 Speaking: Coaching
Role-play (page 51, exercise 9)

Student B

Situation 1

Your job: Assistant manager, sports department
After organizing a big advertising campaign with special offers on mountain bikes for the following week, your boss, the department manager, went on vacation. However, your biggest supplier phoned to say he couldn't supply the bikes. Your boss was unreachable, so you worked all weekend to resolve the problem, which upset your family. Now you expect you're going to be criticized for dealing with the problem yourself without consulting your boss.

Situation 2

Your job: General Manager
You are the General Manager. The manager of your white goods department ran a one-day training session for sales assistants last month. Although you were sceptical, the feedback was excellent and you have heard that the whole store has felt the benefits of the staff's new motivation. Tell your department manager how happy you are with what she/he did.

Situation 3

Your job: Sales assistant
You are the best sales assistant in the toy department, and probably in the whole store (you have won the prize for the salesperson of the month three times in the last year). Your boss wants to see you - this is an opportunity to ask for more flexible working hours. You feel that if you are free to choose to work when there are most customers in the store, you can achieve even more spectacular results than up to now.

Situation 4

Your job: Finance Manager
Despite previous warnings, one of your new young administrative assistants is giving credit to her/his student friends who do not have a regular income. So far there hasn't been a problem, but the risk has become too high. Otherwise, the assistant is doing an excellent job. Make sure she/he understands that she/he has to be careful about who she/he gives credit to.

7.4 Speaking: Communicating in meetings
Role-play (page 91, exercise 8)

David
- You are happy with the idea of changing software because the existing system has never performed very well. However, you want to avoid any extra costs on your department budget.
- You estimate that you will need to employ two external computer engineers on the project for at least six months. You would like Mahler to pay for this
- You would also like Mahler to pay for training for your staff on the new software. However, you may have to compromise.

5.6 Case study: Backchat Communications
Negotiation (page 69, exercise 7)

Buyers

Follow the instructions below to calculate your score.

	Score
Give yourself 1 point for every Plus contract bought.	
Give yourself 2 points for every Basic contract bought.	
Give yourself 1 point for every 18-month contract bought	
Give yourself 2 points for every 12-month contract bought	
Give yourself 1 point for every extra obtained free	
Deduct 1 point for every extra bought	
Give yourself 1 point for every 5000 won discount obtained	
Total	

8.4 Speaking: Negotiating a compromise
Negotiation (page 103, exercise 7)

Student B

You have a surplus of some commodities and a shortage of others. Relations between your country and Student A's country are very friendly. Negotiate a deal with Student A to get the commodities you need.

	You have	You need	After negotiation, you have:
Coal	1 million tons	2 million tons	
Gas	4 billion cubic meters	4 billion cubic meters	
Oil	300 million barrels	100 million barrels	
Wheat	1 million tons	1.5 million tons	
Coffee	6000 tons	2000 tons	
Tobacco	0	30,000 tons	
Steel	1 million tons	4 million tons	
Gold	0	20 tons	
Aluminium	400,000 tons	350,000 tons	
Chemicals	3 million tons	2.5 million tons	

Grammar and practice

1 Building a career

Tense review

1 Read the dialogue at a party and study the verbs in **bold**. Then answer the questions below.

A: I (1) **haven't seen** you for ages!

B: No, that's right. It's been a long time.

A: What were you doing the last time we met? Let me try to remember. Yes, you (2) **were working** as a sales manager somewhere. You (3) **had** just **finished** University.

B: Exactly.

A: I hope (4) **you're enjoying** the party. And who is the guy you came with? Is he your boyfriend?

B: Yes, he is. Actually, we (5a) **met** while I (5b) **was doing** that sales job. He was in the same department.

A: Really! How long (6) **have** you **been going out** together?

B: About two years.

A: That's great. And do you still work together?

B: No, he (7) **works** at that same company, but I don't. I (8) **decided** to have a change. Now (9) I'm **working** for an advertising agency. What about you?

A: (10) I've **quit** my job. I'm unemployed at the moment.

B: Are you trying to find something else?

A: Oh yes, of course. (11) I've **applied** for lots of jobs over the last few weeks, but it's so difficult to get an interview.

Find an example in the dialogue of each of the following:

a) the present simple to show a permanent situation ☐

b) the present continuous to show a situation in progress right now ☐

c) the present continuous to show a situation in progress around now, but not right at this moment ☐

d) the past simple used alone to show a completed action ☐

e) the past continuous to show a situation in progress in the past ☐

f) the past simple followed by the past continuous to show a completed action and its background situation ☐

g) the past perfect to show a past event that happened before another past event ☐

h) the present perfect to show a situation that goes from the past up to the present ☐

i) the present perfect to show a series of actions from the past up to the present ☐

j) the present perfect to show an event in the past with a result in the present ☐

k) the present perfect continuous to show a situation in progress from the past to the present ☐

2 Put one verb into the past simple (*did*), one into the past continuous (*was/were doing*) and one into the past perfect (*had done*).

1 I _____ (work) in an IT company in Budapest at the time, but I wasn't happy and I _____ (already/decide) to give in my notice. Then, by chance, I _____ (find out) about a job in London.

2 I _____ (sit) at home one evening having my dinner when my friend Andreas _____ (call) me about the London job. He _____ (hear) that there was going to be a vacancy for a systems analyst.

3 Put one verb into the present simple (*do/does*), one into the present continuous (*am/are doing*) and one into the present perfect (*has/have done*).

1 An outside company _____ (design) all our sales materials. We _____ (used) the same one for many years and we're very happy with their services. We _____ (not/think) about changing right now.

2 This year we _____ (exceed) our sales targets by eight per cent. Congratulations everybody. But there is no room for complacency. We _____ (go through) some big changes in the market at the moment, as you _____ (know).

4 Look back at *know* in exercise 3 #2. It is a 'state' verb (not used in a continuous form even for temporary situations). Identify six other state verbs from the list below.

belong	contact	manage	mean	meet	
motivate	seem	transfer	understand	want	
weigh	worry				

5 Put each verb into the most appropriate form, present perfect (*has/have done*) or present perfect continuous (*has/have been doing*).

1 a I _____ (apply for) jobs all week.
   b I _____ (apply for) five jobs this week.

2 a I _____ (write) the report. Here it is.
   b I _____ (write) this report since three o'clock. I need a coffee.

6 In the example below both forms are possible.

I've worked/I've been working here for a year. ✓

Use this example, and exercise 5, to complete the grammar rules below. Compete each sentence 1–4 with an endings a–c.

1 To talk about experiences up to now, use …

2 To focus on the action, not the result, use …

3 To focus on the result, not the action, use …

4 To say 'how many' use …

a) the present perfect

b) the present perfect continuous

c) the present perfect or the present perfect continuous

7 Put each verb in this email into the most appropriate form: present simple, present continuous, past simple or present perfect. The words in **bold** give you a clue.

Hi Estera! How are you? I (1) _____ (sit) in an Internet café in Milan **at the moment** – I'm here in Italy because I (2) _____ (visit) Stefano **for a few days**. I have some news to tell you. **A couple of weeks ago** I (3) _____ (go) to a reunion party of all the alumni from our Business School. **Since leaving**, I (4) _____ (lose) contact with most of them except you, so it was good to see everyone again. We had a great night. As you know, **normally** I (5) _____ (not/like) going to discos, but **that evening** we (6) _____ (go) to a really good one with 70s music like Abba and the Bee Gees.

Zero, first and second conditional

8 Read the dialogue and study the verbs in **bold**. Then answer the questions below.

A: (1) **If you see** Marie-Flore, **will** you **give** her a message?

B: Of course, but I doubt that I'll see her until next week. She usually goes to her parents in Lyon at the weekend and (2) **if** she **goes** there then she **leaves** around 5 p.m. She's probably already left.

A: I need to speak to her as soon as possible. Do you know how I can contact her?

B: I'm really sorry – (3) **I'd help** you **if** I **could**, but I don't have any contact details for her at all.

Find an example in the dialogue of each of the following.

a) a zero conditional for something that is always or generally true □

b) a first conditional for an event that the speaker thinks is likely to happen □

c) a second conditional for an event that is imaginary, unlikely or impossible □

9 Underline the correct form in **bold**.

1 I'm very confident, and of course if **I get/I will get** the job, **it is/it'll be** very convenient for me. It's just a short bus ride from my house to their offices.

2 I'm not very confident, and if **I got/I would get** the job **it will be/it would be** a miracle. I was twenty minutes late for the interview and I answered the questions really badly.

3 If **I know/I will know** that I have an interview coming up, **I go/I will go** to the Internet and do some research on the company beforehand.

10 Put each verb into the most appropriate form.

1 If I _____ (know) the answer, I _____ (tell) you, but it's not my field.

2 It's always the same. If I _____ (forget) my umbrella, it _____ (rain).

3 If you _____ (give) me the address, I _____ (find) it. No problem.

4 If I _____ (not/hear) from you within the next few days, I _____ (assume) you're not coming.

5 Unless I _____ (hear) from you within the next few days, I _____ (assume) you're not coming.

6 I _____ (not/do) that if I _____ (be) you.

7 Let me see. What _____ (I/do) if _____ (I/be) Prime Minister?

8 It's midnight. What _____ (we/do) if _____ (the bus/ not come)? Maybe we should catch a taxi.

Will, be going to and present continuous

11 Match *will* in each sentence 1–5 with the best description of its use a–e below.

1 I imagine I'll get a pay rise in January. □

2 It's getting late. I'll give you a lift to the station. □

3 Next year **will** be the 25th anniversary of our company. □

4 It's hot in here. I'll open the window. □

5 I'll love you forever. □

a) simple fact about the future

b) prediction, often with I *think*, etc.

c) promise

d) offer, or willingness

e) decision made at the moment of speaking

12 Match *be going to* and the present continuous in sentences 1–3 with their use a–c below.

1 I**'m having** an interview with them on Friday. □

2 I**'m going to buy** a new computer in the sales. □

3 Is that the time? We**'re going to miss** the train. □

a) prediction with evidence in the present situation

b) intention, plan

c) fixed arrangement (it's 'in my diary')

Note: the uses given in exercises 11 and 12 are guidelines, not rules. With the future, more than one form is often possible.

13 Underline the most likely form in **bold**.

1 This shop **will be/is going to be closed** on 24 and 25 December.

2 The interview went very well. I think **I'm getting/I'll get** the job.

3 Look out! **It will fall/It's going to fall**.

4 Wait a moment, **I'll open/I'm going to open** the door for you.

5 **I'll play/I'm playing** tennis with Ana on Saturday afternoon. I can meet you afterwards, around 5 p.m.

6 **I will start/I'm going to start** applying for jobs in other parts of the country – there's not much available here.

Comparing solutions

1 Look at the prices of four items in a range: Aqua, Bounti, Cresta and Delite. Then complete each sentence using a form of the word in brackets plus any of these words that are necessary: *and, as, least, less, more, most, than, the.*

Aqua €100
Bounti €150
Cresta €150
Delite €200

1 Cresta is *cheaper than* (cheap) Delite.
2 Cresta is _____ (expensive) Delite.
3 Bounti is just _____ (expensive) Cresta.
4 Cresta is expensive, but not _____ (expensive) Delite.
5 Bounti is _____ (expensive) Aqua.
6 Aqua is _____ (cheap) of all the items.
7 Delite is _____ (expensive) of all the items.
8 Aqua is _____ (expensive) of all the items.
9 As you move from Aqua to Delite, the prices get _____ (expensive).
10 As you move from Delite to Aqua, the prices get _____ (cheap).

2 Complete this table of irregular comparatives and superlatives. Sometimes it is the spelling which is irregular.

		comparative	superlative
1	good	b_____	the b_____
2	bad	w_____	the w_____
3	big	b_____	the b_____
4	healthy	h_____	the h_____
5	far	fu_____	the fu_____

3 Fill in each gap with one of these words: *as, of, than.*

1 X is far more expensive _____ Y
2 X is almost as expensive _____ Y
3 X is a little more expensive _____ Y
4 X is a fraction of the price _____ Y
5 X is slightly more expensive _____ Y
6 X is a lot more expensive _____ Y
7 X is not nearly as expensive _____ Y
8 X is nearly as expensive _____ Y

4 Now match two phrases from exercise 3 with each set of prices below.

a) X costs €300, Y costs €100. ☐☐
b) X costs €120, Y costs €100. ☐☐
c) X costs €90, Y costs €100. ☐☐
d) X costs €30, Y costs €100. ☐☐

5 Underline the correct words in **bold**.

1 Excuse me, where's **the next/the nearest** post office?
2 Get ready – we have to get out at **the next/the nearest** stop.
3 Have you seen this amazing mobile phone? It's **the last/the latest** model.
4 That mobile phone company is being taken over. Your phone is probably **the last/the latest** model they will make using that brand name.

6 We often use a superlative with the present perfect. Rewrite the sentences beginning as shown.

1 I have never been to such a boring meeting.
   That was *the most boring meeting I have ever been to.*
2 I have never used software as user-friendly as this.
   This is _____ .
3 I have never worked with such a friendly team.
   They are _____ .
4 I have never seen documentation as bad as this.
   This is _____ .

7 We can use a comparative form to say that a change in one thing is linked to a change in another. Write a tick (✓) if the form is correct, write a cross (✗) if it is not.

1 The older I get, *less* I want to go to the discotheque.
2 The older I get, *it's less* I want to go to the discotheque.
3 The older I get, *the less* I want to go to the discotheque.
4 The older I get, I want to go to the discotheque *each time less*.

8 Rewrite the sentences using *the … the …*

1 You pay more for your Internet connection depending on how fast it is.
   The faster your Internet connection, the more you pay (for it).
2 We spend less time watching TV as we use the Internet more.

   _____

3 How much can go wrong depends on the complexity of the network.

   _____

4 I don't spend much time with my friends because I work so hard.

   _____

5 The idea becomes less attractive as I think about it more.

   _____

Obtaining help

9 Compare (a) and (b) each time, then study the notes in the box below.

1 a) When *is the meeting*?
   b) Can you tell me when *the meeting is*?
2 a) What time *does* the meeting *start*?
   b) Can you tell me what time *the meeting starts*?
3 a) Which room *will it be* in?
   b) Can you tell me which room *it will be* in?
4 a) *Will the meeting* start on time?
   b) Can you tell me *if/whether the meeting will* start on time?

Indirect questions
- Each example (a) is a direct question.
- Each example (b) is an indirect question. Typical phrases to begin an indirect question are
  Can you tell me …?
  Do you know …?
  Can I just check …?
  Do you think you could let me know …?
  I'm trying to find out …
  I was (just) wondering …
- Notice how the word order changes in the indirect questions. The subject comes before the main verb, just like in a normal statement (The *meeting is* at 10.30; The *meeting starts* at 10:30; *It will be* in room 24; *The meeting will* start on time.)
- Notice also how 2b has no auxiliary verb *does*, again just like in a statement.
- In example 3a and 3b notice the position of the preposition *in*. The preposition comes at the end of a question (both direct and indirect). Be careful: in many other languages you would say *In which room …?*, but this word order is not common in modern English.
- Example 4 is a 'Yes/No' question, whereas the previous three were open 'Wh-' questions. Notice how we use *if* or *whether* with an indirect 'Yes/No' question.

Now rewrite each direct question as an indirect question, beginning as shown.

1 How can I get to the station from here?
  Can you tell me _____ ?
2 What time does the train leave?
  Do you know _____?
3 Which platform will it leave from?
  I'm trying to find out _____.
4 Do I change in Cologne?
  Can I just check _____ ?
5 Can I get something to eat on the train?
  I was wondering _____.

10 Change each 'Yes/No' question into a more open 'Wh-' question.

1 Are you thinking about your presentation?
  What are you thinking about?
2 Did you borrow this from Susan?

3 Is this dress made of linen?

4 Will you share your new office with Miguel?

11 Look at the patterns with 'mind', then study the notes in the box below.

a) **Do** you mind if I **open** the window?
b) **Would** you mind if I **opened** the window?
c) **Do/Would** you mind **opening** the window?

Questions with *mind*
Examples a) and b) are asking for permission: a) is a regular first conditional and b) is a regular second conditional (both have the *if* clause at the end). Example b) is more formal and polite.
Example c) is a request – we want the other person to do something.

Now make questions using the words in brackets.

1 (mind/call you back/later)
  _____ ?
2 (mind/called you back/later)
  _____ ?
3 (Would/calling me back/later)
  _____ ?

12 Study the notes in the box.

Replying to requests
To reply 'yes', simply repeating the auxiliary is not very friendly.
Can you give me a hand?
~~Yes, I can~~ ✗   Yes, of course ✓   Sure ✓
To reply 'no' give an apology and/or a reason.
Can you give me a hand?
I'm sorry, I've got no idea how it works. ✓
Be careful! Questions with *mind* mean 'is it a problem for you?' So 'yes' means 'yes, it's a problem'!
Would you mind giving me a hand?
~~Yes, I would~~ ✗   No, not at all ✓

Now put a tick (✓) by appropriate responses. Put a cross (✗) by inappropriate responses.

1 Can you show me how to use this software?
  a) Sure. No problem.
  b) Yes, I can.
  c) To be honest, I've never used it myself.
2 Would you mind showing me how to use this software?
  a) Yes, I would.
  b) No, not at all.
  c) Actually, I'm a bit busy right now. Perhaps later?

Passive structures: affirmatives

1 Look at the active sentence given first and then write the passive version below.

1 The Board usually takes strategic decisions.
   Strategic decisions _____ by the Board.
2 They announced the date for the talks yesterday.
   The date for the talks _____ yesterday.
3 A health and safety officer will visit the factory next week.
   Next week the factory _____ by a health and safety officer.
4 They are going to completely redesign the product.
   The product _____.
5 They are still considering the matter.
   The matter _____.
6 The garage was servicing my car last week.
   My car _____ last week.
7 The design engineer has finalized the plans.
   The plans _____ by the design engineer.
8 There was no point having the meeting – they had already agreed all the details.
   There was no point having the meeting – all the details _____.

When you have checked your answers, read the information in the box below.

> - In examples 1–8 you formed the passive for each of the most common verb tenses. Notice the similarities: you used *be* + past participle in every case. Also notice how the form of *be* is the same as the tense in the active version.
> - Is the person who does the action (the agent) mentioned in the passive version? Look back. The answer is 'yes' for sentences 1, 3 and 7. In the case of 1 and 3, the agent is necessary in the passive version – otherwise the meaning is not complete. In 7, the agent is not necessary – it could be left out if it is clear from the context (or not important) who finalized the plans.
> - There were adverbs in sentences 1 (*usually*), 4 (*completely*), 5 (*still*) and 8 (*already*). Did you put them in the correct place?

2 Rewrite these active sentences in the passive, making the words in **bold** into the subject. Leave out the agent if it is not necessary.

1 We do **dozens of quality checks** every day.
   Dozens of quality checks are done every day
2 Thousands of people use **our products**.
   _____
3 The secretary's just found **that file you were looking for**.
   _____
4 Last month the bank gave **us** more credit.
   _____
5 We will pay **all senior managers** a bonus at the end of the year.
   _____

6 They are never going to do **that**.
   _____
7 Highly trained inspectors do **our quality checks**.
   _____
8 We are dealing with **the issue**.
   _____

3 Match each example of the passive 1–5 with the best description of its use a–e below.

1 First the beans are separated from the shells and then they are roasted over a low heat for two hours. ☐
2 Don't worry. the conference room was cleaned this morning. ☐
3 Keys and mobile phones must be placed on the trays provided. ☐
4 Yes, I can see that a small mistake was made on the invoice. I'll correct it and send out a new one. ☐
5 It was agreed that Inge should set up a working party to investigate the matter further. ☐

a it is obvious or not important to say who did the action
b avoiding mentioning a name in order to be make the statement less personal
c reporting formally (a decision, what someone said in a meeting, etc.)
d describing a process
e official announcements (often written)

4 Notice in exercise 3 5c above that we often use *It* + passive to report things formally. Complete the sentences below with the words in the box. Several answers may be possible, but one solution uses all the words in the most appropriate way.

> agreed   announced   believed   estimated
> said   reported

1 It was _____ at the press conference that the CEO had resigned.
2 After some discussion it was _____ that Jim should be team leader for the forthcoming negotiations.
3 It is _____ that 'diamonds are a girl's best friend'. But I don't believe it. I think that chocolate is a girl's best friend.
4 It was _____ in yesterday's newspapers that the economy grew by four per cent last year.
5 It has been _____ that fish stocks in the North Atlantic will decline to zero by the year 2050.
6 It is _____ that a gang of four armed men carried out the attack, but police are still unsure of the exact numbers.

Passive structures: negatives

5 Complete the second sentence so that it has the same meaning as the first. Use contractions (*n't* instead of *not*, etc) where possible.

1 No one has serviced the machine since April.
   The machine *hasn't been serviced* since April.
2 They aren't going to pay us until June.
   We _____ until June.
3 The staff had been poorly trained.
   The staff _____ very well.
4 No one is monitoring the process.
   The process _____.
5 We still haven't shipped your order.
   Your order _____ yet.
6 People just don't do things like that around here.
   Things like that _____ around here.

Passive structures: questions

6 Put the words in the correct order to make a question with a passive form.

1 this machine is serviced regularly?
   Is this machine serviced regularly?
2 being at the moment is it serviced?
   _____
3 yesterday it was serviced?
   _____
4 will next week be it serviced?
   _____
5 it recently has serviced been?
   _____
6 it is serviced going to be soon?
   _____

Now use 1–6 above to make corresponding negative questions with a passive form. Use contractions where possible.

7 *Isn't this machine serviced* regularly?
8 _____ at the moment?
9 _____ yesterday?
10 _____ next week?
11 _____ recently?
12 _____ soon?

7 Make the questions below less personal by changing them to a passive form and leaving out the agent.

1 Will you deliver the goods by next week?
   Will the goods be delivered by next week?
2 Has someone changed the password?
   _____
3 Are you using this photocopier?
   _____
4 Are they going to give us a meal when we arrive?
   _____
5 Did Robert give you any options?
   _____

Passive structures: modals

8 Study the active and passive forms in the box. Then rewrite 1–6 below as passives.

Somebody should do it right now.
It should be done right now.

Somebody should have done it yesterday.
It should have been done yesterday.

1 We must find a solution.
   A solution _____.
2 They must have found a solution by now.
   A solution _____ by now.
3 We could postpone the product launch.
   The product launch _____ .
4 We could have postponed the launch, but it's too late.
   The launch _____, but it's too late.
5 The company might design it like that on purpose.
   It _____ on purpose.
6 The company might have designed it like that on purpose.
   It _____ on purpose.

Balance between active and passive

9 Complete this memo by putting the verb in brackets into the present perfect active (*has done*) or present perfect passive (*has been done*).

This memo (1) _____ (write) at the request of the Senior Quality Inspector. Regular checks over the last few weeks (2) _____ (show) that defects (3) _____ (reach) an unacceptable level of three per thousand pieces. It seems that this (4) _____ (cause) by incorrect set-up of the machine tools. The operators involved (5) _____ (now/told) that they must take greater care when preparing their tools for the manufacturing process.
Some operators (6) _____ (ask) us if they can have more time to set up their machines, and we (7) _____ (agree). They now have 30 minutes instead of 20.
You will see that some minor changes (8) _____ (make) to the Defect Report Form to allow us to identify the problems more rapidly.

> Notice the balance between active and passive forms. Too many passives make a text formal and difficult to understand.

have something done

10 When a professional person does some work for us, we can use *have something done*. Rewrite the sentences below using this structure in the same tense as the original.

1 A technician fixed this computer last week.
   I *had this computer fixed* last week.
2 PwC audit our accounts.
   We _____ by PwC.
3 The garage is servicing my car on Friday.
   I'm _____ on Friday.
4 The builders are going to install air conditioning.
   We're _____.
5 A girl at Gina's Salon does my hair.
   I _____ by a girl at Gina's Salon.

Past modals (regrets and speculation)

1 Study the table about how to form modals in the past then do the exercise below.

can do	could have done couldn't have done
may/might do	may/might have done may/might not have done
must do	must have done mustn't have done
ought to do	ought to have done ought not to have done
should do	should have done shouldn't have done
will do	would have done wouldn't have done

A manager is talking about a project team he set up last month. Fill in the gaps using a form of the modal and main verb in brackets. Sometimes a negative is necessary.

'The team isn't working well, and it's my fault. If I had done things differently, we (1) *might not have reached* (might/reach) the situation we are in today. The basic problem is my choice of team leader. I gave the job to Sonia, but I (2) _____ (should/do) that. She doesn't have enough experience. It (3) _____ (will/be) better to give the job to Angela. Yes, that's right, I can see that now – I definitely (4) _____ (ought/give) the job to Angela. What was I thinking at the time? I (5) _____ (must/be) crazy or something. But maybe I'm blaming myself too much. I know I took a risk, but at the time it seemed justified. I (6) _____ (can/know) that things would go so wrong.'

2 In each of 1–5, read the first sentence then complete the sentences using the phrases in the box so that the meaning is the same. Be very careful!

could have been (x2)	ought to have been
might have been	should have been
must have been	would have been

1 I made a mistake when I appointed Sonia. My strong opinion now is that Angela was better for the job of team leader.
   Angela _____ team leader.
   OR
   Angela _____ team leader.
2 Yes, I made a bad choice. Angela, not Sonia, had the real ability to be a good team leader.
   Angela _____ a good team leader.

3 I wonder why I made that mistake. Perhaps I was focused on another project at the time.
   I _____ focused on another project.
   OR
   I _____ focused on another project.
4 I wonder why I made that mistake. Almost certainly I was focused on another project at the time.
   I _____ focused on another project.
5 Yes, I'm certain. Sonia was a terrible choice and Angela was definitely the best choice.
   Angela _____ better than Sonia.

Before you check your answers, read the information in the box below. Then go back and make any necessary changes in the exercise.

- For past regrets – when we are sorry about what happened – use *should have done, ought to have done* and *could have done*.
- These modals keep their normal meanings, so: *should/ought to* are used for strong opinions; *can* (*could* in the past) is used for ability.
- For past speculation – when we are wondering or guessing about what happened – use *may have done, might have done, could have done, must have done* and *would have done*.
- These modals also keep their normal meanings, so: *may/might/could* are used for possibility and uncertainty; *must* is used for very strong possibility, almost certainty; *will* (*would* in the past) is used for certainty.

3 Complete the sentences using an appropriate past modal + a form of the verb in brackets. Sometimes more than one modal is possible (e.g. *could* and *might*).

1 I did an MBA course but I was lazy and got a bad grade. It was a pity. I know I *could have got* (get) a better grade.
2 My parents persuaded me to do business administration at college. But I regret it – I always wanted to be a fireman. I _____ (listen) to them.
3 Imagine that I had decided to travel around the world instead of going to university. I _____ (get) a job anywhere.
4 Who was that in the cinema with Alex last night? No, it wasn't Joelle. Joelle is in Brussels at the moment. It _____ (be) Joelle.
5 Well, if it wasn't Joelle – who was it? You think it was Sandra? Yes, I think you're probably right. It _____ (be) Sandra.
6 Wait a minute! Alex already has a girlfriend, doesn't he? Her name is Ana. Ana _____ (be) very happy if she had seen Alex and Sandra together last night.

4 Make the question forms of past modals using the words in brackets.

1 You say that Angela would have been a better team leader. I'm not so sure. *Would she have consulted* (would/consult) with the rest of the group before taking decisions?
2 I don't think this restaurant is very good. What do you think? _____ (should/go) somewhere else instead?
3 Mike and Sue aren't here yet. I wonder what's happened to them. _____ (could/get) lost?
4 I've made a few mistakes. But _____ (would/do) anything differently if I had another chance? No, I don't think so.

Third conditional

5 Look at four possible situations a–d. Match each situation with the sentences 1–4 below.

a Stefan managed the project. And the result? We reached our targets.
b Stefan managed the project. And the result? We didn't reach our targets.
c Stefan didn't manage the project. And the result? We reached our targets.
d Stefan didn't manage the project. And the result? We didn't reach our targets.

1 If Stefan **had managed** the project, we **would have reached** all our targets. ☐*d*
2 If Stefan **had managed** the project, we **wouldn't have reached** all our targets. ☐
3 If Stefan **hadn't managed** the project, we **would have reached** all our targets. ☐
4 If Stefan **hadn't managed** the project, we **wouldn't have reached** all our targets. ☐

- Notice above how to form the third conditional: *If + past perfect* for the condition clause, *would have + past participle* for the result clause.
- We use the third conditional to talk about something that did not happen in the past. The word *If* means that we are imagining the opposite to what really happened.
- Because the third conditional is imagining the opposite of what happened, a positive clause means this thing didn't happen and a negative clause means this thing did happen.
- The condition and the result can be in the reverse order. In this case there is no comma in writing.
*We **would have reached** all our targets if Stefan **had managed** the project.*

6 Look at each situation in **bold**. Then complete the sentence that follows using the correct form of the third conditional.

1 **I didn't take an umbrella, and so I got wet. But …**
If I _____ (take) an umbrella, I _____ (get) wet.
2 **I did take an umbrella, and so I didn't get wet. But …**
If I _____ (take) an umbrella, I _____ (get) wet.

3 **We didn't have enough people working on the project, and so we didn't meet the deadline. But …**
If we _____ (had) enough people working on the project, we _____ (meet) the deadline.
4 **We had a lot of people working on the project, and so we met the deadline. But …**
If we _____ (had) so many people working on the project, we _____ (meet) the deadline.

7 Underline the correct words in **bold**.

1 Yes, I'm sure. If we had given Murray a different job, he **wouldn't have/might not have** resigned.
2 Well, I'm not sure, but if we had given Murray a different job, he **wouldn't have/might not have** resigned.

Instead of *would*, we can use *might* or *could*. This shows an uncertain result.

used to, be used to, get used to

8 Match sentences 1–3 with their meanings a–c.

1 I **used to give** presentations in my job. ☐
2 I'm **used to giving** presentations in my job. ☐
3 I've **got used to giving** presentations in my job. ☐

a I give presentations in my job. At first it was difficult but now it's OK.
b I give presentations in my job. It's a completely familiar situation to me and there's no problem.
c In the past it was normal for me to give presentations, but now I don't.

- *Used to + infinitive* describes a habit in the past. It suggests that the action or situation is no longer true, and so makes a contrast with the present.
- With negatives and questions, *used to* becomes *use to*.
*Did you **use to** give presentations in your job?*
*I **didn't use** to give presentations in my job.*
- *Be/get used to* are completely different. They mean you have done something many times before and it is no longer difficult.
- *Be/get used to* are followed by *-ing* or a noun, not an infinitive.
*I live in the UK now. **I'm used to driving** on the left, and **I'm** also **used to** the weather.*
- *Be used to* is a state, *get used to* is a process. Compare with:
I'm tired/hungry/fed up etc. (state)
I'm getting tired/hungry/fed up etc. (process)

9 Complete the sentences using *used to, be used to* or *get used to* and the correct form of the verb.

1 I'm beginning to enjoy my new job. Slowly, I _____ (work) with my team.
2 I prefer being in a large company to working as a freelancer. I _____ (work) in a team.
3 Now I'm a freelancer and I prefer it. I'm my own boss. I _____ (work) in a team in my old job, but I got annoyed when other people did a bad job.

Question tags

1 Complete each question by filling the gap with a question tag. Always use contractions where possible, so write *don't* not ~~do not~~.

1   This is the newest model, *isn't* it?
2   This isn't the newest model, _____ it?
3   You're from Latvia, _____ you?
4   You haven't got this available in blue, _____ you?
5   She works in the sales department, _____ she?
6   You give discounts on large orders, _____ you?
7   You don't have this available in a larger size, _____ you?
8   You gave us a discount last time, _____ you?
9   You were selling this for a much lower price in the summer, _____ you?
10 Have you got my travel plans for Scandinavia? I'm going to Copenhagen and Oslo after Stockholm, _____ I?
11 You'll be bringing out a new model next year, _____ you?
12 You won't be late, _____ you?
13 It shouldn't cost more than about €100, _____ it?
14 I'm not late, _____ I?
15 I'm late, _____ I? Sorry!
16 The meeting's been going on for an hour and a half. Let's have a break, _____ we?
17 Turn the lights off, _____ you?
18 Everybody got a copy of the agenda, didn't _____?
19 Somebody will be here on Saturday morning, won't _____?
20 I know there were some problems at the beginning, but everything was OK in the end, wasn't _____?

Before you check in the Answer Key, study the following boxes and then make any necessary changes above.

Question tags: general rules

- a positive sentence has a negative tag, and vice-versa
- if there is an auxiliary verb (*be, have, do*) or modal in the statement, repeat the auxiliary or modal in the tag
- if there is no auxiliary or modal, use a form of *do*
- the tense of the tag agrees with the tense of the main verb
- Question tags are common in British English but are not used in American English. Americans say *right?* for all tags.
- NB It is possible for a positive statement to be followed by a positive tag. This is used to express interest during a conversation.
  So you like working here, do you?
  This use is not practised in this book.

Question tags: special cases

- the tag for *I am* is *aren't I?* However, the tag for *I'm not* is *am I?*
- the tag for *let's* is *shall we?*
- the tag for an imperative is *will you?* It is also possible to use *won't you?*
- after *everybody/everyone* and *somebody/someone* use *they* in the tag (this is to generalize and avoid saying 'he or she')
- after *everything* and *something* use *it* in the tag

---

2 The intonation of a tag is different according to the meaning. Study the information in the box then answer the questions below.

Tags with a rising intonation
If the intonation of the tag rises at the end, then the person is asking for information and it is a real question
A: *You're from Latvia, **aren't you?*** ↗
B: *Yes, that's right. I come from a little town outside Riga. Have you ever been to my country?*

Tags with a falling intonation
If the intonation of the tag falls at the end, then it is not a real question. Instead, the speaker either wants to check information, or to persuade.
Checking:
A: *You're from Latvia, **aren't you?*** ↘
B: *Yes, that's right.*
A: *I thought so. Have you met Ilona? She's from Latvia as well.*
Persuading:
A: *It's not just a question of price, **is it?*** ↘
B: *No.*
A: *I thought not. Quality and design are also important.*

Note that in these two cases speaker A continues after B has made a short reply. This is because A's first line is not a real question.

For each mini-dialogue, write ↗ at the end of A's line if the intonation goes up, and write ↘ if it goes down.

1   A: You haven't seen this kind of quality at such a reasonable price, **have you**?
    B: No, I haven't.
2   A: You don't happen to know where the spare paper for the photocopier is, **do you**?
    B: No, sorry, I don't. Have you looked in that cupboard over there?
3   A: I'm sending this to your main office, not the factory, **aren't I**?
    B: Yes, that's right.

Look at the two answers were the intonation went down. Which one is checking? Which one is persuading?

3 Look at the mini-dialogues and underline the most likely answer in **bold**. Then read the information in the box below.

1 A: The negotiations are going well, aren't they?
    B: **Yes, they are.** / **No, they're not.**
2 A: The negotiations aren't going well, are they?
    B: **Yes, they are.** / **No, they're not.**

- A positive statement with a negative tag often expects the answers *Yes*.
- A negative statement with a positive tag often expects the answer *No*.
- A negative statement with a positive tag is also used to be polite, or indirect, or ask for a favour. The answer could be *Yes* or *No*.
  You haven't by any chance got a spare pen, have you?

4 Complete the sentences using a tag and any other necessary words.

Example:
You thought the meeting was good.
You say: 'That was .. *a good meeting, wasn't it?*'

1 You want to suggest that we go to the bar.
   You say: 'Let's go _____?'
2 You want to check if the train leaves from platform 4.
   You say: 'The train _____?'
3 You want to persuade someone that they can't afford to take a risk.
   You say: 'You can't afford _____?'
4 You want to make sure that the other person will speak to their boss.
   You say: 'You'll speak _____?'
5 You want to make sure your name is on the list.
   You say: 'I'm on _____?'
6 You can't reach the salt and want someone to pass it to you.
   You say: 'Pass _____?'
7 You're worried that the other person will be in danger.
   You say: 'Take care, _____?'
8 You feel a cold current of air.
   You say: 'Someone's left the door open, _____?'
9 You want to know if the other person has met Joelle. You expect the answer is 'no'.
   You say: 'You _____?'
10 You want to know if the other person has met Joelle. You expect the answer is 'yes'.
    You say: 'You _____?'
11 You want to ask a favour – for the other person to get you a sandwich from the shop.
    You say: 'You couldn't get _____?'
12 You want to ask politely if the other person will be passing a post box on their way home.
    You say: 'You won't by any _____?'

Negative questions

5 Match each negative question 1–4 with its use a–d. If several are possible choose the best one.

1 Don't you accept American Express? ☐
2 Don't you agree that anything that saves you time saves you money? ☐
3 Don't you eat meat? ☐
4 Don't you think that this proposal will just lead to increased costs and reduced efficiency? ☐

a negative question to persuade
b negative question to disagree politely
c negative question to show surprise
d negative question in social English to make it easier for the other person to say 'no'.

It is possible to use an uncontracted form with 'not' after the subject. This is formal and intensifies the meaning.
Do you not accept American Express?
Do you not eat meat?
Do you not think that this proposal will just lead to increased costs and reduced efficiency?

6 Using the first sentence, add a tag question for a) and make a negative question for b). Look at the example.

Example: 'There's a deadline'.

a) *There's a deadline, isn't there?*
b) *Isn't there a deadline?*

1 It'll be expensive to use Air Express.
   a) _____
   b) _____
2 It'd be better to ship via Rotterdam.
   a) _____
   b) _____
3 We've met somewhere before.
   a) _____
   b) _____
4 You spoke to our sales agent yesterday.
   a) _____
   b) _____
5 There's always room for compromise.
   a) _____
   b) _____
6 You don't have insurance cover.
   a) _____
   b) _____
7 You haven't seen one of these before.
   a) _____
   b) _____

7 Rewrite 6b and 7b from exercise 6 with an uncontracted form of 'not'. Note how this intensifies the meaning.

1 _____
2 _____

will do (future simple)

1 Match the main uses of *will* 1–5 with examples a–e.

1   simple fact about the future ☐
2   prediction, often with *I think* etc. ☐
3   decision made at the moment of speaking ☐
4   promise ☐
5   offer ☐

a   Are you going to use UPS to deliver the package? I think it'll be cheaper to use DHL.
b   We'll be closed for one week over the Christmas period.
c   Don't worry, I'll be at the airport to meet you.
d   **Will** you stay for lunch?
e   Do we need more copies of the agenda? No problem, I'll photocopy them right now.

> The uses of *will* given above often overlap (eg decisions and promises), but it is helpful to remember that there are two basic categories:
> • *Will* used for information about the future (1 and 2 above).
> • *Will* used for social and functional language (3, 4 and 5 above). This includes announcing decisions, giving refusals (*won't*), making promises and making offers. In these cases, *will* generally expresses 'willingness' or a strong intention.

will be doing (future continuous)

2 Read the notes in the box then do the exercise below.

> • The future continuous is formed with *will be* + *-ing* form of the verb.
> • All the continuous tenses are used for an 'action in progress'. The future continuous is no different. Compare:
> **Past continuous**
> *While I was at University I **was working** part-time in a restaurant.*
> **Present continuous**
> *At the moment I'm **working** part-time in a restaurant. I hope to get a proper job soon.*
> **Future continuous**
> *Next year I'm going to London to learn English. I'll **be working** part-time in the same restaurant where my friend works now.*
> • The future continuous often refers to the middle of an action. Compare:
> *When you arrive we'll **have** the meeting.*
> (You will arrive and then we will start the meeting)
> *When you arrive we'll **be having** the meeting.*
> (You will arrive in the middle of the meeting)
> • The future continuous is often used to show that something is definite. Compare:
> *I'll **speak** to her tomorrow.* (decision, or promise)
> *I'll **be speaking** to her tomorrow.* (definite fact)
> *I'm **going to speak** to her tomorrow.* (intention)
> • The future continuous can be used to ask in a polite way about other people's plans:

> **Will** you **be passing** a post box on your way to the station?
> How long **will** you **be using** the photocopier?
> • Remember that there are no 'rules' for any future tense – just forms that are more common than others in certain circumstances.

Complete each sentence using the most appropriate form of the verb in brackets: either *will* or the future continuous. Use contractions.

1   If you give me the job of team leader, I _____ (work) night and day to make the project a success.
2   I can't go to the cinema on Saturday afternoon – I _____ (work) all day Saturday.
3   We _____ (launch) our new range of clothes at the end of March.
4   Yes, that's a great idea! We _____ (launch) our new range of clothes with an event featuring a footballer and a top model.
5   If you see me at the party tomorrow, I _____ (wear) my little black Gucci dress.
6   What shall I wear at the party tomorrow? I know! I _____ (wear) my little black Gucci dress.
7   No, I _____ (not/give) any more time to writing this assignment. It's good enough as it is.
8   I'll be at the conference, but I _____ (not/give) a talk this year.
9   This time tomorrow I _____ (sit) on an airplane somewhere over the Pacific.
10   Don't worry about your bag and coat while you go to the bathroom. I _____ (sit) here until you come back.

Check your answers before doing the next exercise.

3 In the previous exercise, the *will* form was most appropriate in sentences 1, 4, 6, 7 and 10. Write one of these numbers in each box:

a decision ④ and ☐
a promise ☐
an offer ☐
a refusal ☐

The future continuous form was most appropriate in sentences 2, 3, 5, 8 and 9. Write one of these numbers in each box.

referring to an action in progress ⑨
referring to the middle of an action ☐ and ☐
showing that something is definite ☐ and ☐

4 Rewrite these questions about people's plans using the future continuous.

1   Are you joining us in the bar later?
    _____ in the bar later?
2   Are you going to speak to your boss tomorrow?
    _____ to your boss tomorrow?
3   Will you visit Moscow again next year?
    _____ Moscow again next year?

The future continuous in these cases is more polite. It suggests 'I just want to know your plans – I don't want to put any pressure on you.'

Future perfect

5 Study the notes in the box.

• The future perfect is formed with *will have* + past
participle. It is often used with *by* or *by the time*.
*I'll **have finished** the report by the end of the week.*
*By the time you arrive, the meeting **will** already **have**
started.*

• All the perfect tenses are used for 'looking back'. The
future perfect is no different. Compare:

Past perfect
*When I arrived at their offices, the meeting **had** already*
***started**.*
(looking back from the past to an earlier event in the
past)

Present perfect
*I'm sorry, I'm late. **Has** the sales meeting already **started**?*
(looking back from now to an event in the recent past)

Future perfect
Don't worry if you can't get to our offices until 9.30. The
*meeting **will** already **have started**, but it's scheduled to*
last until lunchtime and your presence will still be useful.
(looking back from the future to an earlier event in the
future)

• The future perfect is not common in English because
it can often be replaced by a simple *will* form. This
is easier and so speakers prefer it. Both of these are
possible and there is no difference in meaning.
*I'll **finish** the report by the end of the week.*
*I'll **have finished** the report by the end of the week.*

Read the information about how a business person is going
to spend her time over the next two weeks. Then answer
the questions below using the future perfect.

*Catherine is marketing director for a firm of publishers
based in the UK. Over the next two weeks she is going
to visit her most important markets in Western Europe:
France, Belgium, the Netherlands, Germany, Switzerland
and Austria. She's flying between the capital cities of
each country, and of course flying out to Paris and back
from Vienna at the end. She expects to have two meetings
a day for each of her ten working days abroad. On trips
like this she eats dinner in the restaurant in the evening
– so that's no home cooking from Monday when she
leaves to Friday afternoon of the following week – not
even at the weekend.*

1 How many countries will she have visited?
   By the end of the trip *she'll have visited six countries*.
2 How many flights will she have taken?
   Altogether _____.
3 How many meetings will she have had?
   When she finally gets to the end _____.
4 How many restaurant dinners will she have eaten?
   By the time she finishes _____.

6 Complete each sentence using the most appropriate
form of the verb in brackets: either the future continuous
(*will be doing*) or the future perfect (*will have done*). Use
contractions.

1 I'm enjoying this course. I _____ (learn) a lot by the
   time it's finished.
2 I'm really looking forward to the course next year. I
   _____ (learn) about the world economy and its impact
   on financial markets.
3 I have to be careful with my money this month. I _____
   (spend) a lot next week when my car is serviced, and I
   also have some bills to pay.
4 I haven't got much money left. If I go on like this, I
   _____ (spend) it all soon.

Future perfect continuous

7 Read the notes in the box then do the exercise below.

• The future perfect continuous is formed with *will have*
been + *-ing* form of the verb.
• The future perfect continuous is used for 'looking
back from the future at an action in progress'. In other
words, it combines the meaning of the future perfect
and the future continuous.
• It is only very rarely that we need to express this
meaning, and when we do it is usually to emphasize
the duration and the repetitive nature of the action:
*By the time he retires, he'll **have been working** here*
for more than thirty years.
*By lunchtime, I'll **have been replying** to emails for over*
two hours.
• Use the future perfect to emphasize a result, and the
future perfect continuous to emphasize an action in
progress:
*By the end of her trip, she'll **have collected** a lot of*
useful market information. (result)
*By the end of her trip, she'll **have been travelling** non-*
stop for twelve days. (action in progress, with emphasis
on the duration and repetitive nature)

Complete each sentence using either the future perfect or
the future perfect continuous. Use contractions.

1 Next year we _____ (make) cars on this same site for
   fifty years.
2 By the end of the year, we _____ (make) profits of over
   €3 million.
3 By Friday I _____ (write) the report. Then maybe I can
   think about something else for a change!
4 By Friday I _____ (write) this stupid report for two
   weeks and it still won't be finished. It's driving me mad.

Cause and effect

1 Each item a)–w) can be used to complete just one of the sentences below. Write each letter in the appropriate box.

a) arose from
b) as
c) as a result
d) as a result of
e) because
f) because of
g) because of that
h) brought about
i) caused
j) consequently
k) developed from
l) due to

m) gave rise to
n) led to
o) on account of
p) originated from
q) owing to
r) resulted from
s) resulted in
t) since
u) stemmed from
v) thanks to
w) was caused by

Cause

1 The successful advertising campaign _____ an increase in sales. [h] ☐ ☐ ☐ ☐

Effect

2 The increase in sales _____ the successful advertising campaign. ☐ ☐ ☐ ☐ ☐ ☐
3 _____ we had a successful advertising campaign, sales increased. ☐ ☐ ☐
4 _____ the successful advertising campaign, sales increased. ☐ ☐ ☐ ☐ ☐ ☐
5 We had a successful advertising campaign and, _____, sales increased. ☐ ☐ ☐

- The verb *caused* can be replaced with *brought about, gave rise to, led to* and *resulted in*.
- The verb *was caused by* can be replaced with *arose from, developed from, originated in, resulted from, stemmed from*. (Do you know the literal meaning of a stem? Check in a dictionary.)
- The linking word *because* can be replaced with *as* and *since*. Note that *as* has a different meaning to its use in comparisons, and that *since* has a different meaning to its use as a time phrase.
- The linking phrase *because of* can be replaced with *as a result of, due to, on account of, owing to, thanks to*. Of these, *because of* is much more common than the others.
- The linking phrase *because of that* can be replaced with *as a result, consequently*.

---

2 Underline the correct words to make usage notes.

1 There is very little difference in meaning between 'because', 'as' and 'since'. However, **because/as and since** can emphasize the reason more strongly, while **because/as and since** can suggest that the reason is obvious.

2 In sentence 3 in the previous exercise, this word order is also possible: 'Sales increased because we had a successful advertising campaign'. In cases like this where 'because' comes in the middle, it is **equally common/much less common** to replace 'because' with 'as' and 'since'.

3 The phrase **owing to/thanks to** is more formal.

4 The phrase **due to/on account of** often refers to a problem or difficulty. For this reason it is **not** very natural in sentence 4 of the previous exercise because there is no problem (something good happened: a successful advertising campaign).

5 The phrase **due to/owing to** cannot come after the verb 'be'. (Example: The increase in sales was _____ the successful advertising campaign).

6 Study the difference between sentence 3 and 4 in the previous exercise. **Because/Because of** is used before a noun phrase (no verb), while **because/because of** is used before a clause (subject + verb).

7 In sentence 5 in the previous exercise the linking phrases come in the middle of a sentence after the word 'and'. It is **also very common/not so common** for them to come right at the beginning of a sentence, followed by a comma.

3 Look back again at sentence 5 in exercise 1. What two-letter word is very common to express the same meaning, is more informal, and is written without commas?

We had a successful advertising campaign _____ sales increased.

4 Complete the sentences with a word or phrase from the box.

arose from	as	as a result	due to	led to	so

1 Changes in the market _____ the collapse of the company.
2 _____ there were so many changes in the market, the company eventually collapsed.
3 _____ the changes in the market, the company eventually collapsed.
4 The market changed completely _____ the company collapsed.
5 There were a lot of changes in the market, and, _____, the company collapsed.
6 The collapse of the company _____ all the changes in the market.

5 Cover all the other exercises on this page with a piece of paper. Complete each sentence below with one of these prepositions: *about, by, from, in, of, to*.

1 Our cashflow problems last year arose _____ late payments by suppliers.
2 Basically, all our cashflow problems have originated _____ late payments by suppliers.
3 On account _____ late payments by suppliers, we had a lot of cashflow problems last year.
4 Late payments by suppliers have brought _____ all our cashflow problems.
5 All those late payments by suppliers have given rise _____ a lot of cashflow problems.
6 Our cashflow problems are largely caused _____ suppliers paying us late.

Describing ability in the past

6 Underline the words in **bold** that are the most natural then read the information in the box.

1 In the old days **we could/we were able to** take our customers out for lunch all the time without worrying about the bill.
2 The new software arrived yesterday. **I could/I was able to** install it quite easily.

> • To talk about general past ability (not limited to one occasion) we use *could*.
> • To talk about one specific past action we use *was/were able to*.
> • To talk about one specific past action we can also use *managed to*, *failed to* and *succeed in*.

7 Complete each sentence with the correct ending, a) or b).

1 I was able   3 I succeeded
2 I managed   4 I failed

a) to install it
b) in installing it

8 Look at the second bullet point in the box above, and then look at the sentence below.

Her presentation was excellent. I could understand everything she said.

This seems to break the rule – is it correct?

> To talk about one specific past action with verbs of the senses and thoughts (*see*, *feel*, *hear*, *think*, *understand* etc) we can use *could* as well as *was/were able to*.

Articles

9 Match the uses a–j in the box to the examples 1–10.

> **a/an**
> a) referring to something for the first time
> b) used when you mean any person or thing of a particular type, but not a specific one
> c) describing a type of job (*a teacher, an accountant*)
> **the**
> d) referring to something mentioned previously
> e) referring to something for the first time when it is clear from the situation which one we mean
> f) when there is only one of something (*the boss, the sun*)
> g) nationalities and other groups (*the English, the young, the poor*)
> **no article**
> h) plural countable nouns (*facts, jobs, machines, animals*) used in a general way
> i) uncountable nouns (*information, work, machinery, nature*) used in a general way
> j) most countries, continents, cities, streets (*Italy, Europe, Geneva, Church Street*)

1 He's finished university and wants to work as **an** electrical engineer. ☐
2 Have you got **a** car? ☐
3 I have **a** suggestion. ☐
4 I've been thinking about **the** suggestion you made at the meeting yesterday. ☐
5 We sell these products all over **the** world. ☐
6 I think there should be more training for **the** unemployed. ☐
7 I think **the** project is going well. ☐
8 For me, football is like life. ☐
9 At our plant in Slovakia we make cars and trucks. ☐
10 Riga is the capital of Latvia. ☐

10 The word *advice* is uncountable. Decide if each sentence is correct (✓) or incorrect (✗).

1 He gave me a good advice.
2 He gave me the good advice.
3 He gave me good advice.
4 He gave me some good advice.
5 The advice he gave me was very good.

> • A common mistake is to use *a* or *the* with uncountable nouns used in a general way. In these cases we sometimes use no article, but it is more common to use *some* or *a lot of*.
> • In sentence 5 *the* is used because it is clear from the situation which advice we mean.

11 The word *computer* is countable. Decide if each sentence is correct (✓) or incorrect (✗).

1 He's a real techie – he loves the computers.
2 He's a real techie – he loves computers.
3 The computers we have at work are a bit out-of-date.

> • A common mistake is to use *the* with plural countable nouns used in a general way. We normally use no article.
> • In sentence 3 *the* is used because it is clear from the situation which computers we mean.

12 If the sentence is correct, write a tick (✓). If it is incorrect, add or delete the articles *the* or *a/an*.

1 In business, the up-to-date information is critical for success.
2 This is a very important information.
3 Thanks for information you gave me – it was useful.
4 I enjoy job I do in the evening.
5 It's hard to find jobs in the finance sector.
6 To become doctor you need to study at university for many years.
7 The love is not rational – you can't explain it.
8 The love I have for my cat is not the same as the love I have for my boyfriend.
9 We need to do a research.
10 We need to do some research.
11 We need to do the research to see if you're right.
12 We need to do a lot of research.

Obligation and permission

1 Match the forms in **bold** to their best descriptions a-e below.

1 You **have to do** it. ☐
2 You **must do** it. ☐
3 You **don't have to do** it. ☐
4 You **mustn't do** it. ☐
5 You **can do** it. ☐
6 You **can't do** it. ☐

a You have permission.
b It is not necessary.
c It is prohibited (forbidden) *or* You do not have permission.
d It is necessary. I am telling you.
e It is necessary. The rules say so.

2 Read the notes in the box then do the exercise below.

> There is no real difference between *must* and *have to* in writing. In speech there is a very small difference:
> *must* can suggest that the speaker decides what is necessary
> *have to* can suggest the necessity comes from the situation.

Complete the sentences with the most likely form, *must* or *have to*. Remember that this is not a 100 per cent rule, and both are possible in all the sentences.

1 I _____ go on a diet – these trousers don't fit any more!
2 I _____ go on a diet – the doctor says that I am overweight.
3 This is the text the teacher gave us. We _____ read it for homework. We're going to discuss it in class tomorrow.
4 This book is really good – you _____ read it.

3 In very formal language (such as legal documents) you can use *shall* to express obligation. Match the words in **bold** below to some words in bold from exercise 1 (so that the meaning is the same).

1 You **shall do** it. _____ and _____ .
2 You **shall not do** it. _____ and _____ .

> The most common use for *shall* is making suggestions, and in this case we only use it with *I/we*: *Shall we stop for lunch?* But in the formal use for obligation mentioned above it can be used with *you/he/she/it/they* as well.

4 The forms in **bold** below are other ways to express obligation and permission. At the end of each sentence write the words in bold from exercise 1 that have the same meaning. You might write the same words twice.

1 You **need to do** it. _____ and _____ .
2 You **needn't do** it. _____ .
3 You**'re allowed to do** it. _____ .
4 You**'re not allowed to do** it. _____ and _____ .
5 You**'ve got to do** it. _____ and _____ .

5 Be careful with the word *may*. It can indicate permission in a formal context, or it can indicate possibility (approximately a 50:50 chance of something happening).

Look at the use of *may* in the sentences below and write 'permission' or 'possibility' at the end.

1 Visitors **may** use the swimming pool between 5.30 and 7.30 p.m. _____
2 There **may** be an easier way of solving the problem. _____
3 **May** I use your phone? _____
4 You **may** go home now if you want. _____
5 You **may** be asked to show your passport. _____
6 Some chemicals **may** cause environmental damage. _____
7 You **may** not use this equipment unless you have been on a training course. _____
8 You **may** not believe me, but it's true. _____

> When *may* is used for possibility (as in 2, 5, 6 and 8 in exercise 5) we can use *might* with the same meaning. We cannot do this for the other sentences.

6 Underline the correct word in **bold**.

1 I'm sorry, this is a non-smoking area – you **haven't got to/can't** smoke here.
2 You **mustn't/don't have to** come if you are busy, but it would be nice to see you.
3 Ethical behaviour is important – you **mustn't/needn't** accept bribes.
4 You **mustn't/needn't** take an umbrella – I've got a spare one in the car.
5 You **don't have to/can't** enter the USA without a visa.
6 This report is confidential – you **mustn't/needn't** show it to anyone.
7 You **must/aren't allowed to** maintain the equipment in good condition.
8 You **mustn't/don't have to** do that, I'll do it tomorrow.
9 You **mustn't/don't have to** do that, it's dangerous.
10 All payments **shall/mustn't** be made within 30 working days.
11 If you want to smoke, you **shall/may** go outside.
12 Don't worry, the law states that you **shall/may** receive all the money that is owing to you.

7 Complete each sentence with a form of *have to*. Choices include *has to, don't have to, had to, didn't have to, 'll have to, won't have to*.

1 If you want to do well in your exams, you _____ work a lot harder this semester.
2 I'm sorry I'm late, I _____ take my daughter to the hospital.
3 It's a drop-in service, you _____ make an appointment.
4 If we redecorate the offices this year, we _____ do it again for another five years.
5 Teresa can't fly direct from Brno. She _____ go via Prague.
6 Oh, you brought your own projector! You _____ – we have one in the conference room.

8 Complete b) and c) so that they have the same meaning each time as a). For b) use a form of *can*, for c) use a form of *allowed*.

1 a When I was young, we had permission to park anywhere in the city centre.
  b When I was young, we _____ anywhere in the city centre.
  c When I was young, we _____ anywhere in the city centre.

2 a I'm sorry, it's prohibited to smoke in here.
  b I'm sorry, _____ in here.
  c I'm sorry, _____ in here.

3 a Yes, that's OK, taking pictures is permitted.
  b Yes, that's OK, _____ pictures.
  c Yes, that's OK, taking _____.

9 Look at the word *got* in these sentences. If it is correct, put a tick (✓). If it is not correct, cross it out.

1 Maria is busy – she's got to finish some work before tomorrow.
2 You could have gone to the restaurant. You didn't have got to wait for us.
3 Is that the time? I've got to go now.
4 What time have we got to be at the meeting?
5 Do I have got to sign in the visitor's book?
6 It's boring to have got to wait so long.

> Both *have to* and *have got to* express necessity. *Have got to* is a little more informal, and is mostly used in the present simple. Also, *have got to* cannot be used in the infinitive form (#6 above).

Inversion

10 Read the information in the box. Then rewrite each sentence 1–6 beginning as shown.

> - In formal speech and writing there is a special construction when the sentence begins with a negative adverb (like those underlined below).
>   *I have never in my life seen such bad service.*
>   → <u>Never in my life</u> **have I** seen such bad service.
>   *You shouldn't do that under any circumstances.*
>   → <u>Under no circumstances</u> **should you** do that.
>   *It is not only bad practice, it is also illegal.*
>   → <u>Not only</u> **is it** bad practice, it is also illegal.
>   *I wasn't able to see a doctor until Monday.*
>   → <u>Not until</u> Monday **was I** able to see a doctor.
> - Notice how the subject and the verb – in bold – are inverted (change places).
> - This structure emphasizes the negative adverb.
> - Words and phrases used with this structure include: *never, no sooner, not once, not only, not since, not until, on no account, only after, only once, only then, rarely, seldom, under no circumstances.*

1 I have rarely tasted coffee as good as this.
  Rarely _____ .
2 You shouldn't accept a bribe under any circumstances.
  Under no _____ .
3 We won't pay them until all the work is completed.
  Not until _____ .
4 The contract is not only badly worded, it is also incomplete.
  Not _____ .
5 You should not talk to the media on any account.
  On no _____ .
6 Work can begin only once safety checks have been carried out.
  Only _____ .

> In 2 and 5 in exercise 10 notice how the word *any* in the first sentence becomes *no* in the second.

11 Look at the list of negative adverbs in italics in the final bullet point of the box above. Complete each explanation below with items from this list:

1 '_____' means 'very rarely'.
2 '_____' and '_____' are both used to emphasize that someone must definitely not do something, for any reason.
3 '_____ had ... than ...' is used to say that something happened almost immediately after something else

Recordings

Unit 1 Building a career

1.1 About business: The education business

🔊 1:01

Speaker 1: I don't care what they say about checks and balances, Harvard is part of a totally elitist, sexist and racist system. If you're not a white American male from a rich family with political connections, you can forget it – you'll never get in to Harvard!

Speaker 2: As Mr Fitzsimmons says, it makes sense to put the best students with the best faculty. Every country needs an intellectual elite to work in its government and key industries.

Speaker 3: Forty thousand dollars a year! It's scandalous! Education should be accessible to everyone, and the government should pay for it. And it's completely absurd paying all those people just to recruit the best students!

Speaker 4: I admire Harvard for practising what they preach. It's high time more schools and universities were run as businesses – they'd be more efficient and save taxpayers money.

1.2 Vocabulary: education and career

🔊 1:02

Speaker 1: I'm thinking of leaving actually. I've worked in China, Argentina, and Alaska, and now they want me to go to South Africa for two years! But even if I resign, they'll make me work at least another three months. I'm just sick of being moved around all the time.

Speaker 2: When the company was modernized, they told me to stay at home for a week or two while they found me a different job – but they never did, so in the end they had to 'let me go', as they say. Replaced by a machine! Actually, I'm grateful – it was probably the best thing that could have happened to me.

Speaker 3: I've just been sent home for a week because I refused to wear a safety helmet – they're too hot and uncomfortable. They keep harassing me – I think they'd like to fire me actually!

Speaker 4: I was on the road for thirty years as a sales rep. Then I was lucky enough to get the job as sales manager here four years ago. I've just been made 'Director of Customer Satisfaction' – or as the boys in sales say, they've kicked me upstairs! Well, at my age, I'm over the moon!

Speaker 5: I'm based in London for the moment – actually, right now I'm doing audits in Paris, for our French subsidiary – but it's just for three months. After that, they've asked me to move to the Vancouver office. It's a fantastic opportunity!

Speaker 6: Well, I'm not actually working at the moment. I'm an actor, and I finished a movie a couple of months ago. I'm thinking about taking a year off to write a book.

🔊 1:03

Hi. My name's Bob. A few years ago I started up an electronics company which has been very successful. So successful in fact that I had to hire a CEO to give me time for my creative work. I brought in Jack, a manager from a completely different business, a soda manufacturer in fact. I thought he would be the right man to help my company grow, but now I know I made a big mistake. Recently we disagreed about strategy. Believe it or not, the Board decided he was right and I was wrong, and stripped me of my duties. Of course, I resigned. Well, what would you have done? I still hold my shares in the company, but I think I'm going to sell them. I don't know what I'll do next. Maybe I'll invest the money from the shares and retire somewhere cheap and sunny? Or I suppose I could start over and build a new company. Or join a competitor. What do you think I should do?

🔊 1:04

Hello, I'm Lucy, and my problem is that I've never really known what sort of career to choose. I studied languages at university, which was great, but it doesn't really qualify you to do anything. After graduating, I worked as a researcher for a charity, then I went abroad and worked as an English teacher for a while. Now I'm a secretary; or should I say I was a secretary, because I've just been fired for writing stories at work! I love writing – but it's not easy to make a living from it. I suppose I'd need to go back to school and do a creative writing course. Perhaps I could work part-time, waitressing or something. Or should I just look for another secretarial job? Or go back to being a researcher, or a teacher maybe, at least that's more creative. What do you think?

🔊 1:05

Hi. I'm Mel. I've wanted to run my own business for as long as I can remember. When I was in high school, a friend and I designed a product which we managed to sell to local government departments. But my parents were really keen on sending me to business school, so now I'm in my third year at a really prestigious, expensive school. The thing is, my friend and I have a fantastic opportunity to start our own business; we have a new product, and a big company is really interested in buying it. But to develop our idea, I'll have to drop out of school, and I know my parents will be really upset. What do you think I should do?

1.3 Grammar: tense review

🔊 1:06

Jess: Fraser Orbell!

Fraser: Oh, hi.

J: Oh my God! Fancy meeting you here! You look great! Do you still go running?

F: Oh, thank you. Yes, I usually run two or three times a week. Um, I'm sorry, I'm afraid I always forget people's names ...

J: It's Jess! Jess Tomey!

F: Oh, Jess, of course! I'm so sorry ...

J: It's alright. People often don't recognize me. Too many business lunches, so I always tend to put on weight!

F: No, no, you look wonderful. As always!

J: Thank you Fraser! So what are you doing these days?

F: Well, actually at the moment I'm not doing very much. Sort of, job-hunting, you know ...

J: Oh, I see. Well I hope you find something soon. But what did you do after graduation?

F: Well, you probably remember that I dropped out in my final year, so I didn't actually graduate. But I worked for ITC in Manchester for twenty years.

J: Oh, did you?!

F: Yes, until they were taken over by Morgan-Hoenshell about a year ago. Twenty years of loyal service, but when Morgan-Hoenshell came along, I was made redundant without so much as a word of thanks.

J: Oh, how awful for you!

F: Yes, well, you know, that's life, isn't it? But, um, actually, I've just got back from Nepal.

J: Nepal? Wow!

F: Yeah, been, um, working on a book.

J: Oh, that's terrific, Fraser! So when can I buy it?

F: Well, I haven't finished it yet, but hopefully it'll be published next year – I promise I'll send you a copy. But anyway, that's enough about me – what have you done since you left Franklin? Did you get that job you wanted in finance?

J: Yes, I did. I worked in several firms, actually; I became a specialist in downsizing – cutting costs, streamlining, restructuring, you know ...

F: I see. A bit like Morgan-Hoenshell!

J: Well, yes, a bit ...

F: So where are you working now?

J: Oh, I'm currently managing one of our subsidiaries, um, up north.

F: Oh yeah – anywhere near Manchester?

J: Um, yes ... but I'm going to move down to London soon.

F: Oh really?

J: Yes, I've just had some rather good news.

F: Uh-huh?

J: Well, if all goes well, I'm taking over as group CEO next year.

F: Wow, congratulations! Which company?

J: Um, you probably wouldn't be interested ...

F: Come on Jess, we go back a long way! No secrets between us, eh?

J: Well, it's Morgan-Hoenshell, actually.

1.4 Speaking: Giving reasons

🔊 1:07

1 Can you tell us why you chose your school or university?

2 Could you explain why you are single or married?

3 I'd like to know the reasons why you are, or are not, a member of a union.

4 Would you mind telling us why you do or don't have children?

5 Do you smoke or drink? Why, or why not?

6 What exactly made you choose to apply to this company?

7 I'd be interested to know why you are, or are not, a vegetarian.

8 Can you tell me where you want to live and work, and why?

DVD-ROM The recordings are available as MP3 files on the DVD-ROM, to be downloaded or played back with interactive script.

Recordings

 1:08

Interviewer: So, Ruth, Could you tell me what motivated you to study business, and why you chose to attend the Franklin School of Business?

Ruth: Um, yes. Um, well, I suppose mainly 'cos my boyfriend was going to Franklin. And I liked economics at school. I thought about some of the better-known business schools, but, you know, they're too expensive anyway … I nearly chose French actually, 'cos my mother's French, but I thought business was better. More money in it, basically. And Franklin was great, you know. Really good school. I had a great time. But as I say, basically it was because my boyfriend was there – well, my ex-boyfriend I should say. And, erm, … the teachers. The teachers were terrific of course.

 1:09

Interviewer: Could you tell me what motivated you to study business, Anais, and why you chose to attend the Franklin School of Business?

Anaïs: Well, as regards choosing business, although I love languages, basically I've always wanted to go into management, and I felt that business was the obvious choice. It not only prepared me to work in more or less any department in a company, but it also means that I can use my language skills in an international career. In addition, a business degree always gets attention, interest and respect. So to sum up, I chose business rather than languages; if not I think it would have been more difficult to get into management.

As far as my choice of business school is concerned, it's true that the big names open doors, but on the other hand, newer schools like Franklin have significant advantages. For one thing, they have better facilities, and for another, they're less expensive. What's more, their curricula are more innovative, their classes are smaller, and their student intake is more diverse. In the end I decided to choose a new university, simply because it represented better value for money overall.

1.6 Case study: Mangalia Business School

 1:10

First of all, I would like to thank you all for coming here today. We hope you will enjoy your visit, and experience for yourselves why Mangalia is such a wonderful place to live and study. As you know, institutions like MBS now compete on a global market. The days when we could rely on our contacts in Romania and Central Europe to fill our school are long gone. Today we compete with giants like Harvard and the London Business School. Small schools like MBS face a difficult choice: either we sit back and watch the brightest students and the best professors fly away to Massachusetts, Paris, Barcelona or London, or we take risks, invest, and develop new ways to be more competitive in the global marketplace. Here in Mangalia, we are not used to sitting back and doing nothing. We have chosen to draw up a five-

year plan to make MBS a truly international business school, and we have invited you here to help us. We are not only relying on your experience, your know-how and your creativity to help us make the right decisions, but we are also counting on you to identify and promote the USPs, the unique selling propositions, that will give us a competitive advantage in attracting the best students and the most influential corporate clients. As far as finance is concerned, some of you will already have heard the excellent news that the prominent businessman and multi-millionaire Ion Bumbescu has offered to sponsor our school. This would have the immediate effect of doubling our budget. However, Mr Bumbescu's business methods are somewhat controversial, and his offer specifies that the school should be known as the Bumbescu Business School; consequently I must ask you to consider carefully all the implications of such a change.

 1:11

In business news, controversial multi-millionaire Ion Bumbescu has again been accused of involvement in defence procurement for developing countries. Mr Bumbescu, who is believed to be travelling in Southeast Asia, was unavailable for comment, but in a short statement made earlier today, a spokesman for Bumbescu Holdings claimed that 'the group's companies had done nothing illegal.' Mr Bumbescu's business methods have been frequently criticized by his competitors. Recently his Bumbescu Foundation has been pouring millions into research and education projects, in what appears to be an attempt to improve his image.

Unit 2 Information

2.1 About business: IT solutions

 1:12

Speaker 1: I'm not sure all this technology is a good thing. Take these Blackberry phones, for example. I was at a meeting last week where three of the six attendees spent most of the time doing email under the table! People get really addicted to it – it's a drug! I heard about one executive whose wife got so fed up with him checking his emails all weekend, she flushed his Blackberry down the toilet!

Speaker 2: IT? Oh, I love it! As soon as there's a new gadget, I have to have it. I think it's just amazing what you can do nowadays. Of course, you don't really save time, but you get so much more done in a day. I just cannot imagine how anyone can manage without a laptop and a mobile.

Speaker 3: As far as I'm concerned, information technology is just another weapon in the class war. Management will use any way they can to exploit the workers, and increasing productivity with computer systems is just another way to get as much as they can. Not to mention the untold damage that the radiation and microwaves from all these electronic devices are doing to our eyes, our backs, and our brains!

Speaker 4: Well, I have to use the computer at

work sometimes, but I wouldn't have one in the house. All those viruses, and spam, and computer crime! Anyway, a lot of people at work seem to spend more time fixing computer problems than actually doing any work. I think we'd be better off without them!

2.2 Vocabulary: information systems and communication

 1:13

Speaker 1: Hello? Mr Skopelitis? Oh. This is Ebony Brooks in Accounts. Something went wrong with the system when I was in the middle of a backup. Everything just stopped. It wasn't just my computer. Do you think you could call me? Give me a ring as soon as you can.

Speaker 2: George, its Maurice. I'm still having that problem making appointments on the website. I log in, then everything seems to freeze, and when I try to escape, I get the famous blue screen. Can you give me an update on what progress you've made on this problem? Just a quick report.

Speaker 3: Yeah, George, it's Martha here. Listen, could you contact me? I want to replace my department's laptops with something more modern. Our old IBMs are getting pretty tired, know what I mean? Please get in touch as soon as you have a moment.

Speaker 4: Hello George. This is Lincoln Thigpen. I hope you can help me out here, I seem to have done something stupid. I was cleaning up my hard disk, and well, now some very important presentation slides seem to have disappeared. I hope you have some way of rescuing them – if you could get back to me with an answer some time today, I'd appreciate it.

Speaker 5: Hi Mr Skopelitis. This is Camilla Ramsey from Customer Services. It's about that little software thingy you sent me? I've edged it into the database program like you told me to, but it doesn't seem to work. I know some other people were having the same problem. Do you think you could include me in the group of people to inform? You know, keep me in the loop. Thanks.

Speaker 6: George – Maurice again. Where the hell are you?! Marketing are hassling me every five minutes because they still can't use the Internet. Will you please tell me when you're going to be able to get them on line?! Let me know asap.

Speaker 7: George, Marvin. Long time no see! Remember how you said you could get that software from the Internet to make my sound card work? Can't work without my music! I guess you're working on it, but can you keep me informed, maybe a regular progress report, OK?

Speaker 8: Good morning Mr Skopelitis. This is Cara Bickerson in Marketing. I'm looking for a quicker way to get information from our market studies into the database – typing it all in is just too slow. I'm interested in voice recognition software – I wonder if you could fill me in on the details of what's available? You can reach me any time today before 4 p.m. Thank you.

2.4 Speaking: Telephoning

 1:14

Lorenzo: Accounts?
Kelly: Lorenzo? It's Kelly, from Sales.
L: Uh-huh.
K: Listen, I'm with a customer, and I need you to give me last year's billing figures.
L: What's the customer account number?
K: Um, I don't have it here. But it's Zimmer, in Warsaw.
L: Well if you don't have the account number, I can't help you.
K: Come on Lorenzo, I really need this! I'm sure you can find it.
L: Look, Kelly, it's the end of the month, and we're closing the accounts; I'd like to help you, but I'm up to my eyes in work here. I really haven't got time to look for your customer's records now. Try Marielle in Sales Administration. I'll put you through.
K: Thanks a million.

 1:15

Cory: Cory Wilks.
Tabetha: Hello Cory. It's Tabetha Pullman here.
C: Oh, hi Tabetha, how are you doing?
T: I'm fine, thanks. How are you?
C: Well you know, mustn't grumble, I suppose. Things'll be a bit easier when the weather improves.
T: Oh yeah, it's been a really long winter, hasn't it? Anyway, have you got a couple of minutes?
C: Yes, sure.
T: Well, do you happen to know how to set up a WiFi connection on a laptop? I would've asked the IT department, but apparently they're all in some big meeting, so I thought you might be able to help me.
C: Oh I'm sorry Tabetha. I wish I could help you, but I don't know that much about it myself. Amanda does all my department's computer stuff, and she's out of the office today. I'm sorry.
T: Don't worry. I just thought you might know, but it doesn't matter. Thank you anyway.
C: No problem.
T: Anyway, I won't keep you any longer – thanks once again.
C: You're welcome – sorry I couldn't help you more.
T: That's alright. Bye.
C: Bye.

 1:16

Lauren: Hello?
Erich: Good afternoon. I wonder if I could speak to Ms Simpson please?
L: Speaking.
E: Excuse me?
L: This is Lauren Simpson.
E: Ah, Ms Simpson. Erich Schrader, calling from Switzerland. We met at the conference in Nice last month.
L: Oh, yes, of course! How are you, Erich?
E: I am very well, thank you Ms Simpson. And how are you?
L: Fine thanks. Um, what can I do for you?
E: Well, I'm very sorry to disturb you, but I was wondering if I could ask you a favour?
L: Yes, of course …
E: Do you think you could possibly send me a copy of the slides you showed at the conference? They were most interesting.
L: Ah. Well, normally I'd be glad to help, but I'm afraid my hard disk crashed last week.
E: Oh dear, how very unfortunate. I trust you didn't lose too much important information.
L: Well, everything actually. But there wasn't too much important stuff on it; except the slides, of course.
E: And you wouldn't happen to have a backup, or a hard copy would you?
L: No, I'm afraid not.
E: I see. Well, I mustn't take up any more of your time. Thank you all the same, Ms Simpson.
L: You're welcome. Goodbye Erich, I mean Mr, um …
E: Schrader.
L: Um, yes, goodbye then.

 1:17

Russell: Russell Pond speaking?
Mike: Hello Russell – Mike.
R: Hello mate. How's life?
M: Not so bad. And you?
R: Fine, fine. Looking forward to the weekend, though!
M: Yeah, me too. Er, Russell, you got a moment?
R: Yes; what's on your mind?
M: Well, I know this is asking a lot, but I've got this presentation on Monday, and my laptop's got a virus. Any chance I could borrow yours for the weekend?
R: Ah. Look, it's not that I don't trust you or anything …
M: OK, just forget it I shouldn't've asked.
R: The thing is, I've got some really important data on it, and the anti-virus isn't up to date …
M: It's alright Russell, I know what you mean. Anyway, I'd better get on. You going to the match on Saturday?
R: Yes, I expect so.
M: OK. I'll see you there, then. Bye.
R: Cheers.

2.5 Writing: Memos

 1:18

Hello, Chris Webster here. I'm at the airport, just about to leave for my holiday, and I've just realized there's something important I've forgotten to do, so I wonder if I could ask you a favour? You know the new procedure we discussed for computer upgrades? Asking people to evaluate their computing needs for the next two years so we can budget for buying new equipment in advance? Well, do you think you could write a memo to everyone in the department, explaining the new system? Remind them that we've been dramatically over budget in the last two years, so, you know, some people who needed laptops didn't get one, while other people got an upgrade they didn't really need. I need to have the information in time for the budget meeting in October, so can you ask people to email me their evaluation as soon as possible, by the end of September at the latest? And make it positive and friendly please, because I know people complain about the amount of paperwork they have to do already. OK, I've got to go now, my plane's boarding. Thanks a lot, I really appreciate your help – and, see you in two weeks!

2.6 Case study: Meteor Bank

 1:19

Look Astrid, we appointed Saul Finley because he's a very bright, very ambitious young man. Alright, he's irritated some of his colleagues – but as he says, you don't make an omelette without breaking eggs. Of course I'm worried about staff turnover and downtime costs, and so is Saul. But you have to remember that our transactions have increased by 40 per cent since he joined us – our subsidiaries in Ivory Coast, Ghana, Cameroon etc. are growing really quickly. We need to invest in the new equipment he's asking for.

1:20

Well if you ask me, I have to say that I think Saul is too ambitious – he's just empire-building. OK, he's increased our capacity, I suppose that's an achievement. But he's made our computer system too centralized – if the main server goes down, we're in trouble – not just in Nigeria, but all over West Africa. The trend today is towards grid computing: that way, if the server in Lagos goes down, we can just redirect transactions via Abidjan, Niamey or Dakar. I say we should decentralize our systems. And another thing; you can't explain the downtime just by component failures and software errors. You have to wonder whether some of it isn't malicious.

1:21

The problem is simple – everybody in IT is exhausted. Mr. Finley is a very demanding manager He works fifteen hours a day, and he expects us to do the same. That's why so many people are leaving! Frankly, I'm not sure that appointing a European IT manager was such a good idea. OK, Mr. Finley has raised salaries. But he's made the job too hard – and it's going to get more complicated if he invests in more sophisticated equipment. So now some people are pleased when the system goes down – you know what I mean? We need to recruit more experienced staff, a lot more.

1:22

Look, I've nothing against Saul Finley, I like him, he's a nice young man, and he's succeeded in getting rid of some older staff who just couldn't adapt to change. Of course he's made mistakes, like not understanding the work culture here, but that's almost inevitable when you bring in a foreign manager. I just want efficient service, and no more downtime – some of our big customers are getting very angry. It seems to me the simple answer is to outsource our IT services. That way we don't have any of the investment, HR or recruitment problems to worry about.

3 Quality

3.1 About business: What quality means

 1:23

Well, over the years, in the household electrical goods industry, or *white goods* as it's often called, there's been a lot of talk about planned or built-in obsolescence. This means making products that are designed to last a limited time. It's true that we are seeing a general trend towards shorter product lifespans. A fridge, for example, that would once have lasted for twenty years, now lasts for around ten on average. However, I wouldn't go as far as to call it planned obsolescence. But it's true that manufacturers these days decide very carefully what build quality they are aiming for. Consumer behaviour is changing and people don't want to keep things forever. They want to upgrade more often, and there's not much point in producing machines that will last for twenty years when people will be tired of them after ten. So, most manufacturers design accordingly. And that's why it's often cheaper to buy something new than to have a product repaired. The cost of the spare parts and the labour time to repair a broken washing machine, for example, may well come to more than the cost price of a new one. I think another factor is recent legislation regarding recycling. This means that today's ethical consumer can buy electrical goods knowing that we can recycle them at the end of their useful life. And, of course, they can also argue that by upgrading regularly, they're investing in more efficient, more environmentally friendly, technology. Now, if you want to buy a quality product that will last, you can still go for the top brands and ...

3.2 Vocabulary: Quality and Standards

 1:24

Speaker 1: Well, most of the time I'm looking for value for money, you know, for everyday things and that. So a balance between quality and the price I'm paying. But, erm, if I'm splashing out on a pair of trainers or the latest MP3 player, I want something reliable that's going to last. And of course, they've got to look great, too, know what I mean?

Speaker 2: My job basically involves ensuring that the process is as efficient as possible and makes the best use of all the resources needed to make the final product. So, I'm constantly looking at ways to improve it, which means not only solving problems that come up, but also looking for new ways to do things even better. I let the design guys worry about pure product quality. Quality for me is really producing a part or a product, which conforms to given technical specifications, in the most cost-effective way.

Speaker 3: Erm, although I believe what I do contributes to the end quality of the product, it's not really my everyday concern. I check that the company has documented quality procedures in place and that they're being followed. So, erm,

I suppose in theory, the company might conform to the quality standards, but might be producing a product that is substandard in some way. We don't live in a perfect world, after all!

3.3 Grammar: Passive structures and *have something done*

 1:25

Willi: Well, thank you all for coming. I know you're all very busy at the moment so we'll see if we can sort this out as quickly as possible. José, perhaps you can start and tell us the background from the Sales side?

José: Sure, Willi. Well, the problem is simple. Airbridge can't fix the pumps to the fuel tanks properly. The reason, it seems, is because they don't fit.

Birgit: What do you mean, they don't fit, José?

J: Basically, Birgit, your Production department put the wrong type of fitting on the pumps!

B: My Production department, José! Hold on! First of all, Sales didn't warn Production that that they wanted this early. That made things very difficult. We had to organize an extra shift.

J: Well, yes, I'm sorry about that. We'll try to give you more warning next time.

B: That was bad enough. And Stock didn't make things any easier. They shouldn't have sent two different parts to the workshop in the same delivery. And, to top it all, they delivered them at the last minute! OK, I'm prepared to admit that there may have been a problem, but you can hardly blame my people in Production if they didn't spot the difference!

W: But wait a minute, Birgit. The Stock department didn't make a mistake. If you remember, at the last Logistics meeting, we, yes, you, me and everybody else, decided to deliver different parts together to reduce stock movements!

B: OK, Willi, OK, I accept that, but Stock did deliver late. And Sales should've given us more warning!

J: More warning! How could we give you more warning? You know that Airbridge only increased their order two weeks before the final delivery date! It's always the same. The customer ...

W: Woah! Now take it easy, both of you. We're not going to find a solution if we spend all our time blaming each other. We've all made mistakes but, as I see it, the underlying cause seems to be customer pressure. So, let's put our heads together and see how we can improve our reaction time without compromising our quality ...

3.4 Speaking: Delivering presentations

 1:26

Speaker 1: Anyway, the ACI has shown an increase on the marginal propensity gradient of 4.5 per cent over and above the CDWLP.

Speaker 2: Well, that's as you can see an increase OK in the rate of sales growth over the quarter and this rate of growth OK continued OK into the new year which was completely unexpected OK and then ...

Speaker 3: As is clear from the graph, there was ... as is clear, there was an important development, erm ... important change in the market structure during the previous ... year.

Speaker 4: Obviously, we aim to do a profit. We always expect to do a profit, and I'm sure we will do a profit. The sales team are really making a great job.

 1:27

So, this graph shows the PFR, that's the Part Failure Rate, per ten thousand over the first ten months of the year. As you can see, it was pretty high for the first four months, around seventy on average. And that's why we set up the quality improvement plan in April. By the way, I'd just like to thank Magda for her input on the plan. I think you'll all agree she did a great job. Anyway, the first results were very promising, with PFR falling to thirty-five in May and then twenty-eight in June. However, since then the rate has got worse again, rising to forty-four in August and forty-seven last month. So, we need to turn things around again. In other words, get the rate back down in the twenties, or better. And basically, that's why we're here today: to look at the reasons and some possible solutions. ... Is that clear so far? ... Good, well, I think that covers the basic problem, so now I'd like to look at some of the reasons we've identified. Let's look at the next table which shows ...

3.5 Writing: Procedures and instructions

 1:28

Max: Hello. Max speaking.

Janice: Hi Max, It's Janice.

M: Oh, hi Jan. How're things? Did you get the same TV stand as me in the end?

J: Well, yes, Max, I did. As a matter of fact, that's why I'm calling. I can't put the thing together and I've lost the assembly instructions. I was wondering if you'd kept yours by any chance?

M: I may just be able to help you out. Hold on a sec (sounds of phone being put down and paper being shuffled). Yep, got them.

J: Great, Max. You're a hero! Everybody's coming round to watch the film this evening and I don't want to put the TV on the floor!

M: But hold on a minute, Jan. You've still got to put it together. Have you got all the parts?

J: Erm, well, erm, I don't really know, 'cause I've lost the parts list, too!

M: Well, never mind about that. I'll read it to you and you can check if you have everything, OK?

J: OK, Max. Go ahead.

M: OK, let's see ... You should have one top panel, two side panels ...

J: One top panel, two side panels ... yeah, this looks like them ...

M: Yeah ... then one cross bar and one shelf ...

J: Cross bar ... one shelf ...

M: Four pegs, eight screws and four castor wheels. You got that?

J: Four pegs, eight screws and four wheels. ...Yes, it looks as if they're all here. If you could just send me the instructions, Max, I think I can manage.

M: I'm afraid that's going to be a little difficult, Jan, 'cause there's just a diagram and I don't have a scanner. But, it looks pretty straightforward. If you want, I can write some assembly instructions and email them to you. How does that sound?

J: That'd be great, Max. Thanks.

M: That's OK, Jan. Glad I can help. Anyway, if you want to watch the film, I'd better get writing.

J: Cheers, Max.

M: Cheers, Jan, and enjoy the film!

3.6 Case study: Zaluski Strawberries

 1:29

Piotr Sieberski: Piotr Sieberski.

Suzanne Van Peeters: Good morning, Mr Sieberski. This is Suzanne Van Peeters from Schuurman in Amsterdam.

P: Ah, morning Ms Van Peeters. I imagine you're calling about the email we got from you yesterday.

S: That's right.

P: Something about a quality audit, wasn't it? Don't think you'll find much wrong with our strawberries, quality-wise!

S: I'm sure you're right, Mr Sieberski. We've always been very happy with your fruit. But, as I mentioned in my e-mail, we're currently running audits with all our fresh fruit suppliers. Basically, it's a matter of looking at a wide range of issues which may impact fruit quality, and seeing where there may be room for improvement. You know, sort of trying to iron out any potential problems before they happen.

P: Well, of course, you're welcome to come and see us if you want but I'm not sure what can be improved really. Your purchasing guy comes here at least once a year and he's never had anything negative to say about our strawberries, apart from the price of course!

S: Yeah, well, in fact I was calling to fix up a visit to you. Our supplier audits generally last a day or two and I was wondering whether you'd be free to see us towards the end of next week?

P: Next week? ... That's rather short notice and we are pretty busy at the moment, but ... hold on ... Let me check my schedule ...Yes, I guess I could see you on Thursday and/or Friday if that suits you?

S: Perfect, Mr Sieberski. Thursday would be fine. We'd probably be arriving the night before, so we could start as early as you like on Thursday morning.

P: Well, I get in around seven most days, Ms Van Peeters. Gives me time to look at the important matters before things really get going and I'm interrupted every five minutes!

S: Seven! Well, we'll give you a bit of breathing space, Mr Sieberski. How about eight-thirty?

P: Suits me fine, Ms Van Peeters. So that's eight-thirty on the fifteenth.

S: Great! Looking forward to seeing you next Thursday.

P: Yeah! See you then. Thank you for calling! Goodbye.

S: Goodbye, Mr Sieberski.

 1:30

Suzanne Van Peeters: Perhaps we could begin with harvesting, Mr Sieberski. Who does that?

Piotr Sieberski: Well, the farms hire their own workers each season, generally students or local people.

S: And, do they get any training?

P: That's the responsibilty of each producer; but I know most of them do some. After all, it's in their own interests.

S: What about supervision and picking bonuses to make sure only sound fruit are picked?

P: Most farms pay a small productivity bonus if daily picking targets are met, but it encourages quantity rather than quality I think. And I must admit, there's little supervision of the picking crews.

S: And how is the fruit packed for transfer to your cooler?

P: The pickers put them in standard wooden trays, 10 cm deep. Then, the trays are placed on trailers and, when the trailer is full, it's pulled to our shed by tractor.

S: Isn't that rather long, Mr Sieberski? I mean, how long do they take to get from the field to your cooler?

P: Oh, um, on average, I reckon, three or four hours. Maybe more if several trailers arrive at the same time. In the cooler, the berries are cooled to a temperature of three degrees. Then, they're placed in the storage shed until we can pack them.

S: I presume the storage shed is chilled too?

P: Well, yes it is. The thermostat is kept on two degrees but to be honest, we haven't got time to keep records. The picking season is always such a mad rush you know, Ms.Van Peeters!

S: Yes, I can imagine.

P: From storage, the strawberries go to the packing shed. But, I'll let Klara tell you about that. She's been our packing shed supervisor for seven years now and she knows the job inside out. Klara.

Klara Solak: Thanks, Piotr. Well, Ms Van Peeters, the packing shed is where we put the berries into the punnets for retail sale in outlets like yours. It's seasonal work, and most people imagine that it's unskilled. But I can tell you that good packers are not easy to find.

S: And what about training and bonuses; things like that?

K: Of course, we give them basic training when they're hired: fruit selection, careful handling to avoid bruising, that sort of thing. But they learn on the job otherwise. They're paid according to what they pack in a day so there aren't any bonuses. In fact, we've been looking at the idea of a bonus based on the quality of packing. You know, making sure that they don't put bruised or decaying berries in the packages, and so on. But, quite honestly, it's not very easy to measure that sort of thing.

S: Yes, but it would certainly be a good idea, I'm sure, and there'd be benefits all along the line. As supervisor, do you check the quality of fruit being packed?

K: Huh! Not as much as I'd like. You see, I'm usually packing too, covering for absent

staff, that sort of thing.

S: I see. Now, what about shipping?

K: Well, the punnets are loaded onto trucks for shipping to customers around Europe. Now, we require the trucks to have refrigeration systems and be cooled to zero before loading, but we don't check them systematically.

S: Hmh, well. Thank you for your explanations, Mrs Solak. Erm, let me see. Ah yes. One last question for the moment, Mr Sieberski. I'm sure you're aware that the use of nitrogen fertilizers can lead to softer fruit, lower sugar content and less flavour. Do your farmers use nitrogen?

P: Yes, I'm aware of the problem, Ms Van Peeters and at the moment a lot of them still use it. But it's an expensive operation anyway, and most of the producers in the region are planting new varieties of strawberry which don't need nitrogen. So, I reckon that the practice will have died out within the next two or three years.

S: Well, that's encouraging! Good, now perhaps we could go and look at ...

Unit 4 Feedback

4.1 About business: The project team

 1:31

OK. I think everyone's here apart from Mr Wong who'll be joining us on the video link in half an hour. So, perhaps we can start? The purpose of today's meeting is to review the dam project schedule to date, look at why things have slipped and see what we can do to get things back on track. First, I'd like to take a look at the original schedule on the Gantt chart here, to put our current situation into perspective. I think you'll all agree, things ran pretty smoothly in Year 1 and we reached the first milestones, completion of the feasibility study and the geological survey, bang on target at the end of August. Unfortunately, we got bogged down in bureaucracy – you know, the usual red tape – at the project approval stage. That set us back four months and we could only begin buying the land in May of Year 2. Land purchase went pretty much according to plan, despite some delays for legal reasons, but it still took twelve months. We were able to start population resettlement on time, but we had to postpone diverting the river for six months as it had to be done in the summer months, when the river was at its lowest, which meant starting June of year 3. So, that's how things stand today. We've just completed the two tunnels to divert the river, so that's almost complete, and we're beginning excavations for the dam foundations next week – one year behind schedule! Which means we won't be able to begin work on the dam wall until at least September of Year 4. Of course, due to this schedule slippage, we're also facing considerable cost overruns. So, I'd like your suggestions on how we can crash the schedule – yes, heuh, I mean, accelerate things – to try to respect the original delivery date at the end of Year 7. Any ideas ...?

4.2 Vocabulary: Managing people and projects

 1:32

Lucy: Well, Andrei, thanks for finding time to see me. I know things are very busy, what with the annual appraisal interviews. Anyway, perhaps you can just give me your impressions of Anna, Bjorn and Katia, before we go through the interview results in a bit more detail.

Andrei: Sure, Lucy. So, first of all, Anna. Well, on the positive side, she's hard-working. But, she's very independent and single-minded: she tends to do her own thing and she'll pass the buck if she feels it's not her problem, so the others in the team see her as selfish and a bit of a loner. They often think she's not pulling her weight and that she's letting the team down, just because she doesn't see things the same way. And she can be pretty direct, which of course the others interpret as being over-critical, but I don't think she means to be.

L: OK, so Anna has her good and bad points. Now, what about Bjorn?

A: Yes, Bjorn! To be honest, he seems very stressed and I'm worried that he may burn out. He works long hours – he's often in the office long after everyone's gone home. He's definitely organized – some of the others would say obsessive – but I'm not sure he's always really clear about what needs doing and what is less important, so he tends to create work for himself. He could certainly do to take it easy sometimes, you know.

L: Yes, sounds as if he needs to learn to pace himself a little better!

A: Yeah, that's right. He could do with some time management training, in fact, and I'd like to come back to that when we look at interview results in detail.

L: Good idea. But first, let's just finish with Katia.

A: Well, Katia. Well, the first thing is she's new but she's settling in really well. She's friendly and easy-going and gets on well with nearly everybody, except Anna! She's really helpful and she knows what it means to pull together in a team; and she's always ready to cover for somebody. On the other hand, she can be a bit messy, but she's definitely not incompetent. And I think she's very cooperative with her colleagues …

4.4 Speaking: Coaching

 1:33

Mrs. Gomez: Rafael!
Rafael: Yes, Ma'am?
G: I want to see you in my office, now.
R: Yes, Mrs Gomez.
G: I don't know what the hell you think you're playing at, but I'm not having it! Are you trying to sabotage this company?
R: I'm sorry, I don't …
G: You've been here for three years now, you should know better. Don't you like your job? There are plenty of other people just waiting for their chance, if you don't want it.
R: I'm very sorry Mrs Gomez, but I don't know …

G: Don't interrupt me! You're insolent and incompetent. I don't know what you did, but Mr Baitan was very upset. Mr Baitan is a very important customer. We can't afford to upset him. If this happens again, you're out!
R: Yes, Mrs Gomez.
G: Alright, I think I've made myself clear. This is your last chance! Now stop wasting my time and get back to work.
R: Yes, Ma'am.

 1:34

Mrs Gomez: Rafael!
Rafael: Yes, Ma'am?
G: Would you step into my office please.
R: Yes, Mrs Gomez.
G: Rafael, I notice you're not wearing a tie today.
R: Well, it's very hot, and um …
G: Always wear a tie, Rafael. If not, your staff will not respect you. Now, sit down please, I want to talk to you about Sundays.
R: Yes?
G: I know you normally attend church on Sunday morning, so I was very pleased to see that you came to work the last three Sundays while Maria was sick.
R: Thank you Ma'am.
G: Maria had better be very careful, this is the third time this year she's been sick – fortunately for her, you took the initiative of covering for her.
R: Yes Ma'am.
G: So this is a good point for you, but a bad point for Maria. Alright, Rafael, that's all.
R: Thank you, Ma'am.
G: Oh, just one other thing, Rafael. You didn't switch off the computer when you left yesterday evening. Be very careful. This kind of carelessness can cause a fire. You must remember to switch off when you leave.
R: I'm sorry, Mrs Gomez. It won't happen again.
G: Alright, see that it doesn't.

 1:35

Mrs Gomez: Rafael!
Rafael: Yes, Ma'am?
G: Could I have a word with you in my office? … Have a seat Rafael. Now, can you tell me exactly what happened with Mr Baitan on Friday?
R: I'm sorry, but I was very tired, and he was being really difficult: I just lost my patience and he wouldn't stop asking me the same questions.
G: Well, Rafael, you have many qualities, but I think there are a few areas where we need to improve your skills, don't you?
R: Yes, definitely.
G: Now, do you have any ideas as to why Mr Baitan was quite so upset?
R: I understand he's an important customer. He wants to get the information that's important to him. I'm afraid I was probably a bit rude to him.
G: So Rafael, do you realize that this kind of problem can have serious consequences?
R: Yes, of course.
G: Alright then, so what do you think we can do to make sure this situation doesn't happen again?
R: It might be useful to do the customer care course. Perhaps Maria could help a bit

more when things are particularly busy.
G: Right. I think that's a good plan. So, before you go, can I just summarize what we have agreed? I'll book you on the course next week, and Maria will give you some help during the really busy periods. OK? And then we'll meet again in one month to see how you're getting on. Is that alright with you?
R: Yes, that's fine Mrs Gomez. Thank you very much.
G: Alright, now let's break the weekly sales records, shall we?
R: Yes Ma'am!

4.6 Case study: Trident Overseas

 1:36

John Thorpe: Abeba, you've been a mechanic in Witu for five and a half years, is that right?
Abeba: Yes, sir, that's right.
JT: So you worked for two other dealers before Mr. Mbugua – and you say that things have got worse since he became the Dealer here?
A: Yes, sir. Before Mr Mbugua arrived, we had a good team, everyone pulled together, and we enjoyed our work. Now, it's not at all the same. Morale is bad, and the customers can see the difference. A lot of our regular customers have stopped coming. Mr Mbugua fired several good colleagues for no reason, just so he could hire his friends and relatives instead. They get the easy shifts, and the rest of us do the hard work.
JT: Have you spoken to the sales rep. about this?
A: Mrs Mohamed? Huh! We never see her. She's too busy with the development project. Anyway, she can't do anything – Mr Mbugua is Mr Wambugu's nephew, didn't you know? To be honest, I'd leave, if there was any choice. But there aren't any other jobs around here, so I just have to put up with it.

 1:37

John Thorpe: Mr Mbugua, I've been hearing accusations of favouritism – and that you've employed friends and members of your family in your service station?
Mr Mbugua: Oh, Don't pay any attention to what Abeba says, Mr Thorpe. She's not a team player – only interested in herself. It would be better for her to leave, and the sooner she leaves, the better.
JT: But is it true that you employ members of your family?
M: Yes, of course it's true. As a Young Dealer, I work my fingers to the bone for Trident, Mr Thorpe, and I get very little thanks for it. I need staff who will work hard for the company too, and it's not easy to find them, I can tell you. I employ two of my cousins and a couple of friends because I know they're hard workers, like me. What's wrong with that?
JT: Does Mrs Mohamed agree with this recruitment policy?
M: I haven't asked her. Anyway, I don't think Mrs Mohamed is interested. Her big development project is far more important! I get absolutely no support from her, or from the company, for that matter. Other

companies look after their dealers much better. I have to do everything myself. Everything!

🔊 1:38

Mrs Mohamed: Thank you for taking the time to see me, Mr Thorpe, I really need to talk to someone; I don't think I can go on much longer like this.

John Thorpe: That's what I'm here for, Mrs Mohamed. The more you can tell me about the problems, the better – and I promise I'll do my best to help.

M: Thank you. It's just – I always wanted to become a sales rep. But it's turned into a nightmare. Mr Wambugu, the District Manager, delegates everything to me, and I just can't cope. He gives me impossible deadlines, then blames me when we fall behind schedule. And that means I have no time to visit the dealers, so they're not getting any support.

JT: Yes, I've just been speaking to Mr Mbugua in Witu.

M: Oh, don't talk to me about Mbugua! The man is a monster! The way he treats his staff is a disgrace, especially the women!

JT: So how did he become a Young Dealer?

M: Didn't you know? He's Mr Wambugu's nephew! I tried to stop his appointment, but there was nothing I could do. I think Mr Wambugu got to hear about it, and he's never forgiven me. I think he's giving me too much work because he hopes I'll quit.

🔊 1:39

Mr Thorpe, this is Mr Wambugu. One of my sales reps, Mrs Mohamed, has just handed me her resignation. I intend to promote Mr Mbugua, currently the Young Dealer in Witu, to the position of sales rep. He is a hard-working young man with energy, ideas and enthusiasm who will do well in the job. As you are no doubt aware, I need you to authorize this appointment with the HR department in Nairobi. Personally, I think Corporate should stop interfering, and let us Kenyans manage our own affairs. However, since that's the procedure, I would appreciate it if you could deal with this matter as soon as possible.

Unit 5 Selling more

5.1 About business: Sales and marketing

🔊 2:01

Elaine: Hey, Marcus, look at this viral ad somebody sent me! It's brilliant!

Marcus: Yeah, I saw it on YouTube. It's quite funny, I suppose.

E: Quite funny? It's hilarious! I think we should get one made for our next campaign instead of a TV ad. People really enjoy a good laugh, so they remember them more easily.

M: Well, personally, I'm not sure virals are really very effective. Now everybody's using them, so I think they're having less impact, not more.

E: Oh come on, Marcus, they reach a huge number of households, and they cost next to nothing!

M: Well that's another thing: apart from teenagers, I'm convinced only a small proportion of the public really watch them. And teenagers don't buy car tyres!

E: But they do influence their parents' choice, you have to admit that.

M: Well, yes, but anyway, just because an ad makes people laugh, it doesn't mean they'll buy the product. So we don't get increased sales.

E: No, but it's all about image. A good viral ad makes a product really cool. And remember, most people don't choose to watch TV ads, so they just ignore them. But when they make a conscious decision to watch a viral, they pay more attention!

5.2 Vocabulary: The marketing mix

🔊 2:02

Speaker 1: Determining market segmentation is essential when using media like TV. Football matches guarantee a large, masculine audience; every four years the World Cup attracts an average 90 million viewers per match. It's the perfect opportunity for advertisers to try to flood the market with razors, deodorants and sports shoes.

Speaker 2: Entering a new market often means a 'hard sell'. If you want to promote your new alarm system to companies in Eastern Europe, don't waste money on TV or newspaper advertising: conduct a market study to identify suitable targets, send out a mail-shot, then call any companies who show an interest in your product.

Speaker 3: New technology is providing new promotional tools; sellers can use electronic databases to select suitable prospects, then address a personalized sales pitch by email or SMS. These techniques are often combined with telemarketing. Don't be surprised if the email you received about investing in a timeshare apartment in Spain is followed up a day or two later by a call on your mobile inviting you on a free holiday!

Speaker 4: In many western countries, tobacco and cigarettes are facing a declining market. Advertising is strictly regulated, so even market leaders have to resort to stealth tactics like getting their products in films. Smoking is all about image, and the subliminal messages delivered by Hollywood movie stars are strong motivators.

Speaker 5: A movie is a product with huge development costs; in order to guarantee successful box office, DVD and TV sales, it is crucial to capture market share in the first days after release. Producers encourage rumours about the love life of their stars in the weeks before they bring the movie to market – nothing attracts public interest more than a little scandal!

Speaker 6: A little market research soon demonstrates that one of the best ways to develop a niche market like skateboarding accessories is by releasing games or video clips featuring the products onto the net. Teenagers circulate them to their friends – it's a perfect 'soft sell' by word of mouth – or word of electronic messaging, to be precise.

5.3 Grammar: Questions for persuading

🔊 2:03

You don't happen to know how many you ordered last year, do you? ↗
You don't really want to run out of components, do you? ↘

🔊 2:04

1 You don't happen to know how many you ordered last year, do you? ↗
2 You don't really want to run out of components, do you? ↘
3 You couldn't possibly give me an order today, could you? ↗
4 You can't afford failure, can you? ↘
5 You'd agree that everybody needs to know how to use the system, wouldn't you? ↘
6 You wouldn't have any idea how many people need training, would you? ↗
7 You really should upgrade your software regularly, shouldn't you? ↘
8 You haven't upgraded to the new version yet, have you? ↗

🔊 2:05

A: You'd enjoy driving a nice new car, wouldn't you?
B: I probably would enjoy it, that's right.
C: I imagine your old car is costing you a lot in repairs, isn't it?
B: It certainly is.
A: And I expect you're going on holiday soon, aren't you?
B: Y … um, that's correct.
C: So this might be a good time to think about buying a new car, right?
B: Well, possibly…
A: Because you wouldn't want to break down in the middle of your holiday, would you?
B: Of course not.
C: You didn't say 'no' then, did you?
B: No, I said 'of course' … OH NO!

5.4 Speaking: Dealing with objections

🔊 2:06

Customer: Listen, your proposal looks great, but I just don't feel ready to, take the plunge!
Salesperson: Well, if you don't sign the contract this week, I'll have to bill you for the study and the plans for the pool.
C: Bill me for the study? You never mentioned that!
S: It's in all our literature. Look, here, in the small print.

🔊 2:07

Customer: $32,000?! How do you justify that?
Salesperson: Simple. To develop software as good as this, you need the best engineers.
C: But I've had another quotation for less than twenty thousand!
S: Well you know what they say; if you pay peanuts, you get monkeys!

🔊 2:08

Customer: Can you give me a discount?
Salesperson: I'm afraid it's not our policy …
C: Oh, come on! I used to work in a health club, so I know you can if you want to.
S: Well, perhaps a five per cent reduction …

C: Ten per cent. Take it or leave it. Now, where do I sign?

2:09

Customer: Listen, your proposal looks great, but I just don't feel ready to take the plunge!

Salesperson: I know exactly what you mean. It's a big decision to make, isn't it?

C: Yeah. I'm just worried that I won't have enough time to do everything.

S: Oh I see. Finding enough time is always a problem, isn't it?

C: Yeah. Things are busy at work, and I don't have time for the garden, let alone a pool.

S: OK. Well, I understand. We all want to get a product we can actually use, don't we?

C: Sure.

S: So, if we include the automatic chlorinator and robot pool cleaner options, I can guarantee that you will spend less than ten minutes a week on maintenance. Are you comfortable with that?

2:10

Customer: $32,000?! How do you justify that?

Salesperson: I understand how you feel. Like you, a lot of our customers felt that this was more than they wanted to spend. However, they soon found they were saving money. After you start using the software, you'll reduce your operating costs by 25–30 per cent.

C: As much as that?!

S: Yes, more in some cases – but that's the average saving. Have I answered your question?

2:11

Customer: Can you give me a discount?

Salesperson: Well I'm glad you asked me that. Our philosophy is that if we gave discounts, we'd have to compromise on quality and service – and I'm sure you'd agree that would be a mistake, wouldn't you?

C: Yes, I suppose it would.

S: So tell me, is the membership fee the only reason you're not ready to sign up now?

C: Yes. I've just bought a new car, you see.

S: Right. So, if I could postpone your first payment to next year, would you be ready to sign up today? Would that make sense?

6.6 Case study: Backchat communications

2:12

Assistant: Mr Lim?

Lim: Yes?

A: I just had a call from Seoul Deliveries, you know, the courier company?

L: Yes?

A: They're interested in mobiles for about two hundred staff.

L: Are they now? Hm, we'd better send somebody to see them.

A: They said they'd like a proposal by fax.

L: Well, yes, but we need to know more about their needs before we can write a proposal. Let me note this down. Who's in charge over there?

A: The Office Manager is a Mr Ibanez. He's French, apparently.

L: Ibanez. Right. Two hundred, you say. Do we know who they want the phones for?

A: Well, there are three categories. Drivers, managers and admin. staff.

L: Admin. staff? Why do they want mobiles?

A: Well it seems that they have to move about a lot between different offices. They only really need to call the drivers when they're out on the road, but they take a lot of calls from customers, and they like the idea of Bluetooth headsets so they can work hands free.

L: I see. Yes, that makes sense – I can imagine it would make their lives a lot easier. What about the managers?

A: They seem quite keen on Blackberries. Email is very important for them.

L: Good. They'll need the high-tech price plan then. Do you think budget will be a problem?

A: They didn't say.

L: Good. We can try to sell some longer contracts – we need to secure our future cash flow, even if we have to give discounts.

A: They did say they were interested in giving the drivers a sophisticated phone to motivate them.

L: Sounds better and better! And the geopositioning system would be really useful – then the office would always know exactly where they were.

A: I don't know if the drivers would like that very much!

L: You're right, I'll make a note – we have met some resistance in the past. But generally once they find out there's an mp3 player, and they can also have TV to keep up with baseball and soccer games, they're happy.

A: Hm. But I guess the managers won't be very happy if they think drivers are wasting time watching TV and playing video games!

L: Well, that's where we come in. The sales team's goal is to show them why they need all these features – and to try to get some longer contracts and sell them some options too, of course! OK, thanks very much, I'll get someone over there as soon as possible.

Unit 6 New Business

6.1 About business: Self-financing

2:13

Presenter: Good morning everyone and welcome to 'Biz Podcast', coming to you from sunny California. I'm your host Karen Guilder and today we're going to be talking about raising finance for new businesses. My guest today is Alex Vecchia, a business angel here on the West Coast. Hi, Alex and welcome!

Alex: Great to be here, Karen.

P: Alex, I was reading an article about do-it-yourself financing for new businesses the other day and it gave the impression that trying to raise finance from venture capitalists or business angels was a complete waste of time.

A: Well, Karen. I think a lot depends on how much money you need. Of course, if you just need a few thousand bucks, you may be able to raise that from friends and family and that's OK for projects

with low start-up costs. But most people underestimate the real costs of setting up a business and even the do-it-yourselfers will probably come knocking on the venture capitalist's or the angel's door at some stage.

P: And what are angels looking to get out of a deal?

A: Of course, the bottom line is ... like for any investor, an angel is in it to make, a profit; typically, we're looking at a high return on investment over a period of, say, five years.

P: And, for all the budding entrepreneurs listening to us today, what key factors would convince you to back them?

A: That's a complex question, Karen, but I think most potential investors will be looking at three broad areas: the team, the business and the deal. First, the team. Many entrepreneurs forget that most seasoned investors 'bet on the jockey, not on the horse'. OK, you must pitch your idea but don't forget to sell yourself and your team. Potential investors want proof of honesty, determination and commitment. Market knowledge and business skills are vital too. The business plan is important, of course, but investors want to be sure you can actually run a business, not just write about it! In terms of the business, financial forecasts must be realistic and the business plan should present both a 'best' and a 'worst-case' scenario. And you may well need to demonstrate a high growth potential too, because static 'lifestyle' businesses, a single restaurant for example, just aren't attractive to investors. Finally, in terms of the deal, an unrealistic business valuation is a classic deal-killer – sometimes they can be too high for the investor, too low for the entrepreneur. Otherwise, make sure you have everything to hand for the due diligence process. Investors will want to check such things as the certificate of incorporation, audited accounts, details of existing contracts, and so on. Oh, and you shouldn't ignore ...

6.2 Vocabulary: Funding a start-up

2:14

Speaker 1: Well, basically the first angel we met turned us down because of the IRR – that's the Internal Rate of Return – we were forecasting; between 30 and 40 per cent. Investors lose money on around 40 per cent of deals and they need to make that up on the others. So, a rate of 50 per cent per annum minimum would've been a 'tastier carrot', you know, a better return on investment.

Speaker 2: The three of us were fresh out of college, full of enthusiasm, with a damn good product. We had checked out the market and drawn up a real good business plan. But there was just one problem. None of us had run a business before and I guess we just didn't have the sort of hands-on experience they were looking for.

Speaker 3: The venture capitalist we contacted went through our business plan in detail. When he'd finished working out the figures, he said that our niche market was just that – too 'niche' – not enough growth potential. Our target customers were specialists in their own field and there would've been a limit to what we could sell them.

Speaker 4: We'd done our homework and we knew that the financials needed to be set out in detail. But, in retrospect, I think we tried to be too realistic, taking all eventualities into account. The projections were peppered with 'if this, then that' and I think they were looking for something more concrete.

6.4 Speaking: Taking questions

🔊 2:15

Last but not least that brings us to the the question of ... Questions! A lot of inexperienced presenters are terrified of the question and answer session. After all, it's the part of the presentation over which, apparently, you have least control. But, with careful preparation, you can come out smiling. Put yourself in your listeners' shoes. What sort of questions could they ask you? What are the worst questions they could come up with and how can you answer them? And preparing for questions involves developing your general question-answering techniques, improving your skills in response to the five basic types of question. There are a couple of general points to remember. The first point to remember when you're fielding questions is listen to the questioner. For example, maintain eye-contact with the questioner and use body-language, nodding for example, to show that you're paying attention. The next thing to remember is don't interrupt. That would make you look rude, and the questioner might feel he or she hasn't had a chance to get their point across. Next, comment on the question before you answer the it. This signals your attitude to the audience, but, equally important, gives you a few seconds of thinking time! The final thing to remember is to reply to the audience. Yes, not just the person who asked the question, but the whole audience. Although one person asked the question, it might have been in everyone's minds. After all, you hope everybody wants to hear the answer! ...

🔊 2:16

That brings me to the five basic question types and how to react to them. First, useful questions. They reinforce or clarify what you're saying. Thank people for asking them. Second, awkward questions. Questions can be awkward for different reasons: they may be loaded – aiming to put you on the spot – aggressive, or just unclear. Or maybe you just don't have the answer. Whatever, you must avoid getting into an argument. Defuse the aggressive ones, clarify the vague ones. Be prepared to explain, reformulate, or reassure. Be fair but firm and don't be aggressive or defensive yourself. And be honest. If you can't, or don't want to answer, say so, or offer to get back to the questioner afterwards. Next, irrelevant questions. Double check quickly that they are irrelevant, comment tactfully and move on. Then there are unnecessary questions, which you've already covered. Point this out, summarize briefly and move on. And finally, 'No questions'. Maybe your

presentation was perfect and your audience is speechless! Unfortunately, in most cases two other scenarios are more common: either, they need a bit of encouragement or you've put them to sleep! In either case, if you don't want to finish on a low, you need to start them off; tell them a question you're often asked and then answer it! The chances are the questions will begin to flow. OK. Let's look in a bit more detail at ...

6.6 Case study: Angels or demons

🔊 2:17

Luis: Kate, if I didn't know you better, I'd say you brought me here to boost my morale. The food's OK, and the decor isn't bad, but if this is the best Montreal can offer, then I think we can do better with Kaluma.

Kate: Shh, Luis, the waitress! Yeah, but you're right, I'm sure we can.

L: Did you bring the executive summary headings – Sorry, I forgot to print them out.

K: Yep! Here you go. Shall we just take it as it comes?

L: Yeah, go for it. Humh, outline ... Kaluma ...

K: Well, we need to say a bit about what Kaluma is. You know, a medium-sized restaurant selling organic food, and so on. We also need to say we have an emphasis on fair trade. I think people think that's more and more important. Now, target customers?

L: Well, I suggest we need to think a bit more about that one, before we define a precise target market. After all, Montreal's a big city and I'm sure if the product is good, the customers will come.

K: OK, let's leave that for later. So, core products? We have to say that we are selling healthy, organic cuisine. But to me it's not just a question of that. We have to also mention the cool atmosphere. So it's not just the food but the whole concept that we're offering, that sort of thing.

L: Yeah, I'll go for that. ...... OK ... Management team. Mmm. Well that's easy really, we can mention that I'm the general manager. That's probably all they need to know about me. And you're the financial manager.

K: Don't forget about Mario though. He's one of the most experienced chefs in town. Let's mention that he's the head chef.

L: OK. Now, what's next? Oh, keys to success. Well, we have to mention the location. We've talked about that a lot, haven't we?

K: Mm. We should definitely emphasize our location, which is excellent. The other thing we should mention is the training we're giving our staff. Good service is everything. So, location and training.

L: Yeah. You know, I think we're gonna be better than the competition. The whole experience is gonna be, well, just so much nicer than a place like this!

K: Shh! The waitress!

L: Sorry, I'm just getting overexcited again!

K: Yeah, well the financials should calm you down. After all, that's why we're here in the first place! I think we should just stick to some basic figures. Let's just

give our predicted turnover. I think we said $380,000 in year one. That was right wasn't it? And then $550,000 by the end of year two.

L: Yeah. $380,000 and $550,000. And lastly our mission. I think we should keep it really simple.

K: I agree. I had two main things in mind. To be a great place to eat, with an engaging atmosphere.

L: That's obvious enough.

K: And to provide great healthy food.

L: Fantastic. With that devil, Mario, in the kitchen, we're gonna be unbeatable.

K: Well, Luis, let's just hope that general manager, Luis Hernandez, with his fifteen years of management experience, and Mario 'the devil' can persuade an angel to part company with 50,000 bucks next week!

L: Shh! Kate. The waitress!

🔊 2:18

Darren: So, to summarize, first, you have to grab your audience with your opening sentence. You may have a fantastic product and a dynamite team, but if you don't get investors' attention, you won't get funded. So make sure you have a great hook.

Then, cut out all the hype or exaggeration. Don't use superlatives like 'cheapest', 'fastest' and so on. Be specific; say fifteen per cent cheaper, ten per cent faster than the competition, and be relevant, 'cause you just don't have time in 60 seconds to go into detail. And of course, make sure your pitch can be delivered in 60 seconds without rushing. That means a maximum of 150 words and probably something nearer 100.

Finally, questions. The angels may have only three minutes to ask them, but those three minutes will seem like an eternity to you if you aren't prepared. So, think about the sort of questions they might ask, the tough ones, and decide how you're gonna respond . Now, I know ...

Unit 7 Financial Control

7.1 About business: Financial control

🔊 2:19

Interviewer: Welcome to Next Steps, the graduate career podcast. I'm joined today by Pedro Avalleneda, a Manchester-based careers consultant who's been researching changing attitudes to the financial services industry, in particular, accountancy. Pedro, why do you think accountancy has had an image problem?

Pedro: Well, it's a stereotype, and in that sense it's unfair. But there's often an element of truth to a stereotype, and the image may have had some basis in fact in the past. There are several reasons why I think the image developed. Firstly, accountancy is seen as based on numbers. Most people aren't that keen on maths, and it's a subject that a lot of people give up as soon as they can. It's a shame people make this association, because these days much of the maths is taken care of by computers and the accountants can focus on analysis and strategy. Another reason is that accountancy is seen as predictable: I guess what people have in mind is that the tasks you have to do are often similar – relating to balance sheets, profit and loss accounts, and so on. This isn't really true any more, since accountants do a lot else besides. Finally, accountancy is seen as a steady job. You might ask what's the problem with that, but for some people it implies that accountants are not risk-takers.

I: And what's changing now? I mean, how would you say the accountancy profession is breaking out of the stereotype?

P: Well, the best way to answer that is to look at the facts. A recent survey into job satisfaction showed that people who entered so-called creative professions like advertising and the media were often the least satisfied with their jobs. Accountancy, however, reported excellent job-satisfaction. Sixty-seven per cent said they wanted to stay in their jobs. So it seems people who pursue accountancy don't find it predictable. Another reason for its changing image is that it's friendly to women. In the US, 60 per cent of public accountants are women, and in the UK levels are also high. So, it's a female-friendly profession, and this has changed some of the negative perception – the stereotypical accountant was often a man. Finally, accountants really are key-decision makers. Accountants today are important figures in the boardroom, and it's often accountants who have the best understanding to make big management decisions. In that sense, it's a very responsible position. As a consequence, I think graduates are recognizing that accountancy is a profession in which they can expect to have real influence on a business.

I: OK, thanks Pedro. Now, I have got some questions for you. We've had some emails …

7.4 Speaking: Communicating in meetings

🔊 2:20

Alice: OK, guys. Your financial reporting system looks to be in good shape, but we're gonna have to make a few changes in terms of when you do things and how often, you know, to bring things into line with US procedures; do a bit of tweaking on the reporting period side. And …

Serge: Euh, sorry, Alice, could you repeat?

A: Sure, Serge. I was saying we need to do a bit of tweaking on the reporting period side. And we need to iron out some issues on the IT side, too, David. But, I reckon we're gonna have to set up a separate meeting to take stock of things cause we don't really have time today, OK?

David: What, Alice? I, erm …

A: Yeh, Dave, a meeting to take stock, maybe with some of your key team members. What about tomorrow morning at eight-thirty?

D: Umh, what? Oh, yes, OK, eight-thirty.

A: So that's all clear then. Great, so what do you say if we break for lunch. I just got off the plane this morning and I didn't have time to grab breakfast. I'm starving! Shall we meet back at two?

S: Euh, two?

D: Yes, OK, two.

A: Great, well, 'bon appetit' as you guys say.

S: David, what the hell is 'tweaking'?

D: I don't know, Serge. All I know is that I've just agreed to a meeting tomorrow morning at half past eight to talk about 'stacks' or 'stocks'!

🔊 2:21

Alice: OK, guys. Your financial reporting system looks to be in good shape, but we're gonna have to make a few changes in terms of when you do things and how often, you know, bring things into line with US procedures; do some tweaking on the reporting period side. And …

Serge: Euh, sorry, Alice, I'm not sure I follow you. Could you be more specific?

A: Sure, Serge. Humh, what I mean is that we need to standardize the procedures, … make the procedures the same as our US ones.

S: Erm, so, what you're saying is that we're going to have to produce financial statements more often, is that right?

A: You got it, Serge. To be precise, every month.

Serge: That's going to mean a lot of extra work, Alice!

A: Well, you're right up to a point but the benefits are worth it. Anyway, we'll look at ways we can allocate more resources to set up the new system later on, OK?

S: OK, Alice.

A: Now, we need to iron out some issues on the IT side, too, David. But, I reckon we're gonna have to set up a separate meeting to take stock of things, cause we don't really have time today, OK?

David: Sorry, Alice. You've lost me. We need to do what?

A: Well, in other words, we need to deal with some IT problems. And to do that, first we need to take stock, erm, see where we are at the moment. Do you see what I mean?

D: Yeah, that's clear now. I could set up a meeting tomorrow morning at half past eight if that suits you?

A: OK. That's great. So, can we go over what we've decided? We're going to standardize the financial reporting, and David and I will meet tomorrow to discuss the IT problems. Does everyone agree with that?

S: Yes, that's fine.

A: OK. Now, I don't know about you guys, but I didn't have time to grab breakfast this morning and I'm starving, erm, very hungry, so what do say if we go eat?

S: Good idea, Alice. Just thinking about monthly reporting has made me hungry.

D: Let's go!

7.5 Writing: Meeting minutes

🔊 2:22

Enzo: OK, François. Thanks for those statistics on late payers. I can see why management want us to cut late payment time by at least fifteen working days. Any ideas on how to do it? Alice?

Alice: Well, it's pretty clear to me, Enzo. We have to put more pressure on the slow payers much sooner than we do at present – I think François will back me on that?

Francois: Absolutely, Alice. In my opinion, we need to do two things. We need to reword our standard chasing emails to make them sound more threatening and …

E: Threatening, François? I don't really want chasing emails sounding like that!

F: OK, let's say more assertive or persuasive. Anyway, they've got to show the customer that we require prompt payment. And the second thing is, we need to send the first reminder out earlier.

E: Right, so that's make the chasing email more assertive and send the first reminder out more quickly. Erm, François, could you look after redrafting the standard email. And Alice, perhaps you could review the current schedule of when we send each chasing email and see how we can reduce the whole timescale. Can you both report back at our next meeting in two weeks?

A: Fine, yeah, erm, OK.

🔊 2:23

Dylan: So, to put it briefly, covering for absent colleagues instead of just leaving their work until they get back is not just a question of efficiency. It will also improve the department's image both inside the company and with our customers and suppliers. Of course, it will mean slightly more work at certain times, but I'm convinced the effort will be worth it.

A: I see your point Dylan, but I'm not sure that the end of the year is the best time to run a major project like this. Staff will need training to be able to do their colleagues' work and you know that the end of the year is always our busiest moment.

E: Alice is right, Dylan. Why don't we give ourselves more time on this point.

D: Oh, I'm quite happy to have more time. If you like, I'll draw up a training schedule for February next year and show it to you at our first meeting in January. How's that?

E: Sounds great, Dylan. We'll look forward to hearing your conclusions in the New Year.

🔊 2:24

F: Let me see. What else? … Electricity saving measures, toner and ink cartridge recycling, reductions in the use of paper, proper sorting of waste into plastics, paper and I think that's about it.

E: Humh, well I think this brainstorming session has been very useful. It's certainly thrown up a whole lot of good ideas. But I get the feeling that we need some outside help on this if we really want a lasting reduction in waste.

A: You're right, Enzo. We should get in touch with an environmental consultant or something for some basic advice.

E: Fine, well, I'll deal with that if you like. I don't think I'll be ready in two weeks so I'll come back to you on it in October, OK?

7.6 Case study: Car-glazer

 2:25

Nina: Hello. Accounts.

Emily: Oh, hello. Is that Nina Kovar?

N: Speaking.

E: Good morning, Nina. This is Emily Wyatt from Car-Glazer in Prague. Robert Smid asked me to call you. It's about an outstanding bill from July.

N: Ah, yes, well, humh. In fact, can I put you through to Mr Miler. I think he'd like to talk to you about this himself.

E: Well, yes, of course.

Jakob: Miler speaking.

E: Good morning, Mr Miler. Emily Wyatt from Car-Glazer. I was calling about the outst ...

J: Yes, yes, I know why you're calling Ms Wyatt. Look, I'm sorry to sound so rude, but this whole matter has made me rather angry. It's that Sales Manager of yours, Filip Novak!

E: Filip Novak, our Sales Manager for the East? I'm sorry, Mr Miler, I'm not sure I follow you?

J: Yes, well, let me explain. He brought his BMW in to the garage to be ...

E: Sorry to interrupt, Mr Miler. You said his BMW?

J: That's right.

E: But our Sales Managers drive company Volkswagens!

J: Well that explains a lot. Anyway, he brought the car in to be repaired at the beginning of July. He'd had an accident and we had to do a lot of work on it. He told us you knew all about it and that Car-Glazer would pay the bill. Here in Brno we trust people. We simply sent you the bill with our normal July claim – for about 81,000 koruna I believe – and thought no more of it. But we still haven't been paid the 378,000 koruna for the work we did on his car. And that's why we haven't paid you. It seemed like the only way of being paid what your Mr Novak owes us! I've been trying to call him for the last three weeks but had no luck.

E: Well, I see what you mean, Mr Miler, and I can understand why you're annoyed. I'll need to talk to my boss, Artur Nemec, about this, but I'll get back to you as soon as I can. I think Filip Novak owes everybody an explanation!

 2:26

Artur: Well, that was our friend, Filip Novak! He's just landed us the biggest deal we've ever made. We're going to be the preferred glass replacement company for the number one insurance company in the Czech Republic! So, where do we go from here?

Unit 8 Fair trade

8.1 About business: Fair trade

 2:27

Oh, yes, hello, this is Margaret, from Cheltenham. I'm phoning to comment on the article 'Why fair trade is a bad deal' which appeared on your website. I just wanted to say that fair trade supporters are not as 'misguided' as the article suggests. It's rather surprising that the writer himself has forgotten to mention that free trade and globalization are all about the survival of the fittest. Free trade is a jungle! It may be true that big producers who sell to Starbucks and Caffé Nero can improve their productivity and command higher prices, but what happens to the small farmers? They're forced out of business altogether. Fair trade may never make small coffee farmers rich, but at least it lets small farmers make a living! And on a larger scale, free trade is dangerous because it encourages unbalanced economies. Take Mr Singleton's example of Mexico. With free trade, Mexico might decide to stop growing coffee, corn, or rice. All their farmers would only grow chilli peppers because it's more profitable, and they would make enough profit to be able to import everything else. But what would happen if the world market for chilli suddenly collapsed? With fair trade, you spread the risk, and you give everybody a chance to make a decent living.

8.2 Vocabulary: Contracts and corporate ethics

 2:28

Speaker 1 Well, talking about unethical behaviour, does the name Victor Lustig ring any bells? He was the man who sold the Eiffel Tower – twice!

Speaker 2 You must know the story about the American CEO who sold her company shares only days before the share price crashed? She said it was 'an unfortunate coincidence'! Like hell it was!

Speaker 3 Paying government officials to avoid red-tape is well-known, but did you know that music companies have been paying radio DJs to play their music since the nineteen-fifties? Might explain why some number one records are so bad!

Speaker 4 Did you hear about the mayor of that small town in Italy? He used his position and influence to get local contractors to build him this enormous castle in the mountains - for nothing! Incredible!

Speaker 5 And there was this Korean scientist, a top researcher, a really famous guy. Anyway, it turned out that he'd been using government research funds to pay for luxury hotels, restaurants, and even a round the world cruise for his wife! Nice work if you can get it, I say!

Speaker 6 A couple of years ago there was an HR Director who managed to hire and promote several of her brothers and sisters to important positions in the same multinational. Keeping it in the family, eh?!

Speaker 7 I heard about these marketing executives who were so desperate to succeed, they planted bombs in their competitors' factories. Fortunately they were caught before they went off – otherwise I suppose they would have had what you'd call a booming market!

Speaker 8 Of course everybody's heard about the offshore banks which process large cash transactions for drug dealers. I just don't understand why governments seem to wash their hands of the matter!

8.3 Grammar: Obligation and permission; inversion

 2:29

Oksana: Right, Eddie, if you go through the main issues in this outsourcing agreement, then I'll get Jan to draft the guidelines tomorrow morning, OK?

Eddie: Sounds good to me, Oksana. It's a question of giving ourselves the right image. Basically, we can't afford the sort of bad publicity we had last year, when the media suggested our suppliers were treating staff badly. We need to look at everything to do with working conditions, minimum age, working hours, safety, that sort of stuff.

O: Yeah, well let's start with minimum age. I guess that'll be the usual over fifteen the day they join the company.

E: Yeah, nobody under sixteen, and I mean nobody!

O: OK, agreed.

E: Regarding working hours, our suppliers need some flexibility, but we need to stick to a maximum of twelve hours in any one shift. And, at least a half hour break every four hours.

O: OK, so that's no more than twelve hours at a stretch and a half hour break every four hours. Now, what about safety?

E: Well, in fact I'm gonna have to get back to you on that, because I don't have details of all the machines they use. But basically, it's a question of ensuring that all the machines have the necessary guards and that the operators use them. The other thing is that they must give all employees protective gloves of course, that sort of thing. Still, you can ask Jan to draft the basic clause and I'll get back to you with the details.

O: Great! Now, let's see ... accommodation? Company dormitories and so on.

E: Well, things are generally improving. They're beginning to see that if you treat people like rabbits, they work like them. But anyway, I reckon we should insist on a minimum personal space of six square metres and …

8.4 Speaking: Negotiating a compromise

 2:30

Leah: I'm sorry, Alfredo, but we can't go as high as $160. Our normal fair-trade premium for top-grade cocoa beans is world market price plus $140 per ton. I can't go higher than $150.

Alfredo: We want $160.

L: Yes, I know that Alfredo, but as I just told you, it's not possible. What about prefinancing?

A: We want advance payments of up to 60 per cent of the value of the contract.

L: Well, OK, but 60 per cent is only possible if at least half of the crop is grown under shade trees.

A: No. Shade trees mean extra cost. And you already want to increase our costs by refusing to let children under fifteen help their parents on the farms. I can't agree to that.

L: Alfredo, you know very well that child labour is totally unacceptable!

A: Well, our children always help on the farms, and we can't afford shade trees. If you're not prepared to negotiate the premium, I don't think you have any right to criticize our culture.

L: Look, Alfredo, I'm not criti … Oh, forget it!

 2:31

Leah: I'm sorry, Alfredo, but we can't go as high as $160. Our normal fair-trade premium for top-grade cocoa beans is world market price plus $140 per ton. But look, I know how important this is to your cooperative; assuming we can reach a compromise on the question of prefinancing, I'm prepared to meet you half way – $150. Is that acceptable?

Alfredo: Alright; that seems fair.

L: Good. So what about prefinancing?

A: We would like to be able to ask for advance payments of up to 60 per cent of the value of the contract.

L: Well, OK, we are willing to agree to 60 per cent, provided that at least half of the crop is grown under shade trees.

A: Leah, as you know, shade trees mean extra cost. I'd be reluctant to make that sort of commitment - unless you can review your position on children under fifteen. You see, it's a tradition in our country that children help their parents on the farms.

L: Alfredo, I think we'll have to agree to disagree on that. Child labour is something that fair trade customers feel very strongly about.

A: Hm. Alright, I understand that. So, at least half the crop under shade trees, and up to 60 per cent of payment in advance.

L: OK. And no more children working on the farms?

A: Alright. I can live with that.

8.6 Case study: **Green Hills Coffee**

 2:32

Magda: Fabio, for God's sake, stop talking about Gordon Hills as if he was some kind of saint! 'Gordon always said this, Gordon always did that!'

Fabio: Listen, Magda, Gordon was my father's best friend; he was a good and generous man, and if it wasn't for him, Granos Cabrera wouldn't be where it is today.

M: A good and generous man? Don't be ridiculous! He was just a clever businessman: he knew your father grew good coffee, and he knew he could make a good profit on it. And unlike his daughter, he wasn't worried about details like pesticides, or children working on the farms

F: Fiona is very fair. She has strong ideas about ecology and human rights, and she wants a fair deal for everyone.

M: Fabio, get real! She doesn't really care about pesticides, or child labour – for her, it's just a good excuse to negotiate even lower prices! She's only interested in the bottom line. Why do you think Green Hills is so profitable?

F: That's not fair! Green Hills is profitable because Fiona is a good manager.

M: Well she's certainly a good negotiator. She always gets the lowest possible prices. She's the reason for all our problems – Green Hills pay us less every year! It's no wonder we're not making any money!

F: Magda, it's not Fiona's fault. Granos Cabrera's problems are due to world market prices - they keep going down. It's very technical.

M: Well I know I'm only from Germany, and we Germans know nothing about the 'very technical' international coffee market; but I do know that if Green Hills paid a fair price, the organic price, the farmers would be able to send their kids to school, instead of sending them out to work!

F: Well, sure, fair-trade, is the future. That and going organic probably would be the solution to our problems. But Magda, we can't afford fair-trade certification, it's just too expensive –

M: Well then, the solution is very simple. Green Hills should pay for fair-trade certification, and lend us some money to invest in new equipment to go organic! It's in everybody's interests.

F: I don't know; it's very difficult. If Dad was still alive he'd just have a friendly chat with Gordon and everything would be OK.

M: Yeah, well, he's not, is he?! He's dead and gone, and so is Gordon Hills. So you'd better start getting tough with Fiona, or she'll eat you alive

Wordlist

Unit 1 Building a career

1.1 About business:
The education business

alumni /əˈlʌmnaɪ/ (singular alumnus) noun [count] MAINLY AMERICAN, FORMAL someone who was a student at a particular school, college or university

applicant /ˈæplɪkənt/ noun [count] someone who applies for something, such as a job or a loan of money: *Successful applicants will be notified by telephone.*

aptitude /ˈæptɪˌtjuːd/ noun natural ability that makes it easy for you to do something well: *an aptitude test.*

budding /ˈbʌdɪŋ/ adjective [only before noun] at the very beginning of a career in writing, politics etc and likely to be successful at it

corny /ˈkɔː(r)ni/ adjective used so much that it seems silly

coveted /ˈkʌvətəd/ adjective FORMAL wanted, in demand

cutthroat /ˈkʌtˌθrəʊt/ adjective [usually before noun] describing an activity in which people compete with each other in an aggressive way

endowment /ɪnˈdaʊmənt/ noun [count] money given to an institution

enlist /ɪnˈlɪst/ verb [transitive] to get someone to help or support you

faculty /ˈfæk(ə)lti/ noun [uncount] AMERICAN all the teachers in a school, college or university: *a meeting for students, faculty and administrators*

fee /fiː/ noun [count usually plural] money that you pay to a professional person or institution for their work: *Tuition fees at Stanford have now reached £9000 a year.*

practise what you preach /ˈpræktɪs wɒt juː ˌpriːtʃ/ to do the things you tell other people to do

remain aloof /rɪˈmeɪn əˌluːf/ verb to not become involved in something

show up /ˌʃəʊ ˈʌp/ phrasal verb [intransitive] INFORMAL to arrive in a place where people are expecting you: *We didn't think Austin would show up.*

sift /sɪft/ verb [transitive] to examine information or documents to find what you are looking for

staggering /ˈstæɡərɪŋ/ adjective extremely surprising

stellar /ˈstelə(r)/ adjective extremely good

step up /ˌstep ˈʌp/ phrasal verb [transitive] to increase

1.2 Vocabulary:
Education and career

drop out /ˌdrɒp ˈaʊt / phrasal verb [intransitive] to leave something such as an activity, school or competition before you have finished what you intended to do

miss out /ˌmɪs ˈaʊt/ phrasal verb [intransitive] to lose an opportunity to do or to have something

start over /ˌstɑː(r)t ˈəʊvə(r)/ phrasal verb [intransitive] AMERICAN to begin doing something again from the beginning

thoroughly /ˈθʌrəli/ adverb very carefully, so that nothing is missed: *The case will be studied thoroughly before any decision is made.*

working party /ˈwɜː(r)kɪŋ pɑː(r)ti/ noun [count] BRITISH a group of people who examine a problem or situation and suggest a way of dealing with it

1.3 Grammar:
Tense review

come along /ˌkʌm əˈlɒŋ/ phrasal verb [intransitive] to arrive or become available

fancy /ˈfænsi/ SPOKEN used when you are very surprised about something

put on weight /ˌput ɒn ˈweɪt/ phrasal verb [transitive] to become fatter

1.4 Speaking:
Giving reasons

intake /ˈɪnteɪk/ noun [singular or uncount] the number of people accepted by a school or university at one time: *this year's intake of students*

1.5 Writing:
Cover letters

accomplishment /əˈkʌmplɪʃmənt/ noun [count or uncount] something difficult that you succeed in doing, especially after working hard over a period of time

brokering /ˈbrəʊkərɪŋ/ noun [uncount] AMERICAN (UK brokerage) the activity of organizing business deals for other people

lead /liːd/ noun [count] a piece of information or a contact that may bring new business

outgoing /ˌaʊtˈɡəʊɪŋ/ adjective someone who is outgoing is friendly and enjoys meeting and talking to people

tender /ˈtendə(r)/ noun [count or uncount] a formal written offer to provide goods or services for a particular price

venue /ˈvenjuː/ noun [count] the place where an activity or event happens: *A popular venue for corporate events.*

1.6 Case study:
Mangalia Business School

campus /ˈkæmpəs/ noun [count or uncount] an area of land containing all the main buildings of a school or university: *We have rooms for 2000 students on campus.*

draw up /ˌdrɔː ˈʌp/ phrasal verb [transitive] to prepare and write something such as a document or a plan

heritage /ˈherɪtɪdʒ/ noun [count or uncount usually singular] the art, buildings, traditions and beliefs that a society considers important to its history and culture: *Ireland's rich musical heritage.*

metropolis /məˈtrɒpəlɪs/ noun [count] a big, exciting city

procurement /prəˈkjʊə(r)mənt/ noun [uncount] the process of buying supplies or equipment for a government department or company

sit back /ˌsɪt ˈbæk/ phrasal verb [intransitive] to relax and stop making the effort to do something

tailor /ˈteɪlə(r)/ verb **tailor something to/for** to make or change something especially for a particular person or purpose

Unit 2 Information

2.1 About business:
IT solutions

bury /'beri/ verb [transitive, often passive] to cover or hide something

cram /kræm/ verb[transitive] to force something into a place that is too small

flush something down the toilet /'flʌʃ sʌmθɪŋ daʊn ðə ˌtɔɪlət/ [transitive] to get rid of something by putting it into the toilet

mad dash /mæd 'dæʃ/ noun [singular] going somewhere very quickly because you are in a hurry in an extremely uncontrolled way: *At the end of the nineties there was a mad dash to buy shares in high-tech companies.*

mess up /ˌmes 'ʌp/ phrasal verb [intransitive or transitive] to do something wrong or spoil something, especially by making mistakes

overhaul /'əʊvə(r)ˌhɔːl/ verb [transitive] to completely change a system to make it work more effectively

pressure-cooker /'preʃə(r) ˌkʊkə(r)/ noun [count] 1 a deep cooking pan for cooking food quickly 2 INFORMAL a difficult situation in which people have to work very hard or experience a lot of strong emotions

quest /kwest/ noun [count] a long difficult search

slick /slɪk/ adjective done in a very impressive way that seems to need very little effort

take a breather /teɪk ə 'briːðə(r)/ phrase INFORMAL to have a rest.

2.2 Vocabulary:
Information systems and communication

snail mail /'sneɪl meɪl/ noun [uncount] COMPUTING letters that are sent by post

2.4 Speaking:
Telephoning

IP address /ˌaɪ piː ə'dres/ noun [count] COMPUTING Internet Protocol address: a code that represents a particular computer and is used to send messages to it on a network or the Internet.

mustn't grumble /ˌmʌs(t)nt 'grʌmb(ə)l/ used as a reply to someone who asks you whether you are well, for saying that you feel alright

small talk /'smɔːltɔːk/ noun [uncount] INFORMAL conversation about things that are not important

trivial /'trɪviəl/ adjective not very interesting, serious or valuable

2.5 Writing:
Memos

alleviate /ə'liːvieɪt/ verb [transitive] to make something less painful, severe or serious

fine /faɪn/ noun [count] an amount of money that you have to pay because you have broken the law: *Firms could face fines of up to £5000.*

forethought /'fɔː(r)θɔːt/ noun [uncount] careful thought and planning that prepares you well for a future event

forthwith /fɔː(r)θ'wɪθ/ adverb FORMAL LEGAL immediately

officialese /əˌfɪʃə'liːz/ noun [uncount] the way of speaking or writing used by people who work in government offices, especially when ordinary people cannot understand it

shareware /'ʃeə(r)weə(r)/ noun [uncount] computer software that you can get on the Internet and use for a period of time before paying for it

time frame /'taɪm ˌfreɪm/ noun [count] the period of time during which something happens or must happen

2.6 Case study:
Meteor Bank

drag someone kicking and screaming /dræg sʌmwʌn 'kɪkɪŋ ən ˌskriːmɪŋ/ to make someone do something that they do not want to do

downtime /'daʊnˌtaɪm/ noun [uncount] time when a computer or other machine is not working

malicious /mə'lɪʃəs/ adjective deliberately wanting to hurt someone or cause damage

Unit 3 Quality

3.1 About business:
What quality means

commitment /kə'mɪtmənt/ noun [singular uncount] a strong belief that something is good and that you should support it: *The government has failed to honour its commitment to the railways.*

craze /kreɪz/ noun [count] something that suddenly becomes very popular, but only for a short time

enchanting /ɪn'tʃɑːntɪŋ/ adjective very interesting and attractive

end /end/ noun [count] the reason for a particular action or the result you want to achieve

fake /feɪk/ verb [transitive] to make an exact copy of something in order to trick people

planned/built-in obsolescence /plænd/ bɪlt ɪn ˌɒbsə'les(ə)ns/ noun [uncount] the practice of making products that will quickly become old-fashioned, or will not last long, so that people will need to replace them

roughly /'rʌfli/ adverb approximately: *The meeting lasted roughly 50 minutes*

sake /seɪk/ noun [count usually singular] the purpose of doing, getting or achieving something: *For clarity's sake, let me explain that again.*

sour /'saʊə(r)/ verb [transitive/intransitive] if a situation sours, it stops being successful or satisfactory

struggle /'strʌg(ə)l/ verb [intransitive] to try hard to do something that you find very difficult *He struggled to open the bottle with a knife*

take for granted /ˌteɪk fə(r) 'grɑːntəd/ to expect something always to exist or happen in a particular way *People take it for granted that the weather in Spain will be sunny*

white goods /'waɪt gʊdz/ noun [count] large pieces of electrical equipment used in people's homes

3.2 Vocabulary:
Quality and Standards

cost-effective /ˌkɒst ɪˈfektɪv/ adjective giving the most profit or advantage in exchange for the amount of money that is spent

fit for purpose /ˌfɪt fə(r) ˈpɜː(r)pəs/ adjective of a good enough standard for a particular use

in the eye of the beholder /ɪn ði ˌaɪ əv ðə bɪˈhəʊldə(r)/ used for saying that different people perceive things differently: *Beauty is in the eye of the beholder.*

machine /məˈʃiːn/ verb [transitive] to give metal, wood or plastic a particular shape by cutting it on a machine

stakeholder /ˈsteɪkˌhəʊldə(r)/ noun [count] somebody who is affected by or who has an interest in the success or activities of a company

3.3 Grammar:
Passive structures and *have something done*

grab /græb/ verb [transitive] INFORMAL take

hassle /ˈhæs(ə)l/ noun [count or uncount] INFORMAL a situation that causes problems for you, or that annoys you very much

round-the-clock /ˈraʊnd ðə ˌklɒk/ adjective happening or done all day or all night

night shift /ˈnaɪt ʃɪft/ noun [count] a period when some people work during the night in a workplace.

3.4 Speaking:
Delivering presentations

make or break /meɪk ɔː ˈbreɪk/ to help someone or something to be very successful or to cause them to fail completely

signposting /ˈsaɪnˌpəʊstɪŋ/ noun clear or noticeable indicators that give structure to speech of writing

3.5 Writing:
Procedures and instructions

drowsiness /ˈdraʊzinəs/ noun [uncount] sleepiness

garment /ˈgɑː(r)mənt/ noun [count] FORMAL a piece of clothing

groove /gruːv/ noun [count] a line cut into a surface

peg /peg/ noun [count] an object used for fastening things together *The furniture is built using wooden pegs instead of nails*

upside down /ˌʌpsaɪd ˈdaʊn/ adverb with the top part at the bottom or lower than the bottom part *The car landed upside down in the ditch*

3.6 Case study:
Zaluski Strawberries

bulk /bʌlk/ noun [count usually singular] the bulk of something is the majority or largest part of something: *Women still do the bulk of domestic work.*

bruise /bruːz/ verb [transitive] to damage a piece of fruit and cause a soft brown area to appear on its surface: *Fallen apples are often bruised*

harvest /ˈhɑː(r)vɪst/ noun [count] the activity of collecting a crop *the corn harvest*

outlet /ˈaʊtlet/ noun [count] a shop or place where a particular product is sold *Most of the sales are through traditional retail outlets*

punnet /ˈpʌnɪt/ noun [count] BRITISH a small container like a basket, in which fruit such as strawberries are sold

shallow /ˈʃæləʊ/ adjective with only a short distance from the top or surface to the bottom; the opposite of *deep*.

shed /ʃed/ noun [count] a building, usually made of wood, in which you store things

shelf life /ˈʃelf ˌlaɪf/ noun [singular] the amount of time that a food, medicine or similar product can be kept in a shop before it is too old to sell

sound /saʊnd/ adjective healthy or in good condition

squash /skwɒʃ/ verb [transitive] to damage something by pressing or crushing it and making it lose its normal shape

stack /stæk/ verb [transitive] to arrange things so they stand one on top of another *She began stacking plates on the trolley*

straw /strɔː/ noun [uncount] the yellow stems of dried crops such as wheat *a straw hat*

tray /treɪ/ noun [count] a flat open container with raised edges used for holding or carrying things.

Unit 4 Feedback

4.1 About business:
The project team

accomplish /əˈkʌmplɪʃ/ verb [transitive] to succeed in doing something: *We accomplished a lot at work this week*

apathy /ˈæpəθi/ noun [uncount] a feeling of having no interest in or enthusiasm about anything, or not being willing to make any effort to change things

aspiring /əˈspaɪrɪŋ/ adjective hoping and trying to be successful at something, especially in your career

better off /ˈbetə(r) ɒf/ adjective in a better situation

blindfold /ˈblaɪn(d)ˌfəʊld/ noun [count] something that is tied over someone's eyes so that they cannot see

bunch /bʌntʃ/ noun [singular] a group of people

buy into /ˌbaɪ ˈɪntuː/ phrasal verb [transitive] INFORMAL to believe something that a lot of other people believe

milestone /ˈmaɪlstəʊn/ noun [count] an event or achievement that marks an important stage in a process

offend /əˈfend/ verb [transitive] to make someone upset and angry by doing or saying something.

scope /skəʊp/ noun [uncount] the things that a particular activity, organization, subject, etc deals with: *These issues are beyond the scope of this book.*

silly /ˈsɪli/ adjective not intelligent, serious, important or practical.

start from scratch /ˌstɑːt frəm ˈskrætʃ/ to start from the beginning again

4.2 Vocabulary:
Managing people and projects

appraisal interview /əˈpreɪz(ə)l ˌɪntə(r)vjuː/ noun [count] BRITISH an interview between a manager and an employee designed to evaluate how well the employee is doing their job

hectic /ˈhektɪk/ adjective full of busy activity

loner /ˈləʊnə(r)/ noun [count] someone who likes to be alone and has few friends

4.4 Speaking:
Coaching

elicit /ɪˈlɪsɪt/ verb [transitive] FORMAL to obtain information by encouraging someone to talk

insolent /ˈɪnsələnt/ adjective rude, especially when you should be showing respect

overdo /ˌəʊvə(r)ˈduː/ verb [transitive] to do, say, use etc. more of something than you should: **overdo it**: to work too hard, making yourself tired or ill

praise /preɪz/ noun [uncount] an expression of strong approval or admiration: *Give your child plenty of praise and encouragement*

4.5 Writing:
Reports

foster /ˈfɒstə(r)/ verb [transitive] to help something to develop over a period of time: *This approach will foster an understanding of environmental issues.*

4.6 Case study:
Trident Overseas

could do with something /kʊd ˈduː wɪð ˌsʌmθɪŋ/ SPOKEN used for saying that you want or need something

dealer /ˈdiːlə(r)/ noun [count] a person or company that buys and sells a particular product: *a car dealer*

forecourt /ˈfɔː(r)kɔː(r)t/ noun [count] an open area in front of a large building or service station

handle someone with kid gloves /ˈhænd(ə)l sʌmwʌn wɪð ˌkɪd glʌvz/ to treat someone in a very careful or gentle way

mess /mes/ noun [singular] a difficult situation with lots of problems, especially because people have made mistakes; *an economic mess*

put up with /ˌpʊt ˈʌp wɪð/ phrasal verb [transitive] to accept something or someone unpleasant in a patient way

sort out /sɔː(r)t ˈaʊt/ phrasal verb [transitive] to solve a problem or deal with a difficult situation successfully

top up /ˈtɒp ʌp/ phrasal verb [transitive] to completely fill a container that is already partly full

windscreen /ˈwɪn(d)skriːn/ noun [count] BRITISH the large glass window at the front of a vehicle

work your fingers to the bone /wɜːk jə ˈfɪŋɡə(r)z tʊ ðə ˌbəʊn/ to work very hard, especially doing something that involves a lot of physical effort

Unit 5 Selling more
5.1 About business:
Sales and marketing

blog /blɒg/ noun [count] COMPUTING a biographical web log: a personal web page or diary

bucks /bʌks/ noun [plural] AMERICAN INFORMAL money

edge /edʒ/ noun [singular] an advantage that makes someone or something more successful than other people or things: *training can give you the edge over your competitors*

lure /ljʊə(r)/ verb [transitive] to persuade someone to do something by making it look very attractive

raft /ræft/ noun [count] a small light boat made of rubber or plastic

stifle /ˈstaɪf(ə)l/ verb [transitive] to stop something from developing normally

5.2 Vocabulary:
The marketing mix

blend /blend/ verb [transitive] to mix different foods, styles or qualities together in a way that is attractive or effective

coupon /ˈkuːpɒn/ noun [count] a piece of paper that allows you to buy something at a reduced price: *This coupon gives £2 off the price of a meal.*

quantitative /ˈkwɒntɪtətɪv/ adjective FORMAL involving amounts, or involving measuring things as amounts

razor /ˈreɪzə(r)/ noun [count] a small tool used for shaving

SMS noun [uncount] TECHNICAL Short Message Service: a method of sending a text message to a mobile phone

spare /speə(r)/ adjective [only before noun] a spare object is one that you keep in addition to other similar objects in case you need it: *a spare key/battery/pair of glasses*

stealth /stelθ/ noun [uncount] a quiet and secret way of behaving so that no one sees or hears you

subliminal /sʌbˈlɪmɪn(ə)l/ adjective a subliminal influence is one that may affect you even though you do not notice or think about it

5.3 Grammar:
Questions for persuading

luncheon voucher /ˈlʌntʃ(ə)n ˌvaʊtʃə(r)/ noun [count] a piece of paper given by an employer that can be used for buying lunch in some restaurants and shops

timeshare /ˈtaɪmʃeə(r)/ noun [count] a flat or house that you buy with other people so that you can each use it for a particular amount of time every year

5.4 Speaking:
Dealing with objections

peanuts /ˈpiːnʌts/ noun [uncount] INFORMAL a very small amount of money

plunge /plʌndʒ/ noun [count] **take the plunge** to finally do something important, difficult or dangerous after thinking about it

small print /smɔːl ˌprɪnt/ noun [uncount] the details of a contract that are printed in very small letters and often contain conditions that limit your rights

5.5 Writing:
Mail shots and sales letters

grab someone's attention /ˌgræb sʌmwʌnz əˈtenʃ(ə)n/ to succeed in getting someone to listen or be interested: *It's often the bad characters in a story who grab our attention.*

handling /ˈhændlɪŋ/ noun [uncount] the handling of a vehicle is how easy it is to control

trawl through /trɔːl ˈθruː/ verb [intransitive or transitive] to look for someone or something, for example by searching through a large amount of information

5.6 Case study:
Backchat Communications

Bluetooth /ˈbluːtuːθ/ TRADEMARK radio technology which allows electronic devices to communicate with each other

courier /ˈkʊriə(r)/ noun [count] someone whose job is to deliver documents or parcels

flat /flæt/ adjective a flat battery does not have enough power left in it

fleet /fliːt/ noun [count] a group of vehicles or machines, especially when they are owned by one organization or person: *the company's fleet of vehicles*

geopositioning /ˌdʒiːəʊpəˈzɪʃ(ə)nɪŋ/ noun [uncount] defining the exact location of someone or something on the planet

handset /ˈhæn(d)set/ noun [count] the part of a telephone which you hold next to your ear

keep up with /ˌkiːp ˈʌp wɪð/ phrasal verb [intransitive] to continue to learn what's happening

Won /wɒn/ the currency of South Korea: 1 US$ = approx. 950 Won

Unit 6 New Business

6.1 About business:
Self-financing

beg /beg/ verb [intransitive or transitive] to ask people for money, usually because you are very poor

bottom line /ˌbɒtəm ˈlaɪn/ noun [count] the most basic fact or issue in a situation

dip into /ˌdɪp ˈɪntʊ/ phrasal verb [transitive] to take some money from an amount you have saved: *You'd better stop dipping into your savings.*

drag on /ˌdræg ˈɒn/ phrasal verb [intransitive] to continue for longer than you want or think is necessary

mortgage /ˈmɔː(r)gɪdʒ/ noun [count] a legal agreement in which you borrow money from a bank in order to buy a house: *On my present salary I can't get a mortgage.*

odds /ɒdz/ noun [plural] the chances of something happening: *The odds are they won't succeed.*

pitch /pɪtʃ/ noun [count] a very short presentation of a company or a new business idea to potential investors

premises /ˈpremɪsɪz/ noun [plural] the buildings or land that a business or organization uses: *The charity is going to move into new premises next year.*

stake /steɪk/ noun [count] BUSINESS the part of a business you own because you have invested money in it: *They took a 40% stake in the business.*

6.2 Vocabulary:
Funding a start-up

asset /ˈæset/ noun [count] something such as money or property that a person or company owns: *The business has assets totalling £5.1 million.*

household /ˈhaʊshəʊld/ adjective [only before nouns] relating to homes

outstanding /ˌaʊtˈstændɪŋ/ adjective a job or action that is outstanding has not yet been completed or dealt with

raw materials /rɔː məˈtɪəriəlz/ noun [plural] substances such as coal or iron that are in their natural state before being processed or made into something: *The raw materials are stored in silos.*

track record /træk ˈrekɔː(r)d/ noun [count] your reputation, based on things you have done or not done.

6.3 Grammar:
Future perfect and future continuous

float /fləʊt/ verb [transitive] BUSINESS to start to sell a company's shares on the stock market: *The company was floated in 1993.*

6.4 Speaking:
Taking questions

awkward /ˈɔːkwə(r)d/ adjective difficult to deal with and embarassing: *After he spoke there was an awkward silence.*

bluff /blʌf/ verb [intransitive/transitive] to deliberately give a false idea to someone about what you intend to do or about the facts of a situation, especially in order to gain an advantage.

do your homework /ˌduː jə(r) ˈhəʊmwɜː(r)k/ to prepare for something by learning as much as you can about it

field /fiːld/ verb [transitive] to deal with something such as a question or a telephone call, especially a difficult one

nod /nɒd/ verb [intransitive/transitive] to move your head up and down to answer 'Yes' to a question or to show that you agree, approve or understand. *The manager nodded in agreement.*

recap /ˌriːˈkæp/ verb [intransitive/transitive] to describe what has already been done or decided, without repeating the details

6.5 Writing:
An executive summary

core /kɔː(r)/ adjective most important or most basic. *We need to focus on our core activities.*

organic /ɔː(r)ˈgænɪk/ adjective used for describing methods of farming and food production that do not use artificial chemicals: *They only buy organic wine.*

sustainable /səˈsteɪnəb(ə)l/ adjective using methods that do not harm the environment

upkeep /ˈʌpkiːp/ noun [singular/uncount] the process or cost of keeping a building or piece of land in good condition

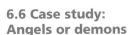

6.6 Case study:
Angels or demons

cunning /'kʌnɪŋ/ adjective used to describe behaviour in which people use their intelligence to get what they want, especially by tricking or cheating people

drop someone a line /'drɒp sʌmwʌn ə ˌlaɪn/ to contact somebody by writing to them or phoning them

grab /græb/ verb [transitive] to interest someone and make them feel enthusiastic

hype /haɪp/ noun [uncount] INFORMAL the use of a lot of advertisements and other publicity to influence or interest people

upbeat /'ʌpbiːt/ adjective INFORMAL happy and positive

Unit 7 Financial Control

7.1 About business:
Financial control

bribery /'braɪb(ə)ri/ noun [uncount] the crime of giving money or presents to someone so that they will help you by doing something dishonest or illegal.

forefront /'fɔː(r)ˌfrʌnt/ noun a leading or important position

fraudster /'frɔːdstə(r)/ noun [count] someone who commits the crime of fraud

litigation /ˌlɪtɪ'ɡeɪʃ(ə)n/ noun [uncount] use of the legal system to settle a disagreement

makeover /'meɪkˌəʊvə(r)/ noun [count] a set of changes that make a person or thing look better

policy-maker /'pɒlɪsi ˌmeɪkə(r)/ noun [count] a person responsible for deciding on a set of plans or actions for a government, political party, business or other group

protection racket /prə'tekʃ(ə)n ˌrækɪt/ noun [count] an illegal system in which criminals threaten to harm you or your property if you do not give them money

scam /skæm/ noun [count] INFORMAL a dishonest plan, especially for getting money

tax evasion /'tæks ɪˌveɪʒ(ə)n/ noun [uncount] the use of illegal methods to pay less tax or no tax at all

undercover /ˌʌndə(r)'kʌvə(r)/ adjective working or done secretly in order to catch criminals, get secret information, etc

white-collar crime /'waɪt ˌkɒlə(r) kraɪm/ crimes in which people who work in offices steal money from the company they work for.

7.2 Vocabulary:
Financial documents and regulation

run out of /ˌrʌn 'aʊt əv/ phrasal verb [intransitive] to use all of something and not have any left

snapshot /'snæpʃɒt/ noun a short explanation or description that tells you what a particular situation or place is like

7.4 Speaking:
Communicating in meetings

in good shape /ɪn 'ɡʊd ʃeɪp/ in good condition

iron out /ˌaɪ(r)ən 'aʊt/ phrasal verb [transitive] to deal successfully with a disagreement or problem, especially by removing the last remaining difficulties

starving /'stɑː(r)vɪŋ/ adjective INFORMAL very hungry

take stock /teɪk 'stɒk/ verb [intransitive] to review your position

tweak /twiːk/ verb [transitive] INFORMAL to make small changes to improve something

7.5 Writing:
Meeting minutes

open-plan office /ˌəʊpən 'plæn ɒfɪs/ noun [count] an office with few walls and a lot of space

partition /ˌpɑː(r)'tɪʃ(ə)n/ noun [count] a wall, screen, or piece of glass used to separate one from another in a room or vehicles

7.6 Case study:
Car-glazer

bodyshop /'bɒdiˌʃɒp/ noun [count] a place where cars are repaired, especially after an accident

chasing letter /'tʃeɪsɪŋ ˌletə(r)/ noun [count] a reminder to pay an outstanding invoice

dent /dent/ noun [count] a place where a surface has been pushed or knocked inwards

embezzle /ɪmˈbez(ə)l/ verb [intransitive/transitive] to steal money that people trust you to look after as part of your work

petty cash /ˌpeti 'kæʃ/ noun [uncount] a small amount of money in coins or notes that an organization or company keeps available to pay for small things

reprimand /'reprɪˌmænd/ verb [transitive] to tell someone officially and in a serious way that something they have done is wrong

scratch /skrætʃ/ noun [count] a thin mark on a surface
There were some nasty scratches on the paintwork

sickie /'sɪki/ noun [count] BRITISH ENGLISH VERY INFORMAL a day when you say you are ill because you do not want to go to work

suspension /sə'spenʃ(ə)n/ noun [count/uncount] a punishment in which someone is removed from a team, job or school, for a short time: *Beckham is back after a two-match supension.*

Unit 8 Fair trade

8.1 About business:
Fair trade

affluent /'æflu:ənt/ adjective rich enough to buy things for pleasure

altruism /'æltru:ɪz(ə)m/ noun [uncount] a way of thinking and behaving that shows you care more about other people and their interests than about yourself

crop /krɒp/ noun [count] a plant grown for food, usually on a farm: *they're all out planting the crops today*

ignore /ɪg'nɔ:(r)/ verb [transitive] to not consider something or not let it influence you: *This ignores the complexity of modern business.*

illiteracy /ɪ'lɪtərəsi/ noun [uncount] the state of not being able to read or write

magic wand /'mædʒɪk ˌwɒnd/ noun [count] a short thin stick used for performing magic or magic tricks **wave a magic wand** find an easy and immediate solution to a problem

naive /naɪ'i:v/ adjective a naive person lacks experience of life and tends to believe things too easily

pursue /pə(r)sju:/ [verb] to follow a course of activity: *They have continued to pursue a policy or repression.*

relieve /rɪ'li:v/ verb to make pain or another feeling less unpleasant.

threaten /'θret(ə)n/ verb to be likely to harm or destroy something: *Their actions threaten the stability and security of the region.*

toil /tɔɪl/ verb [intransitive] LITERARY to work very hard doing something difficult and tiring, especially physical work

8.2 Vocabulary:
Contracts and corporate ethics

lapse /læps/ verb [intransitive] if an official document, decision or right lapses it is no longer effective

like hell /laɪk 'hel/ VERY INFORMAL used for showing that you doubt something or do not believe it

litigation /ˌlɪtɪ'geɪʃ(ə)n/ noun [uncount] use of the legal system to settle a disagreement

offshore /'ɒfʃɔ:(r)/ adjective [only before noun] an offshore bank or company is not in your own country but in a country where the law is different

part and parcel /ˌpɑ:(r)t ən 'pɑ:(r)səl/ an aspect of something that has to be accepted

renege /rɪneɪg/ verb [intransitive] FORMAL **renege on:** to decide not to do something that you promised to do

take out a contract on someone /teɪk aʊt ə 'kɒntrækt ɒn ˌsʌmwʌn/ INFORMAL to make an agreement by which you pay someone to kill another person for you

vote down /vəʊt 'daʊn/ phrasal verb [transitive] to stop or end something as a result of a vote

warranty /'wɒrənti/ noun [count] a company's written promise to repair or replace a product if it does not work, usually for a specific period of time

wash your hands of /ˌwɒʃ jɔ: 'hændz ɒv/ to say or show that you do not want to be involved with someone or something and that you are not responsible for them

8.4 Speaking:
Negotiating a compromise

premium /'pri:miəm/ noun [count] an amount of money paid in addition to the normal amount: *customers are prepared to pay a premium for fair-trade goods; growers receive a premium to be used for community projects like schools and hospitals.*

shade tree /'ʃeɪd tri:/ noun [count] a tree which grows above other plants, protecting them from the sun and providing a natural habitat for birds and animals.

8.5 Writing:
Assertive writing

assertive /ə's3:(r)tɪv/ adjective behaving in a confident way in which you are quick to express your opinions and feelings

evasive /ɪ'veɪsɪv/ adjective not talking or answering questions in an honest way

refer /rɪ'f3:(r)/ verb [transitive] to transfer to another person or place for appropriate action

sue /su:/ verb [intransitive or transitive] to make a legal claim against someone: *Burnett sued the newspaper for libel and won.*

8.6 Case study:
Green Hills Coffee

binding /'baɪndɪŋ/ adjective if an agreement, contract, decision etc. is binding you must do what it says: **legally binding:** *remember that this is a legally binding document*

breach /bri:tʃ/ noun [count] a failure to follow a law or a rule: **be in breach of something:** *the company was found to be in breach of environmental regulations*

jeopardize /'dʒepə(r)daɪz/ verb [transitive] to risk damaging or destroying something important

practice /'præktɪs/ noun [count or uncount] a way of doing something, especially as a result of habit, custom or tradition

Macmillan Education
Between Towns Road, Oxford OX4 3PP
A division of Macmillan Publishers Limited
Companies and representatives throughout the world

ISBN 978-1-4050-8193-1

Original design by Keith Shaw, Threefold Design Ltd
Illustrated by Mark Duffin, Koichi Fujii, Peter Harper and Sarah Nayler
Cover design by Keith Shaw, Threefold Design Ltd
Cover photograph by Getty Images/ Stuart McClymont

Authors' acknowledgements
We would like to thank: our editor, Nick Canham, for patience and
persistence beyond the call of duty; our publisher, Anna Cowper, for
unfailing support and encouragement; Erika Green, because the whole
project was her baby; all the wonderful people at Macmillan Oxford,
especially Steve Hall, Will Capel, Karen White, Balvir Koura, Cindy
Kauss, Jo Greig, Cathy Smith and Claire Chad; the designer, Keith
Shaw, and the audio producer, Jeff Capel; our colleagues and friends at
Infolangues, especially Tessa Wisely and Peter Wheeler, and last, but
definitely not least, enormous thanks from Jeremy to Pascale, Alexis, Loïc
and Jessica for their support and encouragement to somebody who was
present in body but not always in spirit for the best part of a year, and
from John to Brigitte, Lucie, Jeremy, Emily and Julie for accepting that a
jungle is an interesting alternative to a garden.

The publishers would like to thank Annette Nolan, Folkuniversitetet,
Sweden; Elena Ivanova Angelova, Pharos School of Languages and
Computing, Bulgaria; Sabine Schumann, Berufsakademie (University
of Co-operative Education), Germany; Vladimir Krasnopolsky, East
Ukrainian National University, Ukraine.

The authors and publishers would like to thank the following for
permission to reproduce their material: Extracts from 'Are you capable of
minding your own business?' by Barbara Oaff, copyright © Barbara Oaff
2004, first published in The Observer 27.06.04, reprinted by permission
of the author; Extract from 'Turn It Off' by Gil Gordon, copyright © Gil
Gordon, reprinted by permission of Nicholas Brealey Publishers, London;
Extract from 'Raising the Bar on Viral Web Ads' by Catherine Holohan,
copyright © Catherine Holohan, first published in BusinessWeek online
23.07.06, reprinted by permission of the publisher; Extract from 'How
Harvard Gets its Best and Brightest' by William Symonds, copyright ©
William Symonds, first published in BusinessWeek online 21.08.06,
reprinted by permission of the publisher; Extract from 'The Art of Doing It
Yourself' by Vivek Wadhwa, copyright © Vivek Wadhwa, first published in
BusinessWeek online 14.02.06, reprinted by permission of the publisher;
Extracts from 'Smells Like Team Spirit' & 'Delivering Two Kinds of Quality'
by Keith McFarland both copyright © Keith McFarland, first published
in BusinessWeek online 17.05.06 & 15.02.06 respectively, reprinted by
permission of the publisher; Material from 'For Entrepreneurs' copyright ©
New York Angels 2005, reprinted by permission of the publisher; Extract
from 'Why 'fair' trade is a bad deal for poorest farmers' by Alex Singleton,
copyright © Alex Singleton, first published in The Business 12.03.06,
reprinted by permission of the publisher.

The authors and publishers would like to thank the following for
permission to reproduce their photographs:
Alamy/J. Baker p13(l), U. Baumgarten p32(t), D. Hallinan p40(l), Image
State p44, C. Lovell p49(t), Foodfolio p58, M. Solis p94; Corbis/R.
Cummins p27, H. Neleman p29(mr), Artiga Photo p29(r), Bettmann p35,
R. faris p38, H. King p46(l), Grace p49(b), J. Feingersh p81(l), C. Devan
p81(m), B. Sporrer p81(r); Getty Images/D. Anschutz p9(m), L. Peardon
p11, A. Bush p12, R. Beck p15(r), S. Layda pp16, 17, H. Magee p18(l), A.
Chu p18(r), Dr R Muntefering p19, J. Mind p20, B. Hamill p22(t), A & W.
Stringer p22(tm), Hulton Archive p22(mb), Keystone p22(b), R. Lockyer
p24, J. McBride p25(l), J. Ambrose p25(r), N. Kai p29(l), T. Schierlitz
p32(m), N. Vision p32(b), K. Slade p33, G. Hunter p34(b), S. Gallup
p37(b), A. Meshkinyar p39(t), L. Trovato p39(b), First Light p40(r), T. S.
Kennedy pp 42, 43, I. Waldie p45, J. Naughten p46(r), S. Barbour p50, B.
Heinsohn p51, S. Twin p52, J. Culbertson p54, B. Schmidt p55(m), LWA
p55(b), L. Monneret p61(b), J. Knowles p64(r), Panoramic images p65,
W. T. Cain p67, A. Incrocci p68(l), G. Pease p68(r), T. Kitamura p69(t),
R. Price 69(bl), Quill p69(br), H. Reinhart p71, C. Hondros p78(l), M.
Schreiber p78(ml), M. Harmel p78(mr), M. Rakusen p78(r), Altrendo p85,
P. Souders p87(t), Yellow Dog Productions p87(b), B. Van der Meeer p90,
C. Lyttle p95, Z. Sekizawa p97(r), J. Blair p103(m), H. Sorensen pp106,
107, S. Stafford p106(t), S. Hoeck p106(b); Lonely Planet/N. Setchfield
p105; Masterfile p76, D. Mendelsohn p15(l), S. Craft p37(t), R. Fehling
p 61(t), G. Contorakes p 64(l), K. Neale p 72, N. Hendrickson p 89(b), P.
Rostron p100 Masterfile RFpp28(t), 29(ml); Panos Pictures/S. Torfinn
p55(t); Photolibrary/V. Vidler p7, J. Feingersh p9(l), D. Schneider p28, M.
Gilsdorf p32(mt), T. Robins p32(bm), J. Zoiner p34(t), V. Leblic p39(m),
Nonstock inc p40(m), BSIP61(m), R. Sutcliffe p75, D. Bishop p80, I. Scott
p87(m), H. Ashford p89(t), B. Andre p98, Juniors Bildarchiv p102, S.
Sergio p103(l), S. Satushek p103(r); Reuters/Bea Martinez p13(r); Rex
Features p68(t); The Fairtrade Foundation page 97(l).

Picture Research by Sally Cole at Perseverance Works

Splitting Heirs and Checking Out courtesy of BBC motion.

Printed and bound in Thailand

2014 2013 2012
10 9 8 7 6 5